CONTROVERSIES RELATED TO BUDDHISM

CONTROVERSIES RELATED TO BUDDHISM

N.A.De S. AMARATUNGA

MOTILAL BANARSIDASS INTERNATIONAL
DELHI

First Edition: Delhi, 2022

© **MOTILAL BANARSIDASS INTERNATIONAL**
All Rights Reserved

ISBN : 978-93-92510-40-3 (HB)
ISBN : 978-93-92510-33-5 (PB)

Also available at

MOTILAL BANARSIDASS INTERNATIONAL
H. O. : 41 U.A. Bungalow Road, (Back Lane)Jawahar Nagar, Delhi - 110 007
4261 (basement) Lane #3,Ansari Road, Darya Ganj, New Delhi - 110 002
203 Royapettah High Road, Mylapore, Chennai - 600 004
12/1A, 2nd Floor, Bankim Chatterjee Street, Kolkata - 700 073
Stockist : Motilal Books, Ashok Rajpath, Near Kali Mandir, Patna - 800 004

No part of this book may be reproduced in any form or by any electronic or mechanical means including information storage and retrieval systems without permission in writing from the publishers, excepts by a reviewer who may quote brief passages in a review.

Printed & Bound by
MOTILAL BANARSIDASS INTERNATIONAL

This Book is dedicated

to the memory of my parents

May they attain Nibbana

Contents

Preface	ix
Acknowledgement	xi
Introduction	1-8

Controversies related to the following:-

Chapter 1 Anicca, Dukha, Anatta	11-15
Chapter 2 Concept of Existence in Buddhism	16-21
Chapter 3 Concept of Mind and Psychology	22-28
Chapter 4 Knowledge	29-40
Chapter 5 Buddhist Morals	41-47
Chapter 6 Karma and Rebirth	48-62
Chapter 7 Theory of Causality, "Paticcasamuppada"	63-77
Chapter 8 Concept of Reality	78-85
Chapter 9 Matter	86-93
Chapter 10 Universe	94-98
Chapter 11 Creation	99-105
Chapter 12 God	106-111
Chapter 13 Truth	112-116
Chapter 14 Religious Rituals	117-122
Chapter 15 "Sunyatava"	123-131
Chapter 16 Path of Enlightenment	132-142
Chapter 17 Concept of Bodhisatta	143-147
Chapter 18 Nibbana	148-155
Chapter 19 Buddhahood	156-161
Chapter 20 "Parinirvana"	162-163
Chapter 21 "Arahath"	164-166
Chapter 22 Ven. Nagarjuna	167-171
Chapter 23 Important differences between Theravada and Mahayana	172-179

Chapter 24	Idealism in Buddhism	180-186
Chapter 25	Comparison of "Puggalavada", "Sarvasthivada" and "Sauthantrica"	187-198
Chapter 26	Buddhist Logic	199-209
Chapter 27	Ven. Buddhagosa	210-216
Chapter 28	Arahath Mahinda and Ven. Buddhagosa	217-220
Chapter 29	Abhidhamma	221-232
Chapter 30	Silence of the Buddha	233-237
Chapter 31	Early Buddhism in Sri Lanka	238-248
Chapter 32	Translations of Sinhalese Commentaries	249-254
Chapter 33	Vajrayana	255-260
Chapter 34	Relationship between Buddhism and Science	261-266
Chapter 35	Dhamma Sangayana	267-274
Chapter 36	Decline 0f Buddhism in India and its survival in other countries	275-283
Bibilography		284-296

Preface

I am very pleased that a person whose basic academic training is not in Buddhist Studies, but in an applied science like Dentistry, has taken such deep interest in the study of Buddhism, and produced a really informative and impressive work on the controversies that resulted in the emergence of a number of different Buddhist Schools in the history of the development of Buddhist thought. Confirming a basic principle of the teaching of the Buddha that everything is subject to change and transformation, even his teaching is seen to have branched off into numerous schools of thought within just a period of about three centuries. This process continued even through many centuries that followed due to the influence of, and interaction with, other non-Buddhist systems of Indian thought. The consequence of such transformation was the emergence of even interpretations that seemed to contradict each other moving away from the primarily pragmatic concern that was characteristic of the original teaching of the Buddha.

Early Buddhist teachings preserved in the Pāli Nikāya sources and the corresponding Chinese Āgamas gave priority to the message of the founder that emphasized the urgency of attaining liberation from the miseries of repeated existence in the cyclic process of birth and death paying very little attention to theoretical precision of the language and concepts utilized in those teachings. From the perspective of profound conceptual analysis those early teachings could be subjected to diverse interpretations in order to draw out their theoretical implications. This appeared to be the case with the gradually diminishing practical commitment to the teaching and the developing enthusiasm for achieving theoretical precision due partly to the need to defend the system in the midst of a host of teachings inherited from the orthodox Vedic and Brahmanical traditions. There is no doubt that some of the notable controversies within Buddhism were a result of the influence of non-Buddhist Indian philosophical and religious traditions.

In the thirty-six chapters of this work dealing with Buddhist controversies attention has been paid to the most notable developments in sectarian Buddhism touching on the principal Buddhist doctrines such as the three characteristics of being, kamma and rebirth, causality, Nirvāṇa, and the ultimate goal of Buddhism taking into account the doctrinal differences observable in the theoretical standpoints of different Schools. The work helps the reader to gain a thorough understanding of the divergent Buddhist traditions in relation to both the original teaching of the Buddha as well as other non-Buddhist systems of Indian thought. It has also focused attention on certain major figures in the history of Buddhism such as Nāgārjuna, Vasubandhu, Asaṅga, Dignāga, Moggalīputtatissa and Buddhaghosa responsible for developing novel and intellectually stimulating interpretations of the early teaching. In this attempt some notable developments such as the Buddhist Realism of the Sarvāstivāda School, the Emptiness Doctrine of the Madhyamaka School, and the Idealism of the Yogācāra School have been discussed. It helps the reader to gain a total picture of the historical process of the development of Buddhist Philosophy within the different schools of Buddhist thought that emerged after the Buddha's demise.

I am pleased to recommend this work to readers who wish to gain a comprehensive understanding of Buddhism from a doctrinal as well as a historical perspective, noting the major components of the system in terms of the diverse interpretations by the most illustrious teachers known to the tradition. The work is an admirable attempt to synthesize the numerous areas of interest related to the understanding of Buddhism as a system of thought that had a lasting and universal impact on philosophical, ethical and religious ideology in the history of humankind.

P.D. Premasiri

Emeritus Professor of Pali and Buddhist Studies,

University of Peradeniya   Sri Lanka

Acknowledgements

I am indebted to several people for helping me to write this book. Mr. Sumeda Weerawardena, senior lecturer of the Department of Philosophy, University of Peradeniya unhesitatingly gave his valuable advice on matters of the Buddha Dhamma and helped me to get a clear idea of complex issues related to it. He also provided me with information on relevant references and Buddhist texts.

Professor P. Premasiri Professor Emeritus University of Peradeniya and Buddhist Scholar was kind enough to write a preface for the book and also helped me with the spelling of Pāli and Sanscrit words.

Professor G. H. Peiris, Professor Emeritus, University of Peradeniya read sections of the manuscript and made valuable suggestions on improvements. I have tried to follow his advice and apply it to the whole text but I am not sure how far I have succeeded.

Ms. Geethani Attanayake, Senior Assistant Librarian, Postgraduate Institute of Pāli and Buddhist Studies, University of Kelaniya was most generous in supplying me with books on Buddhism going out of her way in looking for these books in book shops and libraries. I had never met her and had only spoken to her on the telephone, yet she was so very helpful. I was fortunate to have made her acquaintance through the kind assistance of Professor Ven. M. Dhammajoti, Director Cultural Centre University of Kelaniya who was introduced to me by Mr. Sanath Nanayakkara author of an excellent publication that traces the evolution of Buddhism from Early Buddhism to Vajarayāna.

I was fortunate to have made contact with Professor Asaṅga Tillekeratne Professor Emeritus University of Kelaniya and

Buddhist Scholar with whom I have spoken, not specifically about this book, but of other issues on Buddhism and he was kind and patient to clarify for me those problems which has helped in avoiding mistakes when drafting this book. Professor Y. Karunadasa, Professor Emeritus of the University of Kelaniya and Visiting Professor, University of Hong Kong helped me in a similar manner. He had gifted me two of his excellent works, one on "Matter" and the other on "Early Buddhist Teachings".

My grand-daughter Anjalika Peiris helped me with the intricacies of word processing in the computer and her father Dr. Manjula Peiris designed the cover page.

The reputed publishing company Motilal Banarsidass International, New Delhi, very kindly came forward to publish the book. Their professional approach to such undertaking is evident in the final product.

I am grateful to all these people without whose assistance and expertise I would not be able to complete this work. May the Triple Gem bless these kind hearted people.

N.A.de S. Amaratunga
47/4, Louis Peiris Mawatha,
Kandy

Introduction

Buddhism is an Indian religion based on the teachings of Gautama Buddha who was born in 623 BC and died at 80 years of age. During his time there was tremendous intellectual activity and several religious and life philosophies were being discoursed. Most of these ideas and views in the final analysis could be broadly divided into two categories; one was eternalist and the other nihilist. The Vedic tradition and also other theistic philosophies propounded eternalism while Materialists and Sceptics tended towards nihilism. However, the common characteristic of these two groups was the tendency towards the seeking of an absolute truth regarding the world and the life on it (Kalupahana, 2006). Buddha before he attained enlightenment, as Prince Siddhārtha had studied all these philosophies and had come to think that the endeavour to look for an absolute truth as the answer to the question on the life on Earth was wasteful and moreover there may not be an absolute truth. Siddhārtha was more interested in the human predicament, the fact that human life was one of suffering and he wanted to find relief from suffering. He gave up lay life and went in search of a way to end suffering. Realizing the inadequacy of his teachers he went on his own path, found the cause of suffering and discovered the method to eliminate the cause and attained Nibbāna, freedom from all attachments.

Buddha's teachings had not been written down until it happened in Sri Lanka in the 1st Century AD at Aluvihare (Adikaram, 1946). Before that the Dhamma was preserved by a well-organized oral tradition with periodical recitals and handing down from generation to generation. This method of preservation of the preaching was not unique to Buddhism, it was the practice in the Vedic tradition and most other religions of that time due to the scarcity of writing material. The system was organized and structured at the First Dhamma Saṅgāyanā (Council) held three months after Buddha's demise. The First Dhamma Saṅgāyanā held at Rājagaha was headed by

Mahākassapa Thera and had lasted six months. Buddha's teachings of the doctrines were recited, revised and were collected into several "Suttas" according to their length and compiled as the "Sutta Piṭaka". All his advice to monks on how they should behave was compiled into the "Vinaya Piṭaka". Further analyses of the Dhamma by leading monks comprised the beginnings of the Abhidhamma. The monks were formed into several groups each headed by a senior monk and were given the responsibility of preserving the three categories of Buddha's teachings by memorizing them. The monks who specialized in this activity were known as Bhāṇakas. Thus was founded the Tipiṭaka, considered to be canonical and written in Pāli, the language of the Buddha. The four major Nikāyas in the Sutta Piṭaka, Dīgha, Majjhima, Aṅguttara and Saṃyutta are considered to be close to Buddha's teachings and could be accepted as consisting of authentic Buddha Dhamma.

Such a method of preservation of Buddha's preaching by memory and transmitting them from generation to generation is bound to have caused changes. Errors may have crept in before they were written down which was done more than four centuries later.

Nevertheless the teachings of Buddha which went into the four major Nikāya are identified as Early Buddhism in order to distinguish them from later additions by leading philosophers of Buddhism. For instance, the discourse known as "Kathāvatthu" which was delivered by Ven. Moggalīputtatissa at the third Dhamma Saṅgāyanā is included in the "Abhidhamma" but obviously does not belong to Early Buddhism. So are "Theragāthā" and "Therīgāthā" which are included in the "Sutta Piṭaka". Though Buddha's teachings have been written in other languages such as Sanskrit, Tibetan etc. only the scriptures known as Chinese Āgama are considered close to Buddha's teachings and matching in content the four major Nikāya though there are differences and some discourses are missing. Hence the discourses in the four major Nikāya and the content in the Chinese Āgama are considered as comprising Early Buddhism.

Dissent in Buddhism had been present even during Buddha's time and had surfaced more strongly after his death (Mahāsīhanāda sutta, Majjima Nikāya). The elder monks had focused their attention more on the study and propagation of Dhamma while the younger monks saddened by the loss of their teacher had attempted to popularize Buddha's virtues often exceeding the boundaries of reality. They encouraged and sponsored the building of stūpas and monuments in memory of the Buddha and started worshiping practices and rituals. They may have been influenced by other religious traditions that practice veneration, worshiping and rituals. The historical Buddha was thus made into a larger than life phenomenon. These developments were resented by the elder monks and this grew into a major conflict. These conflicts had continued even after the First Dhamma Saṅgāyanā. As the differences could not be ironed out a Second Dhamma Saṅgāyanā was held hundred years after the first. At this convention some of the younger monks broke away as a group and formed their own sect called "Mahāsaṅghika". The elder monks who concentrated their mind on the Dhamma formed their own school which came to be known as Theravāda which means elders' views. The word Thera refers to older and mature monks who may have attained "maggaphala", the various fruits in the stages of the path to the final goal.

The effort of the younger monks to create a larger-than-life Buddha resulted in the introduction of elements of transcendentalism into Buddhism very early in its history. Transcendentalism remains as a major controversial core factor in Buddhism up to the present times and has given rise to many controversies. While the word transcend means beyond limits transcendentalism entails phenomena beyond reality and the realm of this empirical world. In the sphere of religion transcendentalism is a philosophy that asserts the primacy of the spiritual over the material and the empirical. Buddha depended on empirical methods to gain knowledge and his theories are based on empirical evidence. Therefore transcendentalism could be a controversial issue when considered in the context of Buddhism. However this factor comes into reckoning when discussing the intricacies of concepts like Nibbāna.

Mahāsaṅghika school of Buddhism may have later contributed to the development of Mahāyāna Buddhism. Within Theravāda too there had been differences and groups breaking away and forming their own schools while remaining as Theravādins. Sarvāstivāda came into being in the 3rd Century BC and Sautrāntika a breakaway group of the former developed in the 1st Century AD. Several controversies in Theravāda theory occurred due to the development of these schools of Buddhism. To some degree Sarvāstivādins were eternalists while Sautrāntikavādins were nihilists which positions were considered extremist by Buddha who adopted a middle path.

Several other Buddhist philosophers such as Nāgārjuna, Vasubandhu, Asaṅga, Dignāga, Moggalīputtatissa and also commentators like Candrakīrti, Buddhagosa have contributed immensely to the later development of Buddhism. The interpretations of their views and analyses have led to the formation of controversy some of which have been so serious that they had caused rupture of some Schools of Buddhism.

There was a plethora of religious philosophies during Buddha's time and also later which tended to influence Buddhism sometimes forcefully. This happened during the development of Early Buddhism and also when leading philosopher monks were engaged in further analysis and development of Buddhism in later years. Brahmanism and later Hinduism tended to forcefully introduce their beliefs and theories into Buddhism. The founder of Jainism Mahāvīra was a friend of the Buddha and there were several inputs by that religion into Buddhism. Mahāyāna due to its transcendentalism and mysticism was vulnerable to encroachment by other doctrines and it was easy for Hinduism to introduce several of its concepts and tenets into Mahāyāna. The latter with these new weapons made a strong attempt to influence Theravāda. There was a special effort by Mahāyāna to enter into Sri Lanka and consequently Mahāyāna was the predominant religion in Sri Lanka from the 5th to the 10th Century AD. The effect of this on the theory and practice of Buddhism in Sri Lanka has been far reaching and the consequences felt even in present times are quite substantial and critical.

There are notable and significant differences in dealing with the same concept in different "Suttas" and these also had led to the formation of controversial ideas and viewpoints. Further the use of certain words in different contexts also had led to the creation of different viewpoints. For instance Buddha had used the word "suñña" to mean that life and matter on earth has no Self or anything like Self or "attā". But in certain instances he comes very close to using the word "suñña" to mean the final goal. For instance he has said that he dwells in "suññatā" very often. This has resulted in the development of an entire school of Buddhism known as the "Madhyamaka" branch of Mahāyāna. Here is an instance where the misinterpretation of a concept had led to the formation of a new sect in Buddhism. "Śūnyatāvāda" has caused confusion and its author Ven.Nāgārjuna has been totally misinterpreted and labelled as Mahāyānist (Kalupahana 2008). Similarly several other Buddhist philosophers who lived long after Buddha's time had been misinterpreted. For example Vasubandhu's important work "Vijñaptimātratāsiddhi" has been interpreted as belonging to Mahāyāna Buddhism.

Linguistic abilities of Buddha were immense and he had coined several words to give meaning to his preaching. Commentators may not have understood the correct meaning of these words and may have caused controversy. For instance the term for cause was "hetu" but Buddha used the term "paccaya" as its synonym. This had later given rise to differences of opinion regarding what Buddha meant.

Introduction

There are several major doctrines in Buddhism which have been the subject of controversy. These doctrines are unique to Buddhism though some of them may have its origin in Vedic tradition. The Four Noble Truths define the basis of the ultimate goal in Buddhism. Though "Dukkha" and "Sukha" (Sorrow and Happiness) have been discussed in the Veda what is meant by "Dukkha" in the Four Noble Truths is different and the cause and its eradication are unique creations by the Buddha. Nibbāna (Pāli) is a concept which is difficult to comprehend for even Buddha had been silent about some queries that had arisen during his time. His silence also had led to controversy. Further when the Buddha was asked whether or not a person who has attained Nibbāna exists after death he had said that the question does not arise. This answer had given rise to controversial understanding of the concept. The Noble Eight-fold Path is the method of attaining Nibbāna that Buddha discovered and is unique to Buddhism. This doctrine is clearly described in the Ariyapariyasena Sutta yet sectarianism in Buddhism has resulted in the modification of it.

Survival after death had been a subject of much interest during Buddha's time. The eternalists said there was a self or something like it that survives death and finds birth in a physical form in the next generation. In contrast the nihilists said there is no life after death. Buddha's view on rebirth was different and its interpretation had given rise to inconclusive debate regarding what exactly links present life with its past.

Buddha's theory of karma also tended to take the middle path in that it was neither deterministic nor indeterministic. Due to the fact that there was no self or anything like it in Buddha's teachings the problems arise in relation to theories of both rebirth and karma. The discussion of these theories though interesting is not conclusive and these issues have again led to the formation of breakaway schools.

The Buddha, though not very much interested in advancing theories about the universe had to deal with the physical reality of matter, whether what we perceive really exists or is a construct of the mind. His views on reality were different from those of his contemporaries. Different interpretation of his views on reality has led to the formation of different theories and even the development of new schools of Buddhism. Idealism in the form of Yogācāra branch of Mahāyāna developed due to these differences of view.

Buddha's point of view has to be examined keeping in mind that he always avoided the two extreme views on life, eternalism and nihilism and adopted a middle path. In the background is the fact that he was not going in search of an absolute truth that explained life on earth and the fact that he was more interested in finding relief from suffering which to him appeared to be much more important and acute.

This book attempts to discuss the controversies in Buddhism taking Early Buddhism as the basis for verification. In this effort it recognizes the fact that Buddhism is built on the foundation of "Anicca, Dukkha, Anatta" which attempts to describe the nature of life. While leading such a precarious life the human being commits deeds cumulative effect of which results in "Karma". Karma ensures the survival after death and Rebirth results completing the cycle of "Saṃsāra". Buddha's theory on causality "Paṭiccasamuppāda" explains how this cycle works where "viññāṇa" or consciousness plays an important role. Buddha was of the view that the cycle of Saṃsāra has to be stopped in order to be free of Dukkha. He found that greed was a key factor in the cycle and was the cause of suffering. If greed could be got rid of the āāSaṃsāra cycle would cease and suffering would stop. The Four Noble Truths define this theory and the Ariyaṭṭhaṅgikamagga describes the method of spewing out greed and other defilements that bind a person to the cycle of Saṃsāra. Buddhist theory mainly pertains to human life and its predicament as described above but apart from the main theory it deals with several other important aspects of life and phenomena of the world.

Introduction

Thus Buddha had theories on the main aspects of life such as birth, suffering, greed, morals, ethics, karma, rebirth, reality, causality, self, mind etc. and finally on relief from suffering. These theories have been analysed by eminent philosophers, both ancient and modern and of both East and West. Some of the major theories would be examined here with the intention of focusing on the controversies that had arisen in relation to these theories. It would be necessary to go into the causes of rupture in major Schools of Buddhism and formation of breakaway groups. The discussion would focus on the major theories and concepts and their interpretations by different schools and individuals with the intention of highlighting the controversies. Reference would also be made to the Vedic tradition which preceded Buddhism and had a profound influence on it, mainly to show how Buddha differed and showed its weaknesses and developed his own theories. The discussion would also touch on Western philosophy to draw the differences and similarities where it is relevant. The decline of Buddhism in India, its relationship with science and its early history in Sri Lanka are also discussed. As there is an overlap of content between the various subjects discussed here some repetition was unavoidable. We apologise for this and hope it will not make the reading of the book cumbersome.

Chapter 1

Controversies related to the Theory of Anicca, Dukka, Anatta (Pāli)

Impermanence (Anicca) is a character that we experience in everything around us. There is nothing permanent in the world including huge rocks and the vast sea. We can see rocks being gradually eroded and the sea undergoing change in size and behaviour. By Anicca what is meant is that everything is subject to change. Elements of matter and mind arise, decline and disappear and arise again. They are in a state of flux and never stable in one state. Buddha said everything that arises as conditioned phenomenon is impermanent. Conditioned phenomenon means something that arises due to causes other than itself. How conditioned phenomena arise and undergo decay and finally die is described in the "Patikka- Samuppada".

Before Buddha's time the Vedic scripture, which are the oldest extant religious texts (1500 BCE), had spoken about impermanence. There are four Vedas; Rgveda, Yajurveda, Samaveda and Atharvaveda. Each of these has four subdivisions called Samhita, Aranyaka, Brahmana and Upanishad. Vedas are identified as "sruti" which means "what is heard" and which differentiates these from texts of other religions which are called "smrti" which means "what is remembered". Hindus consider Vedas as devine in origin. Vedas had directly developed into Hinduism and their philosophy may have had an important impact on the birth of religions like Jainism and Buddhism.

In the Veda texts, however, "anithya" (Sanskrit word for Anicca) was seen as "mithya" or not something real. What undergoes change was considered as not true or "sathya". Things that are true do not undergo change. "Anithya" was considered as an opportunity to find "Nithya" which dwells inside every person's mind. "Nithya" that exists inside the person is Brahman and finding "Nithya" was establishing the union of Atman with Brahman which is the final goal in life or "Moksha" (Katha Upanishad, Mukthika Canon 3).

What is impermanent cannot give satisfaction. That is the experience of life. Buddha had by empirical means realized that what is impermanent do not give lasting satisfaction. To him there was nothing in lay life that could give happiness. Life was suffering. The momentary happiness that one experiences invariably lead to sorrow irrespective of the activity or event. Thus he described another feature of life as "Dukka".

Vedic tradition, however, had a different view on suffering. It said suffering is temporary and happiness could be found by looking into the mind and seeking union with Brahman. Happiness is to be found within oneself. The reality of Atman-Brahman was to be found in oneself. Thus according to Veda life is not characterized by suffering.

Buddha was of the view that in life and matter there was no permanent element which could be identified as Self. There was nothing that could be recognized as "I, me, mine" in life. This theory of No-self as well as Suffering originates from the theory of Impermanence. Buddha delivered his Second Sermon (Anattalakhana Sutta, Samyutta Nikāya) on the fifth day of his arrival at the Deer Park in Isipathana near Benares after he had attained Nibbāna, to the five ascetics who had been his companions in the early days of his journey in quest of a solution to the problem of human suffering. In this sermon he spoke about the absence of a Self in the Five Aggregates of the human form, "Rupa, Vedanā, Saññā, Saṅkara, Viññāna".

Vedic tradition on the other hand recognizes a Self within life, an "Atman" that is permanent and travels from one birth to the next. It is indestructible and decides what form the individual would take in the next birth. It is "Atman" that survives death (Katha Upanishad).

Controversies related to the Theory of Anicca, Dukka, Anatta (Pāli)

Buddhism defines life and all phenomena within these three features, the "Trilakhana". Buddha described life as "Anicca, Dukka, Anatta" whereas Hinduism which developed from Vedic tradition described life as "Nithya, Sukha, Atman", the exact opposite view from that of Buddhism. In other words in Buddhism the characteristics of life are impermanence, suffering and no-self, while in Hinduism they are the exact opposite; it is permanent, there is happiness in it and it has a Self.

Buddhist doctrines are based on these "Trilakhana" and all ideas and views had to conform to these basic tenets. As Buddha relied on empirical evidence and not on metaphysical speculation he believed in the impermanence of life and the world which he could experience and was in a position to refute the views of Vedic tradition. Whenever a diversion from these basics was attempted within Buddhism a serious conflict arose and often led to splits and formation of new schools. Of the three characters it was in relation to "Anatta" or No-Self theory that conflicts often arose. The question that arose was; if there is no Self or anything like it who or what would take responsibility for one's actions? This question becomes more relevant when Karma gets into the picture. If there is no self who would be the recipient of the effects of Karma in this birth or next?

Neither Mahāyāna nor its two main branches, Madhyamaka and Yogācāra, had spoken about the "Thrilakhana". They accept the Four Noble Truths and it is probable that they had agreed with the principles of the "Anicca, Dukha, Anatta" theory also.

Jainism originated in Maghada State before Buddhism and it has similarities and differences with the latter. Jainism like Buddhism is atheistic but believes in a permanent Self that travels from one birth to the next combined with Karma. The three pillars on which it stands are non-violence, asceticism and non-absolutism. It is silent on the question of "Anicca" which is understandable as it subscribes to a theory of a permanent Self.

But Jainism has a meditation system for salvation which could mean that it believes in the phenomenon of "Dukha". However salvation is achieved by discovering the inner Self by means of meditation, which would be the attaining of "Moksha" (Pathmanabh, 1998).

Several theories were put forward by groups of monks to solve the problem concerning the Anatta concept and some of these groups developed into important Schools of Buddhism that enjoyed royal patronage and existed for long periods of time.

One such school was the "Puggalavāda" which arose in the 3rd Century BC (Warder, 1991). "Puggalavāda" was started by a senior monk by the name of Vatsiputra (3rd Century BC). Their view was that though there is no Atman there is a Puggala ("person") in the composition of the human being which is neither conditioned nor-unconditioned. This Puggala travels from one birth to the next, takes responsibility for "Karma" and is the component that experiences Nibbāna. Their contention was that Buddha in his discourses had spoken about a "person" (Samyutta Nikāya, Salayatana Vagga). "Kathāvatthu" of the Theravāda Abhidhamma says that the basis for the theory put forward by Puggalavādins was the statement attributed to Buddha; "there is a person who exerts for his own good", "there appears a person who is reborn for the good and happiness of many for showing compassion to the world of beings".

According to this School the "person" is neither the same as the five aggregates nor different. It is this "person" who experiences Nibbāna which the "Puggalavādins" say is transcendental and inexplicable. The "person" who experiences Nibbāna is not subject to the law of impermanence. Here the influence of transcendentalism, which had encroached Buddhism soon after Buddha's demise, is clearly discernible.

One of the first to reject the Personalist ("Puggalavāda") theory was Ven Moggalliputtatissa, who presided at the third Dhamma Saṅgāyanāwa in the 3rd Century BC. The 3rd Saṅgāyanāwa had been sponsored by King Dharmasoka in order to get rid of the impurities that had crept into the Dhamma before he ventured into the ardous task of spreading it. Ven Moggalliputtatissa's discourse at this convention is known as "Kathāvatthu" and is included in the Abhidhamma Piṭaka. These aspects are discussed in detail in Chapter 25.

Vasubandhu one of the prominent Buddhist philosophers who lived around the 4th Century CE, seven centuries after Ven Moggalliputtatissa, criticized the views of "Puggalavādins". The concept of "person" suggests that there is something in the human composition in addition to the five aggregates ("panchaskanda"). Vasubandhu in his "Abhidhammakosa" says that if there is a "person" one should be able to perceive the "person" either directly or by perceiving the five aggregates. If it is the latter the "person" is nothing but a label for aggregates. On the other hand if the "person" could be perceived directly the five aggregates would be based on the "person" and not the other way about. This may be in total contradiction with the basic tenet of Buddhism concerning the five aggregates. The five aggregates are conditioned Dhamma and therefore it cannot be based on something that is neither conditioned nor unconditioned (Emanuel, 2013).

However there are modern commentators like Dan Lusthaus (1999) who tend to differ. He says "Puggalavāda" was simply an attempt to explain what other Buddhist traditions leave unsaid and assumed; mainly what it is that undergoes rebirth and has moral responsibility and attains enlightenment. However there is no evidence in the TriPiṭaka to support a Personalist theory.

"Puggalavāda" later broke up into several groups. One of these groups known as "Sammitiyas" became prominent and was second only to Mahāyāna when the latter was popular. Puggalavādins existed for about thousand years from the 3rd Century BC till about the 7th Century CE in Gujarat and other areas and their teaching institute in Valabhi University rivalled

Nalanda. Puggalavādins in the 6th Century surpassed Sarvāsthivādins in popularity in the area of Saranath.

Sarvāsthivādins had also come into being in the 3rd Century BC, about the same time as Puggalavādins, and prospered in the North-West of India under the patronage of King Kanishka (Williams, 2005). This School of Buddhism also attempted to get over the problem of No-Self, i.e.; if there is no Self what survives after death and who is responsible for karma. To solve the above mentioned problem connected with the "Anatta" theory they put forward the "svabhāva" concept which said there is something apart from "nama-rupa" complex which they called "svabhāva" that could explain rebirth, "karma" etc. This Dhamma called the "svabhāva" would be present not only in the present but also in the past and the future. Sarvāstivāda is discussed in detail in Chapter 25.

Sautrāntikavada was a breakaway group of Sarvāstivāda and came into being in the 1st Century CE (Dutt, 1970, Warder, 1991). Sautrāntikavadins vehemently opposed the theory of "svabhāva" of the Sarvāsthavāda and in the process got involved in the controversy about existence and "Anicca". They questioned the possibility of four phenomena - "utpāda" "sthithi" "jarā" and "tithassa anganatha" - occurring in a "kshana" or moment. Their argument was that if all four stages occurred together they would nullify each other and if they occurred separately the "kshana", which is a concept of time, has to be divided into four. This showed their ability of thinking and rational argument. Their theory of existence was thus changed and there are only two stages; "jathi" and "vyaya" or birth and death which could be applied to all phenomena. There is no time for the phenomena to undergo change but would immediately disappear no sooner they appear. Further they said what is meant by change is appearance and disappearance and there is nothing in between that could undergo change. One could talk about change not in relation to one Dhamma but an entire system of Dhammas. This whole idea however is questionable for when a phenomenon occurs it has to exist even for a moment (Nanayakkara, 2003).

These two Schools of Buddhism, Sarvāstivāda and Sautrāntika, had opposing views on several doctrinal aspects of Buddhism but for the present discussion their views on existence is relevant as those would indicate whether their theories point to a permanent existence or an impermanent one. Apart from its substantialist view on account of the theory on "svabhāva" which tends to oppose the "Anatta" concept of Early Buddhism, Sarvāstivāda also appears to be eternalist due to its Dhamma theory where the Dhammas exist throughout time which may be in contradiction with the "Anicca" or Impermanence theory. In contrast the theory of existence of Sauthantrika appears to be nihilist as there is only "jathi" and "vyaya" or birth and death of Dhammas and there doesn't seem to be time for existence. The concept of impermanence seems to have been taken to the other extreme of nihilism or anihilationism by Sautrāntikavadins which is totally different from Buddha's theory on existence and impermanence.

These opposing views of Sarvāstivāda and Sautrāntika on Self and Existence were methodically refuted by the great Buddhist philosopher Ven Nāgārjuna who lived in the 1st Century CE. He was particularly focused on the theory of no-self and also on the attempt by various sects and thinkers to make Buddha, Arahath and Nibbāna transcendental concepts. He wrote six treatises and of these "Mulamadhyamaka- karikā" takes pride of place. It is a work that attempted to refute the views of eternalists and annihilationists and also the views of Brahmanism which was raising its head taking advantage of the controversies that plagued Buddhism (Kalupahana 1991). These aspects are discussed in Chapter 22 on Nāgārjuna.

Chapter 2

Controversies related to the Concept of Existence in Buddhism

Human existence had been a matter that had interested man from earliest times. The main interest was in finding answers to questions like how did we arrive here, why we are here and what happens after death. Religions and philosophies may have originated from the thinking and discussions that would have taken place about these questions. These religions and philosophies would have discoursed these issues further and theorized on them. A division of these philosophies and religions into theistic and atheistic types may have occurred when answers to these questions tended to be based on a creator god. A creator god had to come in as some of these questions proved to be difficult to answer. A concept of a creator god who is omnipotent could provide answers to most of these questions.

However there were thinkers who could not accept the metaphysical concept of god. They prefered to rely on empirical evidence and formulated their theories based on experience. Buddha belonged to this group and he did not attempt to find answers to problems that did not come within the scope of the empirical sphere. He did not attempt to answer questions that could only be answered by sepeculative inference.

Buddha was more concerned about the nature of existence as he knew that the problem of suffering is closely linked to it. Several Buddhist doctrines attempt to explain the nature of existence. The Trilakhana concept comprising "Anicca, Dukha, Anatta" is one method of explaining the nature of human existence and we have discussed the controversies related to it in the previous chapter. Given below are few other methods of analysis of existence.

As mentioned earlier the Buddha said there are those who say that everything exists and others who say nothing exists. His view was that the physical world neither exists permanently nor non-exists. The two views, eternalism and nihilism were avoided by the Buddha and to expound his point of view on the middle path he put forward the theory of Dependent Co-origination or "Paticcasamuppādaya" which explained the origin, existence and decline and death of all phenomena in the Universe. All phenomena thus caused are conditioned in the sense they are caused not by themselves. Ignorance or "Avidya" is the root cause of all conditioned phenomena. It is due to ignorance of the true nature of the world and its phenomena that one tends to reconstruct what one perceives via the function called "saṅkāra" (volitional construction / dispositions) and then grasp what was wrongly perceived which finally results in birth followed by suffering, decay and death.

Buddha in the Madupundika Sutta (Majjima Nikāya) explains the process of perception in order to illustrate the functioning of the "Paticcasamuppādaya". In the case of vision for example the eye comes into contact with the physical object and that produces a "saññā" (sign) which is modified by "saṅkāra" (volitional construction) according to past experience the observer may have in relation to the perceived object. Visual consciousness (viññāna) is thus produced. Consciousness would act as Condition for the arising of Materiality-mentality which would be the Condition for Contact followed by Feeling, Craving, Clinging, Existence, Birth, Decay and Death.

Buddhism also explains existence by an analysis of the composition of the Mentality-materiality complex. First it is analysed into the Five Aggregates, "Rupa, Vedana, Saññā, Saṅkāra, Viññāna". Here "Rupa" is materiality and is divisible into four "Mahabhuta'"; "Apo, Thejo, Vayo, Patavi". This is the physical aspect of existence. Mental component is given greater importance as it is composed of four functional parts as against the single "Rupa" in the physical component. All these components are further analysed in the Dhamma Theory of the Abhidhamma.

A further analysis is possible on the basis of the six sense organs; eye, ear, nose, taste, body and mind. Each of the six sense organs has three components related to it, the sense organ, its function and the object of perception. For example the eye would have the eye organ, sight and the physical object of perception. Thus the analysis would result in eighteen elements. Hence it could be seen that in Buddhism existence is defined as a mental phenomenon with the physical component playing a supportive role.

This theory is further supported by the analysis given in the "Mulapariyaya Sutta" (Majjima Nikāya). The word "Mulapariyaya" means Root of Existence. This discourse vividly explains how the human mental function driven by the Self-ego comprising "I, Me and Mine" feelings, conceives what it perceives as "mine". The Discourse identifies twenty four Bases ("vattu") and describes how the mind conceives each Base that it perceives. For example the Earth, which is one of the Bases is first perceived by the individual as Earth, and then he conceives Earth and goes on to conceive "on Earth" and finally to conceive as "Earth is mine". This cognitive process, however, is dependent on the mental state of the individual who perceives. In this regard four types of individuals are identified, the uninstructed Worldling, the Learner of Dhamma, the Arahath and Thathāgatha. The Worldling ignorant of the unsubstantial nature of phenomena and driven by Self-ego perceives an object as something he could conceive as "mine". The Learner of the Dhamma, on the other hand, has some control over his Self-ego and could refrain from conceiving what he perceives as an object that he could take possession of. Arahath and Thathāgatha would have full control of their Self-ego and would have no problem in perceiving the true nature of an object. What is meant by conceive here is formation of "I, Me, Mine" concepts regarding the perceived object. Thus according to "Mulapariyaya Sutta" the root of human existence is the Self-ego which keeps the individual bound to the "samsaric cycle". This explains why Buddha made a special effort to debunk the theories of Self put forward by his contemporary religions and philosophers.

Vedic tradition and Hinduism which evolved from it, subscribe to the view that human existence is characterised by the presence of a Self that is permanent and travels from one birth to the next. Bhagavadgita speaks about a limited Self and a universal Self. The former is the impure ego of the individual whereas the latter is the purest ego of the God. Bhagavadgita says suffering and feeling of emotion is due to ego. In the perceptual world it is the source of all our knowledge, perceptions, feelings and experience.

In the Bhagavadgita subjective and objective aspects of ego are personified as Krishna and Arjuna. Lord Krishna personifies the Universal Self with the purest and indistinguishable Ego, whereas Arjuna stands symbolically for the limited Self or the impure Ego consciousness which is responsible for the feelings of individuality. But in truth it is a reflection of the purest reality or pure consciousness which however remains enveloped by the Nature's impure realities. As a result the individual acts as a separate reality, separate from the purest Self that is God (Fowler, 2012).

Further according to Bhagavadgita the Ego makes us feel that we are the doers of our action and responsible for them. Because of that we engage in actions driven by desire and we crave for their fruit and we incur Karma and remain bound to the mortal world.

Here some similarity between the Bhagavadgita and Buddhist theories on Self and Ego is discernible. The root of existence according to Bhagavadgita seems to be self and ego as it is in Buddhism. However in Bhagavadgita the Self is a permanent phenomenon and part of the human form, almost physiological, whereas in Buddhism it is an intrusion that has invaded the mind due to ignorance. For there is no Self in Buddhism and in fact No-self theory ("Anatta") is one of the main features in the Trilakhana concept that defines life. There has been a Self in Vedic tradition and finally it has been accepted and included in the Bhagavadgita, the most important Hindu text.

When discussing the Buddhist theory on human existence the relationship between Self and Greed/Craving may have to be considered. Greed/Craving features in "Paticcasamuppāda", which is supposed to be capable of explaining all issues in Buddhism, but Self does not. Arahath and Thathgatha who have breached the "Paticcasamuppāda" cycle by eliminating "Loba, Dvesha, Moha" (Greed, Aversion, Ignorence) has the ability to control their Self-ego and moreover "I, Me, Mine" feelings are not evoked in their mind (Mulapariyaya-sutta, Majjima Nikāya). They do not conceive what they cognize as composed of substance that evoke such Self-ego feelings. It seems that when Greed/Craving is under control Self-ego feelings are also under control. No special effort is required to get rid of Self-ego while such an effort is needed to spew out Greed/Craving. Thus it appears that Greed/Craving is a primary factor while Self-ego is secondary, this may be the reason why Self-ego does not feature in the "Paticcasamuppāda".

In the Bhagavadgita however Self and Ego are given primacy over Greed. This is shown by the fact that Greed is a characteristic feature of Arjuna who is the personification of the impure Self and Krishna who is the personification of pure Self is without Greed. Self is present even when Greed is absent which shows Self is the primary factor while Ego is secondary. This is understandable for Bhagavadgita and Hinduism has a profound Self theory.

In Buddhism Self-ego is an undesirable and harmful factor which needs to be controled whereas in Hinduism Self is a means of gaining union with God. Bhagavadgita suggests that one must attempt to dissolve or merge one's limited Self in the purest Self of God, then one's life would be taken over by God himself and He becomes responsible for all one's actions.

Jainism is atheistic, yet it believes in the presence of a Self in human existence. Jain texts say Soul exists "clothed in material body" and it fills up the whole body. Karma is seen as a subtle matter that could bind with the Soul and travel with it in rebirth (Padmanabh, 1988). It appears that in Jainism also, though atheistic, Soul may form a component of the basis of existence. Though there are several similarities between Buddhism and Jainism they differ in relation to the theory on Self.

As mentioned earlier Buddha had not spoken on the subject of the purpose of existence. He avoided discussions on subjects which were not understandable by empirical means. He did not engage in speculation, rational or otherwise, but was more concerned about finding solutions to problems that could be experienced in everyday life. On the other hand theistic religions asserted that the purpose of human existence is ultimate union with God which is permanent happiness. This proposition could hold only if the omnipotent creator God's existence could be proved. This matter will be discussed in Chapters 11 and 12 on Creation and God.

Chapter 3

Controversies related to the concept of Mind and Psychology

Controversies in relation to the mind is discussed here as the concept of mind significantly came into the picture in the discussions on Existence in the previous Chapter. Buddha had placed great emphasis on the mind. Of the five aggregates that the human being is composed of, four deal with the functions of the mind. Further, of the six agents ("salayathana") of perception one is the mind. Thus mind has several functions, apart from the functions involved in "vedana", "saññā", "saṅkāra" "viññāna" it has to function as one of the agents of perception as well. What is perceived by the mind when it functions as one of the six agents of perception are feelings.

From the Buddhist point of view consciousness is central to any discussion on mind and psychology. Consciousness is not a thing that is present somewhere in the body and come into function when something is perceived. It arises dependently in the process of cognition. Visual consciousness arises dependent on eye contact followed by feeling (vedana), sign (saññā) and volitional construction (saṅkāra). Further, consciousness does not exist as an independent phenomenon, it always occurs with the other four aggregates of the human form; "rupa, vedana, saññā, saṅkāra".

The essence of Buddhist psychology is the contention that objects which have no substantiality or self are made into either attractive or repulsive objects by the cognitive process involving the six agents ("salayatana") or organs of perception and the mental process involving "vedana, saññā, saṅkāra, viññāna". In this process the Self which comprises "I", "Me" and "Mine" expression has a vital role to play (Saratchandra, 1952, Nanananda 1971, Kalupahana, 1992,). In the absence of the expression of Self-ego psychological construction of attractive or repulsive objects out of what is perceived does not take place. An object of carnal desire, for instance, is a construct of the mind, there is nothing substantial in the object itself. For example a man might see a woman as an object of pleasure, while a tiger might see the woman as an object of food, whereas an Arahath may see her as a "panchaskanda" filled with impurities. While both the man and the tiger with Self-ego feelings of "I", "Me" and "Mine" have constructed two different objects of attachment out of the "panchaskanda" of the woman the Arahath whose ego is under control has seen the reality and remained unattached. The major Schools of Buddhism generally agree with this basic psychology of Early Buddhism

In early Buddhism three Pāli terms were used to refer to the mind; "citta", "mano" and "viññāna". There could be minor differences in the use of these words in different contexts. The word "viññāna" could mean the awareness of existence apart from its meaning in the context of the five aggregates. In the explanation of rebirth also the word "viññāna" is used. "Viññāna" may have another function, that of coordinating the functions of the other components in the mental function. The word "citta" is used in the description of death consciousness and rebirth linking consciousness ("cuti-citta", "patisandi-citta"). The word "mano" is used to refer to the mind when it functions as one of the six sense organs ("salayatana").

Volitional construction or dispositions (saṅkāra) is the most dynamic of the five aggregates. Its nature and intensity could vary depending on the kind of feeling that the object generates. The object could generate pleasure, sorrow or neutral feelings. If it is pleasure the percipient may want to be attached to the object, if it is sorrow a repulsive response may be the result and if it is neutral there may not be any response. Here neutral feeling doesn't mean that the percipient has realized the reality, i.e. that the object has nothing substantial or self, but there is indecision regarding whether the object would give happiness or sorrow (Karunadasa, 2013).

A discussion on Buddhist psychology and the mind is incomplete without reference to Abhidhamma. Theravāda Abhidhamma attempts to systematize the Buddha's teachings about the dynamics of moment-to-moment experience as it unfolds in the stream of consciousness. In the Abhidhammic analysis of the Five Aggregates ("Panchaskanda"), the Six Agents ("Salayatana") and the Eighteen Elements ("Dhatus") the mind which is the major component is further analyzed. The five aggregates for example are further analysed on the basis of various considerations, for example all the functional components of visual perception are further divided according to whether they are pleasant, unpleasant or neutral. Similarly all other aggregates are subdivided repeatedly until they cannot be analysed any further (Karunadasa, 2013).

Sarvāstivāda theory on mind did not differ very much from that of Early Buddhism. However they had different views in regard to its analysis in the Abhidhamma. The Abhidhamma of the Theravādins had 82 Dahammas while the Sarvāsthavāda Abhidhamma had 75. The details are given below;

	Theravāda	Sarvāstivāda
Citta	01	01
Cetasika	52	46
Rupa	28	11
"Citta viprautta sanscara"	--	14
Unconditioned/ Nibbāna	01	03
Total	82	75

As one can see of the four groups in Theravāda and five groups in Sarvāstivāda three in the former and four in the latter are concerned with the mind. This is in keeping with the theory on the five aggregates ("panchaskanda") in Early Buddhism where the emphasis was on the mind in comparison to the physical body. Of the 82 Dhammas 54 were in the domain of the mind in the Theravāda while in Sarvāstivāda 64 out of 75 were concerned with the mind. If proportions are considered a larger proportion is allocated to the mind in Sarvāstivāda compared to Theravāda.

Sarvāsthivādins were keen on the Abhidhamma and had very profound discourses on it. Apart from the difference in numbers the Sarvāstivāda had an extra group of Dhammas, 14 in number called "Citta viprautta sanscara". One of these Dhammas called "prapthi" has binding properties, for instance the ability to bind greed or aversion with the individual who perceives. There is also another opposing Dhamma called "aprapthi" which has the ability to break such bonds. The process where one "cetasika" declines and another arises is thus facilitated by these "prapthi" and "aprapthi" Dhammas. In Theravāda Abhidhamma this process is carried out by "bavanga-citta" (Nanayakkara, 2003) .

Sautrāntikavadins did not believe in the importance of Abhidhamma. They criticised Sarvasthivadin's attitude towards Abhidhamma. Only the "sūthras" were important to them and not the "sāsthras" which was another term for Abhidhamma. Therefore they did not analyse mind and matter into Dhammas. In their doctrines there was no reference to "vedana", "saññā", in the analysis of the functioning of the mind. They said these are manifestations of "chethana" and that "viññāna" was the main pervasive phenomenon which travelled from one birth to the next carrying all good and bad "karma". Their theory of existence, which we have discussed in the previous chapter, created a problem for the perception of objects by the mind. If objects arise and disappear without time for existence how would the system of perception function? What would be the impact of this on the psychology central to Buddhism that involves the function of "sañkāra" or volitional construction which creates objects of attachment or aversion out of unsubstantial objects?

Sautrāntikavadins attempted to solve this problem by saying that when the perceptive organ establishes contact with the object, there forms a rudimentary portrayal of the object in the mind of the observer and this further develops into the image due to volitional construction. However they accepted the theory of reality of the Theravāda and Sarvāstivāda.

Mahāyāna accepts the basic Theravāda concepts like "thri-lakhana" and Four Noble Truths but differ in the concepts of Buddhahood and the method of attaining enlightenment. In its early major works like "Astasahsrikaprññāparamitha" Mahāyāna attempts to refute the substantialist, absolutist concepts of Sarvāstivāda and Sautrāntika. These "sūthra" put forward the "śūnya" theory to disprove the substantialist ideas. Analysis of the mind and psychology were developed in its two major branches, Madhayamaka and Yogācāra.

The school of Madhayamaka Buddhism concentrated on the "śūnya" concept and it was applied in the theory of perception, but there was no emphasis on volitional construction ("sañkāra"). What is perceived exists in a state of "śūnya" and the mind that perceives the object also exists in a state of "śūnya".

The theory of perception that Yogācāra puts forward is somewhat similar to the one espoused by Sautrāntika where a rudimentary portrayal of the object occurs as the object arises and disappears. Mahāyāna and its branches had come under the influence of Sautrāntikavadins whose nihilistic ideas may have impressed the "śūnya" theorists of Mahāyāna.

However Yogācāra had a much more complex theory regarding the nature of "viññāna" (consciousness). Yogācāra theorists had analysed the consciousness into eight components as follows; the aspects of the consciousness concerned with the six agents ("salayatana" consisting of the five organs of perception and mind), the mind that contains defilements and an eighth called the "alaya-viññāna". These eight components are not discrete entities but comprise the evolution of consciousness. This was a theory formulated by Vasubandu. All the "kusala-akusala" karma are carried in the "alaya-viññāna". This matter would be discussed in detail in Chapter 24 on Idealism.

Buddhist psychology is based on Buddha's preaching on the functioning of the mind, particularly its tendency, due to Self-ego (expression of "I", "Me", "Mine"), to volitionally construct objects of attachment or aversion out of things which have no substance to warrant such an action. Whether this thesis had any impact on the two schools of Mahāyāna is not clear. How the "śūnyathavada" of Madhyamaka viewed the psychology of Early Buddhism and whether it adopted the theory to suit its philosophy is not clear. Yogācāra had developed an idealism out of the No-self theory of Early Buddhism and whether it could accommodate the psychological considerations is also debatable.

Vedic scripture describes mind as constituted of five components; "manas, ahankara, citta, buddhi and atman". These components cannot be further reduced to gross elements. Functionally the "manas" collect sensary impressions that come from the sense perception of sight, sound, smell, taste and touch. "Ahankara" is responsible for the feeling of "I" and taking perceptions to a subjective center and making them "personal". After this the "buddhi", the intelect component evaluate the perceptions that has been made "personal" and make decisions regarding them. The "citta" is the repository of memories but it also functions as the creater of primitive urges and emotions based on memory in relation to what is perceived. Atman is at the center of this complex and is nothing but the Self and is the Brahman within too (Subash Kak, 2016).

The process of perception in the Veda as described above has some similarity with that of Early Buddhism. Functions of "Ahankāra" seems to be similar to those of "Sañkāra" a functional component of mind. But "Ahankāra" is considered to be same as Ego. In Buddhism Self and Ego are synonyms. In the Veda they are separate entities. However the presence of Self in the mind complex as a permanent entity and its equation with Atman and the final goal, Brhaman, are anathematic to Buddhist thought.

Vedic and Hindu theory on mind and psychology is based on the metaphysical concept ofā a creator god which is inextricably linked with Self. Whereas in Buddhism there is no creator god, the Self is considered an intrusion and is undesirable and its elimination is required for liberation.

Chapter 4

Controversies related to Knowledge

Theory of knowledge is an important consideration for any religion. How the knowledge with regard to the doctrines was derived is crucial. Moreover in Buddhism the state of the mind when it has achieved the final goal is a form of higher knowledge. Further the human beings may have several sources of knowledge and these may have been interpreted differently according to the basic beliefs and tenets of religions and philosophies. For instance theistic religions may claim that knowledge in their scriptures come from a divine source. In this context it is significant that the word Veda means knowledge and Hindus believe Veda has a divine origin.

Historically in India, perhaps parallel with the happenings in Greece, in the Middle and Late Upanishad period (600 BCE – 100 CE) intense interest was developed regarding knowledge. Questions started to be raised with regard to the source, nature, scope and validity of knowledge. This resulted in the emergence of several philosophical traditions such as Scepticism, Materialism, and Theism. Several religious philosophies such as Ajivikism, Jainism, Buddhism and Hinduism also were developed during this time (Jayatilake, 1975).

Some Sceptics thought gaining knowledge of the world is not possible. Theists were of the opinion that knowledge was divine in origin. In the Brahmanas, which are Vedic texts, it is categorically stated that the scriptures are based on the knowledge that comes from a divine origin.

During this period Materialism grew in intense opposition to Vedic tradition. However Materialism may have had its origins in the Early Upanishad thought. The view that self is identical to the body which the Materialists subscribed to may have had its beginnings in the Early Upanishads. Materialism and its views on knowledge have had a profound impact on the growth of Buddhist philosophy. However Buddha had attempted to avoid the extremist views of Materialists.

Buddha wanted to avoid extremist viewpoints on life and the universe and therefore had to adopt a middle path regarding the source of knowledge. He had found the higher knowledge of enlightenment by his own effort without any help from divine powers. There were in his time Theists like Makkhali Gōsāla and Brahmins of the Vedic tradition who said their knowledge was of divine origin and Sceptics like Sanjaya Bellattiputta who said no one could hold firm views on after-life, moral responsibility and ultimate salvation (Jayatilake, 1975).

Such a middle path for Buddha was possible for he relied on himself to gain knowledge and his method was based on experience. In the "Sangarava sutta" (Samyutta Nikāya) Buddha says there are three methods of deriving knowledge that teachers and philosophers of his day employ. Firstly there are the Revelationists who believe in revelation of knowledge by divine powers. Secondly there are the rational metaphysicians who depend on reason for knowledge. Thirdly there are those who derive their knowledge by sensory and extra-sensory perception. And Buddha said he belongs in the third group. This is very significant as Buddha confirms that he is an empiricist. He also cautions that one has to be very careful in being reliant on rational thinking alone for it could lead to metaphysical thought without a basis on experience.

Buddha was unequivocal in expressing his stand on epistemology when he preached to the Kālāmas (Kessaputtiya sutta, Aṅguttara Nikāya). He advised them not to depend mainly on the sources of knowledge recommended during that time. He said that they should not be led by scripture, hearsay, a-priori reasoning, or out of respect for the recluse who preaches, but by their own examination and then come to a realization whether or not something is bad and would cause suffering.

Scepticism which vigorously questioned and criticized the Veda had an influence on Early Buddhism. The Sceptics were of the view that knowledge of the world is not possible. They may have come to this conclusion because the methods of gaining knowledge were of a contradictory nature to one another. While the view of Sceptics cast doubts about knowledge itself there were thinkers who claimed omniscience. The leader of Jainism, Mahawira was one such person and also Purāna Kassapa and Makhali Gōsāla belonged in this group. Skeptics had developed thorough arguments against these claims. Their argument basically was that human intellect was limited and therefore omniscience is not possible within that limited intellect. All metaphysical views based on such omniscience cannot be true for even the methods used to arrive at such views were contradictory to one another. No new theory could be true as it is bound to contradict an existing view and therefore knowledge of the world was not possible. This was their scepticism (Jayatilake, 1963).

Buddha in the Brhammajala sutta (Diga Nikāya) recognizes several types of sceptics. One type is those who wriggle out of a question without answering it one way or the other because they are ignorant. There are other Sceptics who believe that knowledge was not only impossible but was a danger to moral development and salvation. Some modern day thinkers are of the view that such sceptic views may have influenced the occurrence of Indeterminate Questions ("avyakatas") in Buddhism.

According to Brhammajāla sutta there were other sceptics who said they did not pass judgment on any issue because they did not want to engage in arguments and be subjected to interrogation that may cause worry to themselves. Further Brhammajāla sutta says there are other Sceptics who due to their stupidity did not give definitive answer to any question. Sanjaya Bellattiputta was supposed to have belonged to this group of Sceptics. Both Samannapahāla and Brhammajāla suttas have spoken about the stupidity of Sanjaya. However

Ven. Sāriputta and Ven. Moggallāna the chief disciples of Buddha had been pupils of Sanjaya before they were converted to Buddhism. It was Sanjaya who developed the four-fold logic that takes into consideration the possibility of four alternatives regarding any issue which could be as follows; 'there is', 'there is not', 'there is and there is not', 'neither there is nor there is not'. This four-fold logic has been adopted by Buddha in his explanation of the question whether the Arahath exists after death. Nāgārjuna also uses this method to nullify various views in his "Mulamadhyamaka-karikā".

Another group of religious teachers who contributed to the development of epistemology during Buddha's time was the Ājīvikas. Makkhali Gōsāla was believed to be their leader. The Ājīvikas may have been influenced both by the rational tradition of the Early Upanishads as well as intuitive methods of gaining knowledge of the Late Upanishad thinkers. Buddha had not relied heavily on reason or intuition as means of gaining knowledge. Further the Ājīvikas had a three-fold logic as against the four-fold system adopted by Sceptics and Buddhists. The three-fold logic analysed all phenomena on the basis of the following alternatives; "there is", "there is not", and "there is and there is not". If this analysis is applied to "being" for instance the three alternative possibilities would be "being", "non-being" and "being and non-being". If it is applied to "world" the analysis would have the following alternative possibilities, "world", "non-world" and "world and non-world". This shows that Ājīvikas had a three-fold mode of predication. Predication would mean the act of making something the subject or the predicate of a proposition. When applied to the subject of "world" there would be three possibilities as shown above. They also had a three-fold set of standpoints as follows, substantial, the modal and the dual. When this set of standpoints is applied to the subject of soul there would be the substantial which is "soul", the modal which is "non-soul" and the dual which is "both soul and non-soul" (Jayatilake, 1963).

At this stage it may be worthwhile to see what Buddha thought about the Ājīvikas. Buddha had rejected the views of Ājīvikas on several subjects like soul, survival etc. In the Brhammajāla sutta Buddha speaks about the epistemology of the Ājīvikas. He says by mere reasoning higher knowledge cannot be gained. Further, reasoning would lead to speculation and arrival at knowledge not supported by facts.

Jainism was another religious philosophy that dates back to pre-Buddhist times. However its texts have appeared after Buddhist Pāli "suttas" and therefore one cannot say with conviction that Jaina thought had influenced Buddhism. Yet the presence of several distinctly Jainist tenets in Buddhism makes it possible that there had been inputs from Jainism into Buddhism and perhaps vice versa too. The methods of gaining knowledge according to Jainism are perception, which could be either sensory or extra-sensory, and inference and scripture. Extra-sensory perception included omniscience. Buddha too employed extra-sensory methods to gain knowledge but he did not believe in omniscience which is clearly stated in the Tevijja-Vacchagotta-sutta (Majjima Nikāya) thus taking the opposite position to that of Mahavir the leader of Jainism.

Jainism also had a system of logic which propounded seven alternate possibilities starting from the most general to the most specific. Buddha was not interested in such an elaborate set of possibilities for every phenomenon. He instead used the "chatuskoti" or four-fold method for logical analysis of important phenomena such as whether the Arahath exists or not after death,

whether the Universe is infinite or not etc.

Thus the contemporary religious thinkers of Buddha could be categorized into three groups according to their epistemological theories;

The Traditionalists who derived their knowledge from scripture. These included the Brahmins who depended mainly on the Vedas.

The Rationalists who derived their knowledge from reasoning and speculation. Sceptics, Materialists and most of Ājīvikas fell into this group.

The Experientialists who depended on personal experience for gaining knowledge. Jains and some Ājīvikas belong to this group.

Buddha agreed with this classification and identified himself with the third category. In the address to Kālāmas Buddha had mentioned tradition or dependence on scripture as the first out of ten methods of gaining knowledge that should be avoided. Six out of these ten are related to authority as a means of gaining knowledge pointing to the need to consider it in detail probably because the belief of divine origin of knowledge was something that Buddha wanted to eliminate from the society. In this regard an important consideration is the fact that the Vedas have been given a divine origin. God Prajapati is considered as the creator of the Vedas in the earliest phase of Upanishads. Later Upanishads are attributed to Brahma.

Buddha in his battle against Vedic thought, particularly the well-entrenched beliefs in a creator god, seems to have realized the need to refute the claim that there could be knowledge that comes from divine sources. In Buddhism even clairvoyance and retro-cognition are considered not as mystic or metaphysical skills but as functions that are possible in the totally purified mind. Therefore such extrasensory perceptions are considered to be empirical in nature.

Kālāma Sutta (Aṅguttara Nikāya) gives a comprehensive list of forms of knowledge that are based on authority or scripture said to be derived from divine sources. Buddhists have criticized all these in a thorough manner. The details of all that criticism cannot be mentioned here as it is beyond the scope of this work. However it should be mentioned that omniscience which the scriptures claim as a source of knowledge has received special and heavy criticism in the Kalama Sutta (Añguttara Nikāya). The list has ten types of methods of gaining knowledge and six of them are on the basis of authority or scripture, the remaining four are claims to knowledge on the basis of reasoning.

Buddha said he does not belong to the class of teachers who are reasoners and speculators. Of the four grounds that form the basis for gaining knowledge by reason and speculation the method known as 'takka' was the main group. 'Takka' means adhering to logic. In Buddha's time there were debaters who had no view of their own but engaged in the attempt to disprove views of others employing the method of 'takka'. Of the sixty two views that were refuted in the Brahmmajala sutta four were based on 'takka'. Sutta Nipāta (Khuddaka Nikāya) speaks about these debaters and identifies sixty three theories authored by them. Their method of gaining knowledge was reason and metaphysical speculation which the Buddha rejected in the Brhammajala-sutta (Dīgha Nikāya).

Some of the subjects debated by these Samanas and Brhamins included the questions left unanswered by the Buddha which are called "avyakatas". As the questions left unanswered is relevant to a discussion of knowledge in Buddhism these are listed below.
1, The world is eternal.
2. The world is not eternal
3. The world is finite
4. The world is infinite
5. The soul is identical with the body
6. The soul is different from the body
7. The thathāgatha exists after death
8. The thathāgatha does not exist after death
9. The thathāgatha does and does not exist after death
10. The Thathāgatha neither exists nor does not exist after death

It may be interesting to see who attempted to debate these subjects and what were their opinion on them as Buddha had avoided answering questions arising from these debates. One group was the Materialists. They have argued that the world is finite in space and time because the observable world is finite. Further the Materialists did not differentiate between soul and body and they said those two were identical. Purāna Kassapa said that with his infinite knowledge he could perceive a finite world. Commentary to Brhammajāla-sutta says Purāna Kassapa's view is an erroneous yogic experience. The Jains had a different point of view. They were of the opinion that the world was infinite (Jayatilalake, 1963).

Brhammajāla-sutta (Dhiga Nikāya) identifies three groups of Eternalists who argued that the soul was separate from the body. Pakudha Kaccāyana who was a thinker who attempted to comprehend man and the world by classifying them into discrete categories also subscribed to this view. Most of the schools which held that the soul was separate from the body and was eternal also thought that the world was eternal. There was nobody who thought that the soul was separate from the body and eternal but the world was finite. There seems to be some value in such thinking because the soul cannot be eternal in a finite world.

The idea that Thathāgatha or saint existed after death was held by those who said soul was eternal. Early Upanishads subscribed to this viewpoint. Materialists of course denied the possibility of a Thathāgatha or saint and therefore the question of the existence of the saint after death may not arise for them. The view that the saint 'does and does not' exist after death was in agreement with the philosophy of Ājīvikas who spoke about 'being and non-being' in a doctrinal sense. Sceptics obviously would agree with the idea that the saint neither exists nor does not exist as they were of the opinion that nothing could be known (Jayatilake, 1963).

It may be relevant at this stage to discuss why Buddha did not answer these ten questions. In this regard there are different points of view, for instance, Theravādins Thathāgatha and Mahāyānists hold different views on this issue. Here it may be relevant to state that Buddha identified four kinds of questions as follows; 1) A question that has to be answered unilaterally, 2) A question that has to be answered analytically, 3) A question that has to be answered with another question and 4) A question that has to be a set aside (Jayatilake, 1963, Tilakaratne, 1993).

An example of a question that needs to be answered with a unilateral answer would be "Are all conditioned phenomena impermanent?" Here the answer has to be "Yes they are". There cannot be an ambiguous answer to this question. A question that needs to be answered analytically would be "Is it the monk or the layman who attains what is right?" Here the answer cannot categorically say either the monk or the layman would attain what is right because it is he who has a good conduct who will attain what is right. "Is consciousness same as a person's soul or are they separate?" would be a question that has to be answered with a counter question. Here the counter question would be "What do you understand by soul?" because according to different thinkers the meaning of the word soul may be different.

That brings us to the unanswered questions. These questions are not unanswerable due to a lack of knowledge necessary to answer the question. Rather these questions are undetermined in the sense it is not known whether the questions could be answered. These questions cannot be answered unilaterally, analytically or by raising another question. That is the position Theravāda Buddhism takes on the issue of unanswered questions (Tilakaratne, 1993).

As mentioned earlier these questions have been debated before Buddha's time and it would have been the practice that these ten questions were presented to all religious leaders during those times. It may be asked what is the reason for the existence of these questions. Ven.Mahāmoggallāna explains that they arise due to the psychological need caused by the self-ego that resides in the mind of those who raise these questions. Another reason why these questions were not answered was that Buddha thought, as he explained to Malunkyaputta, these questions were not relevant to the noble quest of finding a solution to the problem of suffering and attaining Nibbāna (Culamalunkya-sutta, Majjima Nikāya). On this occasion he brings in to the discussion the famous parable of the poisoned arrow. Further the Buddha was of the opinion that these questions are a "wilderness of theoretical views, a vacillation of theoretical views, a bondage of theoretical views" with which the Buddha did not wish to get involved because that would lead to attachment or repugnance and to greed and aversion that Buddha had battled hard to get rid of (Tilakaratne, 1993).

However Transcendentalists and Māhāyana philosophers who attempt to elevate the historical Buddha, his Dhamma and Nibbāna to a transcendental position say that Buddha did not answer these questions because they cannot be explained by the words in the language in use. In other words it is unexplainable as all transcendental phenomena are, for example God. Silence is considered to be an expression of ineffability or unexplainability. However Buddha had not said that these questions are ineffable as could be seen in the above discussion. This subject would be further discussed in Chapter 18 on Nibbāna.

According to Udāna (Khuddaka Nikāya), apart from these ten questions, there were sixteen other theories that were debated during Buddha's time. These may be classified into four groups according to the topics discussed; 1) The duration of the soul and the world, 2) The cause of the soul and the world, 3) The duration of the experiences of pleasure and pain as well as the soul and the world, 4) The cause of the experiences of pleasure and pain, the soul and the world. The logical formation of the sixteen theories in these four groups were similar to that of the ten topics mentioned earlier and appears to be the views that were debated at that time. For example the theses developed under the topic "The duration of the soul and the world" are as follows; a) The soul and the world are eternal, b) The soul and the world are not eternal, c) The soul and the world are both eternal and not eternal, d) The soul and the world are neither eternal nor not eternal. The theses developed under the other three subjects were similar. It could be seen that these theories and the theses are based on reason as the method of gaining and creating knowledge. Further it is seen that the logic employed is the four fold scheme that Buddha also used (Jayatilake, 1963).

The Pancattaya sutta (Discourse on Five Bases, Majjima Nikāya) says that it is not possible to have a perfect knowledge of any theory by reason or upon reflection on them, apart from believing in them out of faith or authority. In the absence of a perfect knowledge a person may acquire a partial knowledge but it would only be an entanglement ("upādāna") of that person. Thus it is seen that one cannot have perfect knowledge of a proposition or theory by the consideration of some reason or by the conviction derived by merely reflecting on it. Belief on the basis of these two kinds of rational reflection is considered as similar to knowledge gained by faith, authority and other subjective considerations such as likes and dislikes. In the Canky Sutta (Majjima Nikāya) it is said that such knowledge would have a two-fold result, that is, they may be proved either true or false in this life itself and that even theories well reflected upon may prove to be false while those not so well reflected upon may prove to be true. Therefore reason could be considered as not a satisfactory method of gaining reliable knowledge (Jayatilake, 1963).

In Buddhism analysis played an important role in arriving at perfect knowledge in certain instances. Buddha used the analytical method in answering certain questions where categorical assertion was not indicated. In certain instances it is not possible to say whether a statement is true or false without analysing the facts available, clearing up ambiguities and making qualifications, but there may be other instances where the Buddha gives a categorical answer. Jainism had a somewhat similar point of view but was different in that the Jains refused to make a categorical judgement on any proposition. This matter is related to the Buddha's way of answering questions and it is discussed above.

A good example where the Buddha does not give a categorical answer is the following; Buddha was asked to give a ruling whether the following statements are true or false; "The householder succeeds in attaining what is right" and "The monk does not succeed in attaining what is right". Buddha said whether or not each of these persons succeeds in attaining what is right depends on whether they are of good or bad conduct. Buddha had refused to make an absolutist judgment without making the necessary qualifications by an analysis of the issue.

Chapter 5

Controversies related to Buddhist Morals

Buddha's philosophy on most aspects of life, society, existence etc. has been influenced by his moral concerns. Whether one is to live as a laymen or a recluse moral behaviour was of importance. These morals for a lay person as well as for someone who has undertaken a greater commitment are of great importance in order to achieve their goals.

Three levels of moral practice is advised in Buddhism. The first level is meant for layman which would consist of virtues like the five precepts. There could be additional virtues up to eight or ten in number which could be practiced by someone committed to higher attainment of moral behaviour in preparation for the greater effort. The second level is the entry into the noble eight-fold path; it is more than the practice of virtues. Right view ("sammā ditti") and right conception ("sammā sañkālpa") have to be established at the very beginning. It is the right view that would show the path and therefore it has to be understood and adopted at the very beginning. Then the virtues practiced earlier such as right speech ("sammā vāchā"), right action ("sammā kammantha"), are to be continued to achieve freedom from physical and mental impurities. In the final stage concentration ("samādhi") and wisdom ("paññā") are achieved. Thus Buddhist morals have the goal of achieving a state beyond good and evil (Kalupahana, 1995).

It could be seen that morals that govern physical behavior are combined with those that aim to clean the mind. Good physical behaviour alone is meaningless without mental cleanliness and the latter cannot be achieved without the former. They complement each other.

Moral life in Buddhism is not just aimed at being good to oneself and to the society though the practice of Buddhist morals would have those benefits as well. Buddhist morals, however, have a greater purpose, that of achieving the final goal of freedom from suffering. Buddhist morals are designed to achieve detachment and get rid of defilements which are the cause of suffering. The defilements identified here are greed, aversion and ignorance (Premasiri, 1975).

In Buddhism the individual is responsible for the practice of morals. He must do it by his own effort. Though Buddha discovered the method to get rid of defilements he cannot make anybody else get rid of these defilements, he can only show the path.

Ancient Greek philosophers Socrates, Plato and Aristotle maintained that "virtue is happiness" (Sachs, 2001). Most of their pupils agreed with this point of view but there was disagreement regarding what is good. Aristotle has asserted that virtue requires habituation which requires law and law requires legislative art which finally depend on politics. It appears that according to Aristotle virtue and morals in the final analysis depend on politics. In this philosophy there doesn't seem to be a higher achievement than gentlemanliness. Unlike in Buddhism there is no attempt to rise above mere goodness.

These Greek philosophers were not bound by Christian theology. The latter holds the view that morals are divine commands. Morals are based on the Biblical pronouncements and have all powerful God as their source. Most of the theistic religions believe that morals are divine in origin.

According to Vedic texts morals have originated from Brahman. The word Brahman should not be confused with Brahma (Hindu God), Brahmana (Vedic texts) and Brahmin (a caste). Vedic Gods were upholders of morals. Moral life or Dharmic life evolved in Vedas and Upanishads which have a divine origin. This has resulted in the formulation of a set of morals consisting of the following five; non-violence ("ahimsā"), self-restraint ("dāma"), non-stealing ("asteya"), inner purity ("saucha") and truthfulness. According to Bhagavadgita these are not absolute and depending on the circumstances could be breached or set aside. For instance during a war started by a foolish person even killing would be allowed and would not have any karmic consequences. The Just War theory mentioned in Bagavadgita attempts to justify war as one's duty (Bagavadgita 1.38-39). In contrast the five precepts in Buddhism cannot be breached without invoking karmic consequences.

Hinduism identifies four goals that an individual must try to achieve which are known as "Purusārtha" which approximately means "soul's purpose". The four goals are as follows; 1) "Artha" which means material and monetary abundance, 2) "Kāma" which means enjoyment of music, dance and sex, 3) "Dharma" which means ethically and ritually correct life according to caste and state of life and 4) "Ashrama" which means renunciation and entering into a life of a recluse in the forest (Prasad, 2008). Most of these goals except "Ashrama" are different to the moral goals of Buddhism, particularly the goal known as "Kāma" which has enjoyment of sex as one of the good deeds worthy of being included as a goal and "Artha" which recommends material and monetary abundance to be accumulated in one's life. Even "Dharma" is based on caste and state of life; people belonging to low caste are expected to do their duty, even if it is niggardly, for caste is determined by God. In contrast Buddhism encourages people to strive and rise up in life irrespective of caste and origin of birth.

The Sceptics in Buddha's time, such as Sanjaya Bellattiputta, held the view that belief in after life, moral responsibility and ultimate salvation cannot be verified and therefore one cannot give any firm opinion about them. One cannot determine with certainty what is good and what is bad. They did not say there is nothing good or bad but that nobody could determine what is good and what is bad. Buddha in Brahmmajāla sutta (Dīgha

Nikāya) has called these Sceptics "eel wrigglers" who wriggle out of an issue without giving an opinion one way or the other.

Somewhat different were the Materialists like Ajita Kesakambala who said everybody terminate their existence at death and there is nothing that could be identified as good deeds or moral life that religions talk about. Purāna Kassapa who was a natural determinist, who believed that everything was determined by natural forces, was of the view that there was nothing good or evil. Niganta Nathaputta the founder of Jainism diplomatically said there is some truth in all these views (Jayatilake, 1963).

According to Ājīvikas there is no cause or basis for sins of living beings and also for their purity. All living beings are without power, strength, virtue or free will but they are the result of destiny and chance. Yet these Ājīvikas lived simple ascetic lives as though such living is good virtue (Jayatilake, 1963).

These views, to some degree, appear to be nihilistic where nobody is responsible for their actions and there is no retribution for misdeeds or merit for wholesome actions. On the contrary in Buddhism the principles that give guidance to moral life rule out a nihilistic approach to the practice of morals. The first principle in this regard is "kammavāda" which recognizes that there is causal relationship between the deed and the consequence, that there is a karmic link between actions and retribution or merit. The second principle is "kiriyavāda" which recognizes the need to do wholesome deeds and avoid doing unwholesome deeds because if one does wholesome deeds one's mind would be purified. Opposite view which the Materialists subscribed to would be that the mind need not be purified and that it is automaticaly purified. The third principle is "viriyavāda" which emphasizes the need for human effort to lead a moral life (Jayatilake, 1963). Thus effort is required in the Arya Astāngika Mārga which defines the moral path of Buddhism and which takes a person to the final goal, Nibbāna.

Though Buddhism recognizes a causal relation between action and its consequences, where good deeds bring about good results which the doer reaps it does not mean that Buddhism is deterministic in the absolute sense. Absolute Karmic determinism is not accepted in Buddhism. How the concept of karma functions is clearly described in Buddhism. This will be discussed in Chapter 6 on Karma.

Mahāyāna which has transcendental features like eternal Buddhahood and metaphysical concepts like Bōdhisattva, had to have differences in its moral precepts and practices also compared to Theravāda or Early Buddhism. Mahāyāna ethics are based on what are called "three kinds of pure precepts"; 1) to prevent all evil, 2) to cultivate all good, 3) to save all beings. Apparently these precepts may be common to all religions but the third precept has a deeper meaning and implications, it is functional in relation to the Bodhisattva, where the latter has sacrificed his/her opportunity to achieve Buddhahood and remains in society to help other sufferers to achieve salvation. An early lay Mahāyāna text, the Updsaka Sūtra gives a good account of this precept. It gives supremacy to compassionate action in society rather than monastic spiritual attainment and it asserts that helping others out of compassion is the highest practice and the best way to attain enlightenment.

It is the Bodhisattva's selfless compassion coupled with wisdom (praññā) and Skillful Means ("upāya") that compel and help him to remain in the world to aid other beings. Bodhisattvas could descend to hell to work for the benefit of dwellers therein. At this stage it is relevant to mention here that the Bohisattva concept in Mahāyāna could have been developed due to the influence of Hinduism. It was not a feature of early Mahāyāna, it was introduced later. This concept would have arisen due to the influence of "Bakthimārga" and "Viññānavada". "Bakthimārga" was introduced into Mahāyāna due to the influence of Hinduism. "Bakthimārga" is the Mahāyāna alternative to "Ñana-mārga" (Path of Wisdom) the path to Nibbāna in Theravāda. These matters will be discussed in detail in Chapters 17 and 18 on Bodhisattva and Nibbāna respectively.

Mahāyāna has ten "paramittās", which define its moral practice, comparable to the Arya Astāngika Mārga. Six of them are similar to the items in the Arya Astāngika Mārga. The ten paramittas are as follows; "dāna, seela, ksanthi (patience), vīrya, samadhi, prañña, upāya, prānadhāna (vow), bala (strength), jhana (knowledge). This matter will be discussed in detail in Chapter 16 and 17.

Nāgārjuna had written a comprehensive treatise on Buddhist morals, titled "Suhrllekha" (Letter to a friend), addressed to his friend the Satavahana king Gautamiputra Satakarni. It deals with every aspect of morals that Buddha had spoken about. Though Nāgārjuna is identified as the author of the Madhayamaka School of Mahāyāna this treatise does not contain any of the moral concepts or precepts found in Mahāyāna such as the "three kinds of pure precepts" or the ten pāramittās. Kalupahana (2008) says Nāgārjuna's treatise on morals is the best discussion of the subject ever made in the East or the West. He is also of the opinion that the Sinhala poem on morals, "LowedAsaṅgarava", has been crafted on the same model as Nāgārjuna's "Suhrllekha".

In any discussion of morals free will has to be taken into consideration. Some Western thinkers are of the opinion that Buddha did not give a definite view on the question of free will (Jayatilake, 1963). On the contrary what Buddha said was that human will is not free because it is entangled in defilements. The mind is controlled by greed, aversion and ignorance and therefore is not free to act on its own. The essence of human action is contained in "cetāna" (volition) a functional component of the mind, it is "cetāna" that decides the karmic consequence and not just the act. Buddha had used three terms "citta", "mano" and "cetāna" to define different functions of the mind. However "cetāna" cannot be equated to free will for it is not free but controlled by defilements.

Further, there were determinists like Purāna Kassapa and also Ājīvikas who said human beings had no free will because human action was pre-determined by natural forces. Indeterminists on the other hand were of the opinion that human beings are completely free to do as they like. Determinism and its relationship to Buddhism will be discussed in Chapter 6 on Karma.

There is also the consideration that if there is no free will a person cannot be held responsible for his actions. If the action is determined by some other agent the doer is not responsible for the action. Hence moral responsibility would be a problem for determinists. The concept of no-self poses a similar problem for Buddhism. Buddhism attempts to resolve this issue by its Theory of Karma. This aspect also will be discussed in Chapter 6 on Karma.

Chapter 6

Controversies related to Karma and Rebirth

Buddhist theory on Karma has to be considered together with its concept on Rebirth for Karma has a bearing on Rebirth. Karmic consequence of acts committed in the present birth can manifest in the next birth. How this is possible and how it happens have to be explained. The fact that Buddhism does not believe in a Self and that No-self theory is one of its key features create problems for Buddhism in its theorizing of both Karma and Rebirth. If there is no permanent Self that travels from one birth to the next how could there be continuity between births? And who receives merit or demerit in the next birth for actions committed in the present birth? These questions have been considered in Chapter 1 on "Anicca, Dukha, Anatta" and would be further discussed here.

Buddhist theory on Karma is different from that of the Vedic tradition, Jainism, and Ajivikism. The word karma has been used in the Vedas. But in Vedic tradition karma is linked to a permanent self which is also responsible for rebirth. The self that is present in the human form and is a permanent feature accounts for rebirth as well as karmic consequence. In Hinduism which has derived its philosophy from the Upanishads the self is called Atman which dwells within the human being. Atman is responsible for rebirth and also for carrying across all karmic actions to the next birth.

Atman is defined in Hinduism as the self-existent essence of human beings, the core consciousness which is different from the ever-evolving individual embodied in material reality and characterized by ego, I-ness, Me-ness, and all the defiling "kleshas" ; habits, prejudices, desires, impulses, delusions, pleasures, suffering, etc. Embodied personality changes with time but not the Atman. Atman is permanent and travels from one birth to the next in samsara.

However some of the schools of Hinduism that developed in the post Upanishad time had different interpretations of the karma-rebirth theory. Some of these schools and their views on karma are as follows; Nyaya School thought that karma and rebirth were central to the doctrines. Vaisesika School thought karma of past lives was not important. Samkhya School was of the opinion that karma is of secondary importance. Mimamsa School opined that karma had a negligible role in human life. Yoga School thought that karma from past lives is of secondary importance and that one's behaviour and psychology in current life is what has consequence and leads to entanglements. Vedanta School says karma and rebirth are not derived from reality and is invalid as it fails to explain evil and inequality. This is not an exhaustive list as there are several sub-schools with different interpretations (C Sharma, 1997).

In Jainism a Soul is present in living as well as non-living objects. It is liable to change, it may expand and contract and at death it contracts into a small "seed" which gives rise to a new life. Soul or "jiva" exists eternally in the āuniverse and they can neither be created nor destroyed. Rebirth in Jainism is made possible by "jiva". Karmic consequence is also made possible by "jiva". Intention ("cetnā") was not given validity in the operation of karma, it is mainly the action that decides whether there would be karmic consequence and in this sense it is a deterministic theory of karma. Action and nothing else decides the consequence (Dundas, 2002). In Buddhism however "cetanā" is the deciding factor in karmic consequence.

Ājīvikas led by Makhali Gosāla were absolute determinists and they said the karma-ethical theory is not acceptable. However they believed in the existence of a Soul and they called it Atman which was different from that of Hinduism. While the Soul in Hinduism had no form that in Ajivikism has material form which could help in meditation and which passes through many births and finally arrives at pre-destined "Nirvāna" (A Basham, 1951).

Karma in Buddhism has been misunderstood due to the presence of all these above mentioned theories. Some commentators say there is no difference between these theories and the Theory of Karma in Buddhism. Further Buddhism on account of its Theory of Karma has been accused of being fatalistic. Others have attempted to interpret Buddhist Theory of Karma in terms of social or biological inheritance of human being.

Before the mechanism of Karma and Rebirth is discussed how Buddha gained knowledge of Karma and Rebirth has to be considered. Buddha did not claim omniscience and he depended on experience to gain knowledge of everything he preached on including karma and rebirth. He did not arrive at this knowledge by pure reason. In his endevour to attain Nibbāna he had acquired the power of retro-cognition ("pubbenivāsanusati) and clairvoyance ("dibbacakkhu"). It is these forms of higher knowledge that enabled Buddha to verify the operation of karma and rebirth. In the Mahasihanada Sutta (Majjima Nikāya) he describes how he tested the Theory of Karma and Rebirth. He describes five destinies where a person could be born in his journey through samsara; 1) The purgatory ("niraya"), 2) The animal 'womb' ("tiracchanayoni"), 3) The sphere of the departed spirits ("pettivisaya"), 4) The human world ("manussaloka") and 5) The world of gods ("devaloka"). When he observes a person, going by his karmic constitution, he could see where that person is going to be born after his death. Later after the person's death Buddha could observe the person born in the destination that Buddha perceived before his death.

One may ask the question is there any evidence to prove that retro-cognition and clairvoyance are possible. The Sceptics and perhaps also the Materialists may say these forms of knowledge are not verifiable and therefore are not valid. The spiritualist might say such claims are mystical and not based on experience. Buddha avoids these extreme views and takes the middle path and he uses whatever knowledge that are available through such means for pragmatic reasons (Kalupahana 2009). Moreover it is not only Buddha who used such means of gaining knowledge but also all Arahaths too had the ability to gain knowledge by these methods.

In Buddhism intention ("cetanā") is central in the mechanics of karma. In the absence of intention there is no consequence due to karma. But intention alone cannot result in consequences except in "mano-kamma" or an act committed by mind such as hatred. There are three types of actions that could result in karmic consequence; 1) acts committed by physical behavior ("kāya-kamma"), 2) acts commited by verbal utterance ("vaci-kamma"), 3) acts committed by mind ("mano-kamma"). These acts could be pleasant, unpleasant or neutral and the consequence would depend on the type. Pleasant acts would result in pleasant consequences and unpleasant acts in unpleasant consequences. Apart from "Cetanā" or intention several other factors have to be fulfilled for a physical or verbal act to be a karmic act with possible consequence. For instance the act of killing would be an act of karma if there is 1) a living being 2) awareness of such a living being 3) the intention of killing 4) means employed to kill and 5) the death of the living being. If a living being is killed due to the action of a person but there was no intention then the offence is one of negligence only (Jayatilake, 1975).

Further, karmic action does not have the sole power of determining the consequence. Several factors operate in the mechanism of determining whether a particular act is to have a consequential effect and karma is just one of these factors. These are natural laws that operate in the universe and laws of karma are part of the system. These laws could be listed as follows; 1) physical laws ("utu-niyāma"), 2) biological laws ("bija-niyāma), 3) psychological laws, 4) karmic laws ("kamma-niyāma) and 5) laws regarding spiritual phenomena ("dhamma-niyāma").

The Buddhist Theory of Karma is neither determinist nor indeterminist. Karma alone does not determine the consequence; it is part of a set of laws that would finally decide on the consequence. Further the intention ("cetanā") is given prime importance, in fact Buddha has said karma is intention. The other distinguishing feature is the total absence of a self or anything like it that travels across births carrying the information about the person's karmic acts. These features make the Buddhist Theory of Karma totally different to those of other religions and life philosophies that were in vogue at that time. Those other theories appear to be metaphysical compared to the Buddhist theory. However the mechanism of transmission of karmic accumulation to the next birth has to be explained. As this is linked to the Theory of Rebirth it is discussed below.

Survival after death had been a subject of interest from early times both in the East as well as the West. Egyptians (3000 BC) believed that the dead would continue to exist in a world very similar to the one they lived in before death. But entry into this world was not guaranteed and one has to battle through many evil forces. Therefore one has to prepare for this battle by acquiring funerary items etc. Mummification is based on such beliefs (Siegfried, 1960).

However the discussion on life after death had never been as intense as it was in India during Buddha's time. There were so many different theories and beliefs and also practices concerned with guaranteeing a good life after death. Some believe that Buddha adopted these theories and accepted them uncritically. This may not be correct for there were so many theories as shown in the Brahammajāla sutta (Dīgha Nikāya) and these were criticized by Buddha. These theories had considered four after death possibilities and explanations as follows; A) survival as discarnate spirit, B) annihilation at death, C) unable to give satisfactory answer, D) rebirth and life continues in this world or some other similar world. There may be several variants of each of these theories. For instance there are thirty two variants in relation to survival as discarnate spirit (Jayatilake, 1975). It is beyond the scope of this book to examine all these theories.

Vedas in its early texts speak about life after death. According to Rgveda Yama was the first human to die and he remains as Lord of the Fathers. It should be the wish of everybody to be born in the world of the Fathers. Similarly other Vedic texts have spoken about life after death with such higher beings like Prajapati, God and Brahmma. These theories spoke about one life after death. Repeated death and intermediate existence was considered in later Upanishads (Gavin Flood, 1996).

According to Vedic texts repeated birth could be avoided by doing good deeds like sacrifice and offering of food and milk. Good moral life could result in birth in a womb of a Brahmin, Kshatriya or Vaisya while evil deeds could result in birth in the womb of dog, swine or outcaste. Thus morality was connected with reincarnation in the later Upanishads. Though this has a similarity with Buddhism the final salvation and escape from repeated birth according to Upanishads is attained by the union of Atman with Brahman. This state is an absolute reality and is transcendental which Buddhism refutes.

In Hinduism as mentioned before there is belief in a self, the Atman, which is permanent and which survives death. It is the Atman that travels from one birth to the next in a cycle of Samsara, evolving and acquiring karma. Thus in Hinduism as elucidated in the later Upanishads like Svetusvatara Upanishad it is the permanent soul or Atman that is responsible for continuity in the travel through Samsara (Gavin Flood, 1966).

Materialists like Purāna Kassapa and Makhali Gosāla denied the validity of the karma-rebirth theory and also the consequence of human action. Ajitha Kesakambala, however, accepted the possibility of rebirth but did not believe that karma has anything to do with rebirth. Purāna Kassapa was an extreme materialist who said even killing human beings has no moral consequence. Makhali Gosāla had a unique theory, he said natural process is based on three factors; fate, species and nature. Beings are subject to go through cycles of birth and death based on these three factors, and are helpless and without control of their destiny until they end their suffering. Purity comes through travelling in the cycle and is not subject to karma (Kalupahana 1992).

In Jainism karma is totally responsible for consequence of human action. This is an extreme view not seen in any other Indian philosophy. Mahavir the leader of Jainism gave equal importance to bodily, verbal and mental actions. He preferred a physical explanation to psychological explanation of human action. He opined that karma existed as material particles in the atmosphere and cover the soul. Apparently there is no intention ("cetanā") and possibly action controls the mind. Hence any action whether intentional or unintentional would have its consequence determined solely by karma. What we experience now is due to actions in the past. One may ask the question if every action, good or bad is invariably followed by consequences good or bad how is it possible to gain freedom from the binding nature of action. Mahavir's answer was that by the practice of extreme self-denial one could remain without committing any action and by this means one could gain freedom (Dundas, 2002).

As mentioned above Buddhism has mentioned five spheres of existence. Rebirth could take place across these spheres. When a being returns to human sphere from some other sphere it may be called rebirth while the word re-becoming ("punarbava") is used to refer to the phenomenon of repetition of births in the human sphere (Jayatilake, 1975).

Buddha's knowledge of karma and rebirth was not based on any previous theory, but something that he discovered at the time of his enlightenment. The methods of knowledge that he gained by acquiring the powers of retro-cognition and clairvoyance enabled him to gain empirical knowledge of karma and rebirth. He was able to perceive the process of karma and rebirth in operation. Buddha with all this knowledge was able to propound the theory of causation or "paticcasamuppāda" which described the conditioned genesis of everything in the universe including man.

Buddhist theory of causality avoids the two extremes of absolute Determinism and Indeterminism. There were three main types of determinism; theistic, naturalistic and karmic. According to the determinism of the theists all events, birth and death and every action happened according to the will of the God. Naturalist determinism held that all events happened strictly according to natural laws. Karmic determinism opinesd that everything happened strictly according to the karma of the person. Indeterminists said that everything happened due to chance and they were haphazard and without a pattern. In both these extreme views there was no possibility of the human being taking control over his destiny. Buddha rejected this view altogether and recommended a method for man to take control over his destiny (Kalupahana, 1992).

Thus in Buddhism rebirth or re-becoming takes place not entirely due to karma or natural laws and certainly not due to a fiat of an all-powerful god. It happens as described in "paticcasamuppāda", (dependent co-origination) in a cycle of birth and death which are conditioned but not determined by karmic and natural laws. This cycle has no beginning or First Cause and no end unless the samsaric cycle is broken by the elimination of defilements; greed, aversion and ignorance. Ignorance is usually taken as the starting point of the dependent co-origination cycle though it certainly is not a first cause.

Ignorance here means lack of knowledge about the true nature of life and matter. Man has beliefs about life and matter which bind him to the samsaric cycle that is sorrowful. As mentioned ignorance is not the first cause and there are factors that condition ignorance also. Obviously for ignorance to be present there has to be a person which in Buddhism is the five aggregates ("panchaskanda"). Ignorance do not exist in isolation, it exists with other conditions.

The question arises, as we have pointed out earlier, that if there is no self or anything like it what travels from one birth to the next in rebirth or re-becoming. The explanation in Buddhism to this problem is based on the functions of the consciousness. This theory is unique to Buddhism and is not found in any other religion or philosophy ancient or modern. Consciousness in Buddhism is not something permanent. It arises and wanes and rises again. It is conditioned by other factors functional in the mind; "vedanā", "saññā", "sañkara"

Though there is no soul or self the continuity of identity was maintained by what was called the stream of consciousness ("viññāna-sota"). It was sometimes called a stream of becoming ("bhava-sota").

In this complex body and mind, which may be called a ball of dispositions ("sañkara-pudja"), there are dispositions which have the potential to give rise to re-becoming ("ponobhaviko bhava-sañkaro"). At the time of death these dispositions could produce a form of viññāna that has the ability to enter into another being in its stage of conception. This form of consciousness is called "prathisandi-viññāna" (Kalupahana, 1992).

In Theravāda there is no intermediate state between death and conception of another being. But in some schools of Buddhism there is a "gandhabba" stage. In Tibetan Buddhism this "Gandhabba" could last for a period of up to 49 days.

Major Schools of Buddhism such as Puggalavāda, Sarvāstivāda, Sautrāntika, Mahāyāna, Madhayamaka and Yogācāra agree on the basic principles of karma and rebirth but may differ with regard to the mechanism. The main difference is mainly due to the presence or absence of something that exists within the human being apart from the five aggregates and which is responsible for karma and rebirth. Puggalavāda had put forward the theory of "Puggala" as the medium that is responsible for karma and rebirth, Sarvāstivāda had "svabhāva" concept, Sautrāntika had the "bīja" concept and Yogācāra had adopted the "bīja" concept and developed it further into the "Alaya-viññāna" concept. These controversies will be discussed in Chapters 23, 24 and 25.

At the time of Buddha most of his contemporary philosophers criticized the Buddhist theory of karma and re-birth. Atmavadins did so on the grounds that if there is no self or anything like it karma and rebirth are not possible. Materialists said death is the final stage of life and there is nothing after death. Sceptics were hesitant to give an opinion except to say that there is no way of verifying these theories.

Further there has been criticism of the theory on karma and re-birth by modern thinkers as well. First is the suggestion that the present knowledge of brain-mind complex rules out the possibility of rebirth. However neuroscience has not solved the mind-matter problem as yet (Taylor, 2010). In very early times there were three theories regarding this problem and those theories remain unresolved. The three theories are; 1) dualism which holds that mind and brain are separate entities. The 16th Century French philosopher Rene Descartes gave credence to this theory by saying that these separate entities are linked in function in the pineal body but there is no proof of this to date. Plato, Aristotle, Hagel, Bertrand Russell were some of the philosophers who subscribed to this view. 2) Idealism which claims that the material world exists in the mind and everything is a creation of the mind. Idealists in

Buddhism were the Viññānavadins or Yogācāras. Asaṅga was a prominent idealist who founded the Yogācāra school of Buddhism. Since then up to the present time there had been philosophers like Emanuel Kant, Arthur Schopenhauer who said the world was a construct of the mind. 3) Physicalism or materialism which says mind and brain are one and the same. Ancient materialists and modern materialists seem to be equally convinced that they are correct.

What could be said at this juncture is that there had been no recent findings in neuroscience which contradict the Buddhist theory of mind and also the karma-rebirth theory. With regard to this issue Buddha avoided all three extreme views and held that the mind and body ("nama-rupa") existed supporting each other like two sheaves of corn leaning on each other.

Quantum physics seems to lend some support to the Buddhist theory of consciousness and perhaps the rebirth theory. In experiments on quantum mechanics where measurement of particles are to be carried out the observer seems to interfere with the process. The requirement that the experiment has to be totally independent of the observer seems to be impossible to fulfil. The observer's presence would cause a change that is called a "wave function collapse". What could be the possible explanation for this phenomenon? Scientists have not found an answer to this problem though there are several theories. One theory asks the question; could it be the consciousness of the observer that causes it? Is it the stream of consciousness that may have the ability to escape from the physical body and travel across and interfere with the experiment (C de M Smith, 2021)?

Is it possible that the stream of consciousness comprise of particles similar to massless subatomic particles such as photons and gluons. The word mass here means resistance to the pull of the Higgs field that is present in space. Electrons, muons and quarts have mass in the sense they are subject to the pull of the Higg's field. Photons and gluons two of the force carrying particles are unaffected by the Higg's field. Massless particles are pure energy. These may play a role in the process of consciousness and other functions of the mind. Karma and rebirth which are explained by the theory of stream of consciousness may be functional due to activity of these massless sub-atomic particles.

Further as neurons consist of atoms, as all matter is, they may be functioning in quantum systems just as all matter does. In this context biophotons which are photons present in biological systems could be of special importance. Recent research suggests that there could be a link between intelligence and the frequency of bio-photons in animals' brains. The findings have been discussed in an article titled "The light of the mind" authored by B.Adams and F. Petruccione, published in the journal "Physicsworld" in its January 2021 issue. The article further hypothesizes that quantum mechanics may be involved in memory, cognition, consciousness etc.

It can be clearly understood that science, especially neuroscience, as it advances steadily, does not contradict Buddha's findings about mind, consciousness, karma and rebirth. Moreover there is continuous addition to the already large volume of evidence on alleged reincarnated persons and also information obtained from experiments employing hypnotic methods which have provided insight into previous births (D.Cockburn, Oct.2008, S.Littlefair May 2018). The work of these researchers supplement the findings of pioneers in these fields such as I. Stevenson (1966), J.Rodney (1955), T. Flournoy (1952), Rev. A.R. Martin (1942) etc (Jayatilake, 1975).

In Kalupahana's (2009) opinion Buddha made use of the theory of karma and rebirth as a wager for the purpose of moral life. What Buddha said was that even if there is no after life moral behaviour in itself is rewarding and if rebirth actually happens and there are good consequence due to the moral behaviour in the previous birth it would be an added benefit. Perhaps the possibility of rebirth in the five destinies including hell, animal womb and the sphere of the departed ancestors described with details of punishments in hell has been preached for the purpose of encouraging moral life.

Chapter 7

Controversies related to "Paticcasamuppāda" - Dependent Co-origination - The Theory of Causality

Causal theory in Buddhism is central to most of its doctrines and is essential to understand its philosophy. It is unique to Buddhism and anything that resembles it cannot be seen in any other contemporary religion or philosophy. It not only explains the causality of empirical life and matter it also provides a basis for the fundamentals of Buddhism that defines suffering, its cause and the moral method to gain freedom from suffering. Further it gives a foundation for the theory of karma and rebirth and the need for a moral life. The word "paticcasamuppāda" is a creation of the Buddha and it is not found in the texts of other contemporary philosophies (Kalupahana, 2006).

In the Kaccayanagotta sutta (Samyutta Nikāya) Buddha in answer to the question asked by Kaccayana "to what extent is there right view?" says that in in the world there are two views; existence and non-existence, these are extreme views, and without agreeing with either of these views he preaches the middle path. And Buddha went on to propound his theory of causality, "paticcasamuppāda". Thus "paticcasamuppāda" paves the way for the middle position between existence and non-existence which as mentioned in the Introduction formed the basis of all philosophies that existed in Buddha's time. "Paticcasamuppāda" also takes the middle position in relation to several such other mutually exclusive pairs of extreme views.

"Paticcasamuppāda" has twelve factors that form into a cycle depicting the cycle of samsara. Twelve-factored cycles have been mentioned in the Vedic tradition but nothing like the "paticcasamuppāda appears in these texts (A Wayman, 1971). Different methods of causation are to be found in Rgveda and other Vedic texts (Kalupahana, 1975).

Though "paticcasamuppāda" has no beginning, in Kaccayanagotta Sutta (Samyutta Nikāya) the description starts with ignorance, "avijja". Each factor is linked to its condition by the word "paccaya", eg: "avijja paccaya sancara", and then "sancara paccaya Viññāna" and so on. The word "paccaya" means "as condition". With ignorance as Condition arise Dispositions, Disposition as Condition arise Consciousness and so on. There is no cause and effect relationship. Ignorance does not cause Disposition, instead it Conditions Disposition.

In the Mahānidāna Sutta (Dīgha Nikāya) Buddha begins the explanation of the cyclic process from decay and death and goes in the opposite direction to what is given in the Kaccāyanagotta Sutta. This Sutta gives a comprehensive account of "paticcasamuppāda" particularly with regard the relationship between condition and effect. Buddha explains to Ven Ananda how in the absence of the Condition the Effect does not arise. For example if there is no birth there is no decay and death. Though each effect acts as the Condition for the next Effect and there is no possibility of a reversal of the process there is a difference regarding Mentality-materiality and Consciousness. Mentality-materiality conditions Consciousness and Consciousness also could condition Mentality-materiality. However in the usual descriptions Consciousness conditions Mentality-materiality. The latter then conditions Contact and Contact could condition Feeling and Feeling could condition Craving and Craving as condition would arise Clinging and Clinging as condition would arise Existence and with Existence as condition would arise Birth and with Birth as condition there is Ageing, Decay and Death. Buddha asks "If there was no Existence of any kind anywhere – that is no Sense-sphere Existence, Fine-material Existence, or Immaterial Existence – then in the complete absence of Existence – with the cessation of Existence would birth be discerned"? Ven. Ananda answers "Certainly not, Venerable Sir". In a similar manner each Condition is analysed in the Mahanidana Sutta (Dīgha Nikāya).

Buddha in Mūlapariyāya sutta (Majjima Nikāya) says, "This being present that arises, this being absent that doesn't arise". This statement further clarifies Buddha's opinion on causation. He has not said "this arises from that". Further no process of evolution is suggested. This is in contrast to the viewpoint of the Samkhāya philosophy which proposes that causation involves evolution. Samkhāya is a School of Hinduism which made its appearance in India in the 1st Century CE, much later than the Buddha's time (C Sharma, 1997). It is believed that Samkhāya, however, was heavily influenced by Buddhism and Jainism which had come into being in the 5th Century BC. Samkhaya philosophy did not believe in a creator God though it had an umbilical relationship with the Vedic tradition. This philosophy suggested the effect is present in the cause and later manifests by a process of evolution (Karl Potter, 1977). Buddhism also had been developing further during that period with its later philosophers like Nāgārjuna (1st to 2nd Century CE), Vāsubandhu (4th to 5th Century CE), Chandrakeerthi (6th Century CE) making significant contributions to the development of Buddhsm. None of these thinkers had spoken about a process of evolution in relation to the Buddhist causal theory. In fact they subscribed to the view that the "effect is not in the womb of the cause".

In early Vedic texts God is mentioned and he is the creator and the force responsible for causation of all phenomena. As Vedic tradition developed into Upanishads the concept of Atman and Brahman was introduced. Atman is the manifestation of Brahman in individual life and is responsible for karma and rebirth which would terminate with the union of Atman and Brahman. Brahman is the ultimate reality and is therefore the final authority on causation. Further development of Veda and Upanishads resulted in the writing of the Mahabharata and one of its episodes Bhagavadgita. The latter brought in the concept of Vishnu as the supreme god who was responsible for causation. Everything on earth was caused by Vishnu (Radhakrishnan, 1957, Swami Bhaskarananda 1994,). All theistic religions including the three Abrahamic religions would have the God as the force responsible for causation.

As mentioned earlier several schools of Hinduism developed in the post Upanishad period and one of them was Mimamsa. According to the latter some form of force is responsible for causation and this theory is called "saktivāda" – Theory of Force. It is this force which causes the effect. Ven. Buddhagosa in his Dhammasaṅgani Atthasalini had said that cause has no force of its own. He may have had this theory, "saktivada", in mind when he made the comment (Gavin Flood, 1996).

According to "paticcasamuppāda" no material passes from the cause to the effect. It is a natural process that occurs according to natural laws. Buddha had said that "paticcasamuppāda" is a natural process and that he did not invent it. He may have discovered it. For example what happens in the causation of suffering could be described as follows; the eye comes into contact with the object and it produces a sign in the mind of the observer and the sign as condition a feeling is produced and feeling as condition disposition results and disposition as condition consciousness of seeing results which eventually leads to grasping of an object which is impermanent and has no substantiality and therefore finally would cause suffering. When the object and the eye are present a sign arises and the process goes on in that manner ending up in suffering. This is how suffering is caused. Thus it is a natural process, though phenomena are not determined by natural laws, they are conditioned by natural laws. Buddha has said whether enlightened ones (Buddha) arise or not this natural process operates (Kaccānagotta sutta, Samyutta Nikāya).

Some thinkers like Kalupahana (2006) are of the opinion that "paticcasamuppāda" is applicable to animate as well as inanimate objects. They think all originations in the world and the universe occur according to the principles of "paticcasamuppāda". This point of view is based on the fact that the world is what we perceive. In the Sabbam sutta (Samyutta Nikāya) Buddha clearly explains that what is meant by everything is all that is perceived by the six sense organs and nothing else. Perception by the six sense organs is subject to the principles of "paticcasamuppāda". In this sense it may be said everything in the world arises according to the principles of "paticcasamuppāda".

As "paticcasamuppāda" deals with the causation of not only animate but also inanimate objects as mentioned above the question might arise whether dispositions (saṅkara) and consciousness (vingana) could be operative in the causation of inanimate objects. What "paticcasamuppāda" describes is the perception of origination of objects by the subject. There is no absolute reality in what is perceived by the process involving the six agents of perception ("salāyatana"). The subject is neither separate nor conjoined with the object and the process of perception involving dispositions and consciousness occur within the subject-object complex. Thus the question whether "saṅkara" and consciousness operates in the causation of inanimate objects may not arise in the context of the Buddhist theory on causation.

Buddha uses the word "saṅkhata" refer to what arises in a process of dispositionally conditioned. The word "saṅkhata" and "paticcasamuppanna" are used together but not as synonyms. Kalupahana (2008) says the reason for this is that the word "saṅkhata" involves human dispositions. He says "All the dispositionally conditioned are dependently arisen but all dependently arisen are not dispositionally conditioned". Does he mean origination of inanimate objects is not dispositionally conditioned? It is possible that Buddha intended to use the paticcasamuppāda with its twelve factors to describe the origination of animate life and its samsaric cycle. Whereas when he said "When this being present that arises, this being absent that doesn't arise" in Mulapariyaya Sutta (Majjima Nikāya") he probably meant both animate as well as inanimate objects.

In Buddha's time there were several theories on causation and Buddha had criticized four of the major theories. The ascetic Acelakassapa (Naked-Kassapa) had questioned the Buddha on these four theories (Acela Sutta, Samyutta Nikāya). He had asked the Buddha whether suffering is 1) self-caused, 2) externally caused, 3) both self and externally caused or 4) neither self nor externally caused. Buddha's reply had been in the negative with regard to all four possibilities. Buddha had said that to say suffering is self-caused is to propose eternalism. If suffering is self-caused the cause and effect are same which suggests a presence of a permanent self. On the other hand to say that suffering is externally caused is nihilism because there is total separation of cause and effect suggesting annihilation. The theory that effect is self-caused was to be found in the Samkhya philosophy (a School of Hinduism which focuses on rational examination – see above in this Chapter). Paticcasamuppāda of Buddhism avoids both extremes and proposes the middle path which is based on Conditionality.

Nāgārjuna in his Mūlamadhyamaka-karikā analyses and refutes the above theories of causation. In Chapter 1 of the Karikā he does an examination of the Conditions (Pāli – "Paccaya", Sanskrit – "Pratyaya") that feature in the process of paticcasamuppāda. In the first verse he refutes the four extreme theories of causation mentioned above. In the second verse he mentions the four Conditions which he says are the only Conditions that operate, namely 1) primary, 2) objective 3) immediate and 4) dominant. These were the four Conditions that were under consideration by the Abhidhamma theorists. Sārvasthivādins in their Abhidhamma had four types of Conditions. Abhidhamma of the Theravādins had developed a very elaborate set of Conditions 24 in number.

After the description of the four Conditions Nāgārjuna attempts to show that the view held by Sārvastivāda that the effect is already present in the cause was flawed for if it already exists there is no use for the Condition. The view held by Sautrāntika, on the other hand, that the effect is totally non-existent in the cause is also not possible for then the arising of the effect cannot be accounted for. Further the Theory of Perception of the Sārvastivāda also came for criticism. In this theory the moments are divided into four stages which also involved 'activity' ("kriya") associated with Condition. Nāgārjuna rejected the possibility of this unobservable metaphysical 'activity' that is supposed to be associated with Condition. Nāgārjuna was attempting to bring Buddhism back to its middle position for it was being dragged towards two extremes by eternalists like Sarvāsthivādins and annihilationists like

Sautrāntikavādins making it possible for the forceful entry of doctrines of other religions like Hinduism.

It can be seen that "paticcasamuppāda" enables Buddhism to assume the middle path in relation to several extreme views. Two of such pairs of extreme views already considered above are; 1) existence and non-existence, 2) self causation and external causation. Another pair of mutually exclusive views is "all are a unity" and "all are a plurality". These are monistic and pluralistic theories. The former suggests that everything could be reduced to one basic factor. The latter holds that everything can be analysed into discrete independent entities. Though Buddhism analyses empirical existence into five aggregates, twelve sense bases and eighteen elements of cognition these are not independent discrete entities. They arise dependent on many other factors. For example ignorance alone does not condition the arising of volitions. Several other factors are present in this process. "Paticcasamuppāda" not only analyses but it also synthesizes these factors. Thus it avoids both monism and pluralism   (Karunadasa, 2013).

Another pair of extreme views that "paticcasamuppāda" avoids is determinism and indeterminism. There are two types of determinism, theistic determinism and karmic determinism. According to the former the creator God determines every phenomenon and the person or any other factor have no role in the matter. In karmic determinism karma is the absolute determinant and again there are no other factors involved. Indeterminism holds that everything happens due to chance and immediate fortuitous circumstances. According to Buddhism phenomena are neither predetermined nor undetermined. They occur as conditioned happening as described in the "paticcasamuppāda". Thus "paticcasamuppāda" assumes the middle position in relation to several mutually exclusive pairs of extreme views.

In "paticcasamuppāda" the effect would act as Condition for the next stage and the process goes on with condition and effect interchanging their role in the cycle. Though one Condition is mentioned there are several factors that act as condition and in the Abhidhamma of the Theravādins twenty four types of Conditions are identified. However it is the main condition that is mentioned. This could be the type called dominant mentioned in the analysis of Nāgārjuna. Similarly there could be several effects also and the main effect is mentioned. Thus there is a conjunction of Conditions and Effects (Karunadasa, 2013).

In the Abhidhamma of the Theravādins this compendium of causation is twofold; 1) The method of dependent arising and 2) the method of conditional relations. However this two-fold theory is combined into one in most of the Discourses where Buddha preached about "paticcasamuppāda". In the first of the above mentioned methods the simple occurrence of a state in dependence on some other state is described while in the second the causal efficacy of conditions in the relations between conditions is highlighted. This efficacy of the condition entails a force that has the power to bring about the effect or the conditioned. Is this contradictory to what is described in the Discourses and their commentaries? As mentioned above Buddhagosa in the DhammAsaṅgani has rejected the possibility of the presence of a force in the cause. This rejection by Buddhagosa was thought to be a refutation of the viewpoint of Mimamsa School of Hinduism that spoke about such a force. Does this Abhidhamma view contradict the view expressed in the Visuddhimagga Tika that nothing material transmits from the cause to the effect? In the Visuddhimagga the twenty four types of Conditions are employed to explain the relationship between each of the pairs of factors in the twelve stages of the paticcasamuppāda. Hence there cannot be a difference of opinion but perhaps what happens is that the Abhidhamma proceeds to fully analyze Conditions and in the process have spoken about a force that has the power to bring about the arising of the effect. For example in the Discourses ignorance is explained as ignorance of the Four Noble Truths whereas in the Abhidhamma ignorance means ignorance of eight things; the Four Noble Truths plus 1) the past before birth, 2) the future after death, 3) both past and future together and 4) the dependent arising. Obviously getting rid of these ignorances would mean achieving higher forms of knowledge such as retro-cognition which are stages in the path to Nibbāna. This is understandable as getting rid of ignorance which is the root cause of suffering must lead the way to Nibbāna. Further, this is nothing but an elaboration of what is given in the Discourses where the first factor in the "paticcasamuppāda", ignorance, is described simply as the ignorance of the Four Noble Truths.

According to the Theravāda Abhidhamma dependent on ignorance arises karmic formations which are analysed into twenty nine volitions divisible into wholesome and unwholesome cittas. These 29 volitions could condition the arising of 32 kinds of consciousness. With regard to rebirth, there are nineteen types of consciousness assigned to rebirth, and at the time of conception one of these arises conditioned by a dominant karmic formation that has been accumulated by the deceased and this consciousness will form part of the karmic constitution of the new being.

These Abhidhammic versions of the explanation of causation differ in the different Schools of Buddhism which had developed their own Abhidhammas. What is given above is the

Theravāda Abhidhamma version on "paticcasamuppāda". Sārvasthivādins had a highly developed Abhidhamma and they were keen expounders of their theories and were capable debaters too. Sārvastivāda also known as "Hetuvada" was founded by Katyayaniputra (150 BC) who put forward a theory of causation consisting of six fold causes (see Chapter 29). He said cause and effect existed simultaneously.

Sarvāstivāda arose as a result of difference of opinion regarding the question; if there is no self who receives the effects of karma and what is responsible for rebirth. Sārvasthivādins developed their "svabhāva" theory as a solution to this problem and they also said "svabhāva" continues through time; the past, the present and the future thus giving a new interpretation to the concept of time. Thus they had to develop a theory of causation also that could incorporate the "svabhāva" concept as well as their interpretation of time. They could not adopt Theravādin's theory of "paticcasamuppāda" as it did not fit in with their "svabhāva" theory and time concept. There had to be a more tangible connection between cause and effect. Hence they said effect is present in the cause and put forward their Theory of Simultaneous Causality ("Sathkaryavada") (Karunadasa, 1983, Tillakaratne, 1995).

Sārvasthivādins argued that the Mango tree develops from the Mango seed because the "Mango-svabhāva" was present in the seed. Due to this assertion the Sārvastivāda was considered to belong to the group of philosophies called "sathkaryavada", This philosophy contends that effect is present in the cause. Samkhaya (one of the Schools of Hinduism) philosophy also strongly subscribed to the "Sathkaryavada".

There seems to be difference of opinion regarding the exact nature of the relationship between the cause and effect as described in the "paticcasamuppāda". Whether the explanation given therein is adequate seems to be the unresolved issue. The Theravādins in their Abhidhamma attempted to analyse the Conditions into twenty four factors and also spoke of the involvement of a force that operated between cause and effect. Sarvāsthivādins also attempted to throw light on this question by their Abhidhammic theorizing and also the "Sathkaravada" concept which said the effect is present in the cause.

Tantrayana is the school of Buddhism which developed mainly in Tibet after the initial beginning in India. According to Guhyasamaja Tantra, which is the most important text of this school of Buddhism, body and mind complex exists in three levels as dependently arisen continuum; 1) gross, 2) subtle and 3) extremely subtle. Thus Tantryana while subscribing to the view that phenomena are dependently arisen, has further analysed phenomena into three levels. One cannot find this analysis anywhere in Nāgārjuna's works though Nāgārjuna's thoughts are said to have influenced the development of Tantrayana (Cummings, 2003).

Causality is a subject that interested philosophers from early times both in the East and the West. Aristotle's theory of causality seems to be still valid and to be able to influence present day thinkers as well. He had identified four types of causes; 1) material. 2) efficient, 3) formal and 4) final. The four types of causes could be illustrated by the consideration of the causation of a chair for instance. Material cause is the wood that goes to form the chair. Efficient cause may be the effort of the carpenter. Formal cause is the form that the chair would take and Final cause would be the finished chair with its utility value. Aristotle seems to have considered mind and matter as one complex, causation of mental phenomena seems to have a material participation (Hankinson,1998).

Later Western philosophers, however, tended to give mind a more important role in the causation of phenomena taking into consideration the mind as the perceiver. For example David Hume (18th CE) Scottish philosopher had said that we do not perceive that one event causes another but we only experience the constant conjunction of events (William & Brown, 2019). To draw causal inference from the past experience it is necessary to presuppose that the future will resemble the past, a presupposition which cannot be grounded in prior experience. Hume was an empiricist who did not believe that knowledge is possible by induction. Does Hume mean that in relation to time causation of present events cannot be linked to the past? Buddha had said that the past is dead and the future is unknown, only the present can be experienced. Hume also said that we cannot guarantee that events are caused by prior events or occur independent of the past either. Is Hume taking a middle position like Buddhism? Does his idea of "constant conjunction of events" have a certain similarity to the causality theory of Buddhism? David Hume was thought to be a sceptic on several aspects of life and world such as causation, existence of a world external to the mind and existence of an enduring Self. Buddhism is not sceptic, it is very much based on empiricism and has positive views on these aspects. However Hume may have been influenced by Eastern philosophy as have been the philosophers like Arthur Schopenhauer (19th CE) and Emanuel Kant (18th CE).

Kant disagreed with Hume and said every event must necessarily have a cause and it is empirically perceived. Schopenhauer had a different view, he said causation is not empirically realized but is an innate process. Ludwig Wittgenstein (18th CE) was another philosopher who had different views on causation. He said all causal laws are understood through experience therefore we cannot ascertain the cause of experience. He said if you give a scientific explanation of a phenomenon you only describe an experience. Causality is actually a description of a style of investigation. There are laws of nature but it turns out that you cannot determine this. Wittgenstein considers that the idea of causality leads to an erroneous perspective in the attempt to understand human fact (Stanford Encyclopaedia of Philosophy, 2021).

Thus it can be seen that while some of these philosophers thought that phenomena have a cause and it can be perceived by empirical means there were others who thought that what is described as cause is our experience and it may not be the actual cause. Nowadays scientists think that the cause and effect relationship must entail the involvement of energy. In modern physics matter is considered energy and brain therefore is also energy and its working involves transmission of energy. All phenomena that involve matter have to contend with the fact that matter could be converted to energy and vice versa. Thus cause could have a link with the effect via energy.

Quantum mechanics may be involved in the cause and effect system, especially if energy is involved. Its possible involvement in the matter of rebirth has been discussed in the Chapter 6 on Karma and Rebirth. Photons and gluons which are energy carrying particles and which are massless may be the particles involved in causation also. Abhidhamma speaks about a force involved in causation though Visuddhimagga has said there is no force involved in causation. Moreover according to the "paṭiccasamuppāda" nothing material passes from cause to effect.

It must be mentioned that Buddhism does not comment on the beginning of the universe and life nor the end of it. The Aggānna sutta (Dīgha Nikāya) speaks about the evolution of life but does not pass a verdict on the First Cause. In the Samyutta Nikāya there are two suttas dealing with the subject of the beginning of the Earth, "Tinakatta" and "Pathavi". In both it is said that the beginning of the earth cannot be known. Therefore the "paticcasamuppāda" does not indicate a beginning and an end to the cycle of samsara. The reciprocally interdependent relationship between consciousness and "nama-rupa" (Mentality-materiality), (see above in this Chapter) as cause and effect makes birth and death possible in a cyclic process. Birth conditions death and death conditions birth. This cyclic process is accepted in most of the Schools of Buddhism though "paticcasamuppāda" as such may not be acceptable to some of the later schools.

Theistic religions both in the East and the West do not subscribe to a causal theory where a cycle is involved. They believe in a linear process. These philosophies believe in a First Cause which is God. Modern science has not solved this problem. The "Big Bang Theory" does not solve it as the question what existed before the "Big Bang" has not been solved.

Chapter 8

Controversies related to the concept of Reality

Whether the phenomena we experience is real is an issue that has been debated from early times. Whether there is a world that really exists independent of the observer was a question that occupied the minds of ancient philosophers as well as modern and also Western as well as Eastern. Ancient philosophers such as Plato and Aristotle had commented on realism and they had looked at it under the categorization of the physical world into Universal and the Particular. The former thought the Universal existed independent of the Particular while the latter thought the Universal depended on the Particular (B Russell, 1945). Arthur Schopenhauer (1818) said the phenomenal world is a product of the "blind noumenal will". He may have been influenced by Buddhism for he sees the link between the vagaries of the mind and what it perceives.

What could be reasoned out by deductive and inductive methods may not be reliable. This had been Buddha's view who depended on experience to gain knowledge. Buddha did not subscribe to an absolute or substantialist theory of reality, he did not see anything absolutely and substantially real in the world and life in it. He would comment only on what could be known by empirical means and not on metaphysical speculation. Thus in Buddhism reality is non-absolutist and non-essentialist.

Vedanta (one of the six Schools of Hinduism based on Upanishads) says the external world that we perceive is a "maya" and the problem arises because we perceive it as real. To solve the problem we must demolish this "maya" or transcend it (Gavin Flood, 1996). However, according to Buddhism the problem is that we perceive the external world as permanent and would want to be emotionally involved and attached to it. The solution is to develop our mind to a state in which it could avoid getting attached to what it perceives.

In Buddhism reality is based on the relationship between subject and object, the perceiving person and what is perceived (A Tillakaratne, 1993). To understand this relationship one must know the Buddhist analysis of the subject and the object. This analysis enables the elucidation of the relationship between subject and object. The subject which is the perceiving person is analysed in two ways, 1) nama-rupa and 2) panchaskanda or five aggregates. In both analyses the psychological aspect is given greater importance. It is the psychological component that is geared to perceive the external world.

The subject-object complex is analysed into twelve bases ("ayatana") comprising the six sensory organs and their corresponding six objects of perception. The six sensory organs are; eye, ear, nose, tongue, body and mind and the corresponding objects are; form, sound, smell, taste, touch and concepts. The six sensory organs are internal to the human being which is the subject while the objects are external. Thus the link between subject and object is explained.

There is a further analysis of this complex into eighteen elements or "dhātu. This analysis when applied to the first sensory organ derives the following three dathu; eye, material form and eye-consciousness. When it is applied to the all six sensory organs it adds up to eighteen dhatus. The analysis of the twelve bases links the internal functions of the observer with the external functions of the universe. The further analysis into eighteen elements ("dhātu") brings in the perception aspect of the subject-object complex. It is the eighteen elements comprising "dhātus" that explains the complexity of the subject.

The analysis of the object takes a similar form. In the Sabbam sutta in the Samyutta Nikāya Buddha explains what could be perceived as everything on earth. What is perceived by the six sensory organs is everything and there is nothing else. Thus the object is nothing else but what is perceived by the human personality using his six sense organs.

In the perception of the world great importance is given to the human psychological function. This is elucidated by the two analyses; the base analysis and the "dhātu" analysis. This explanation shows how the reality of the external world is perceived by the complex psychological process. It also shows the connection between the subject and the object. The psychological function involving "saññā" "saṅkara" and "viññāna" may by volitional construction transform the object into something that the five aggregates could grasp and be attached to. This is the reality that the human personality perceives (Tillakaratne, 1993).

These analyses explain the theory of reality of Buddhism. It is based on empiricism. What cannot be perceived by empirical means is not included in the theory. Moreover Buddhism does not attempt to answer the question whether there is a material world independent of the observer. It does not say whether or not a material world exists independent of the observer. Nor does it say that the world is a construct of the mind. Further it doesn't say the world is not real or that human perception cannot comprehend it. However this middle position that Buddhism takes in relation to reality had resulted in the misinterpretation of the meaning of Buddha's word. Early Buddhism speaks about what could be experienced as the external world and how the mind interprets it as an object of attachment or repulsion.

Early texts of Mahāyāna, the "Praññāparamithā" (1st CE) series claimed that Buddhas and Bodhisathvas attain a deep knowledge of reality, this reality is a transcendent, non-conceptual, non-dual knowledge into the true nature of things. This knowledge was also associated with an insight into the emptiness ("śūnyarta") of phenomena and their illusory nature ("maya"). It perceives that all phenomena have no essential core ("svabhāva") and therefore has no fundamental or real existence. These empty phenomena are also said to be conceptual constructions. These phenomena are unarisen ("anutpata"), unborn ("ajata") and beyond coming and going (Paul Williams, 2008).

The Heart Sūthra ("Praññāpāramithā-hardaya sūthra"), a Mahāyāna text, says phenomena are unproduced and unfilled. The Diamond Sūthra ("Vajaradchedikapraññāpāramithā sūthra") says phenomena are comparable to transient events like shooting star, clouding of the sight, drop of dew, an illusion. Thus it is seen that Mahāyāna had attempted to take the Early Buddhist theory on reality towards a form of idealism making the physical world more or less unreal, non-existent and a creation of the mind.

The two major branches of Mahāyāna, the Madhayamaka School and Yogācāra also developed their kind of idealism. Idealism is a theory that says reality consists of ideas and there is nothing substantial in reality. Early Buddhism did not say reality of phenomena consists of ideas, it said there is no self or soul or anything like it or a permanent substance in phenomena. It very clearly said these phenomena arise, undergo change and disappear. On the other hand Mahāyāna has taken the theory of "anicca" and "anatta", from its middle position to an extreme of non-existence.

Madhayamaka based its theory on the "śūnyatavāda" of Nāgārjuna and said all phenomena are empty and even the mind is empty (Warder, 2000). We have dealt with this issue in Chapter 2 on Existence. Yogācāra which came into being later than Madhayamaka criticized the "śūnyatavāda" of the latter. One of their early sūthras "Sandhinirmocana Sūthra" says "śūnyatāva" is not the final definitive ultimate truth. Phenomena are only the mind ("citta"), consciousness (viññāna) or perceptions ("viññāpti"), and seemingly external objects do not exist apart from the dependently originated flow of mental expressions. Yogācāra criticized the Madhayamaka as descending to nihilism by their "śūnyatavāda".

Sarvāstivāda and Sautrāntika had their views on existence and we have discussed these in Chapter 2 on Existence. These views are applicable to the theories on reality as well. Thus according to Sarvāstivāda the phenomena has a substantial element called "svabhāva" which is permanently present through time, past, present and future, it is responsible for karmic consequence and also rebirth. Thus Sarvāstivāda appears to be believers of an absolute reality. However "svabhāva" is a metaphysical notion and has no empirical basis. Buddha has not perceived it using his extra-sensory perception methods. Thus it cannot have a role in the theory of reality of Early Buddhism.

Sautrāntikavāda was critical of the "svabhāva" theory of Sarvāstivāda. Their theory said phenomena arose and disappeared without existence. This idea of the Sautrāntika earned them the label of nihilist. They also spoke about a transmigrating substratum of consciousness that contains within it seeds of goodness that are in every person. It is believed that these and other Sautrāntika ideas contributed to the development of Yogācāra School to a significant degree particular their "ālaya-viññāna" concept.

In Hinduism Brahman is the ultimate reality, the highest universal principle. The word Brahman should not be confused with Brahma (Hindu God), Brahmana (Veda text), Brahmanism (the religion) or Brahmin (caste). Part of Brahman is present in every human being as the Atman which is also real. In contrast what is perceived by the sensory organs of human beings is "maya", the perceived reality. "Maya" is the effect and it undergoes change, is born and evolves and dies. On the other hand Atman and Brahman are eternal, does not change, are unaffected and are the absolute consciousness.

Controversies related to the concept of Reality

In the earliest Veda like the Samhita (2nd millennium BC) the concept of Brahman is mentioned (Gavin D Flood 1996). In these texts Brahman is the power immanent in the sound, words, and verses in the Vedas. The idea of Brahman evolved in the Vedas and Upanishads and the Brahmen/Atman concept developed in the latter. Later the concept developed further not as a single unified theory but in a variety of themes which were adopted into Hinduism. According to S. Radhakrishnan (1957) the sages of Upanishads teach Brahman as the ultimate essence of material phenomena that cannot be seen or heard but whose nature can be known through the development of self-jhana (self-knowledge). However due to differences of opinion regarding the relationship of Brahman and Atman several Schools of Hinduism came into being. The four major branches are; 1) Vaishnavism – followers worship preserver god Vishnu who had created the creator God Brahman, 2) Shaivism – believers worship Shiva the destroyer, 3) Shaktism – the supreme god is a woman called Mahadevi and 4) Smartism – Smarta movement which rejects theistic sectarianism and believe in all Hindu Gods. Apart from these four major branches there are six other schools of Vedanthic philosophy. These have been mentioned in Chapter 5 on Morality.

Common feature of most of these schools of Hinduism is the opinion on the ultimate reality and the nature of the perceived reality. Ultimate reality is the Brahman/Atman concept and the perceived reality is "maya", an illusion.

Mahāyāna describes Buddha as the body of essence that pervades the whole universe. This point of view seems to be similar to the Hindu conceptualization of Brahman who is supposed to pervade the whole universe. As Mahāyāna originated well after these ideas about Brahman were developed it is probable that Mahāyāna borrowed these ideas from Hinduism. We will discuss the consequences of such intrusions and their impact on Buddhism in Chapter 23.

Western philosophers ancient as well as modern had opined on reality. Plato (423 – 347 BC) the Greek philosopher said the observable Particular is like the shadow on a wall cast by the activities of the Universal which is real but unobservable (Theoder Gomperze, 1905). What we observe is not the real but an image created by the real. We see the Particular phenomenon but the Universal phenomenon is unobservable. In his "Theory of Forms" he speaks of two worlds, one is the real world which cannot be seen and the other an image created by the former which can be seen and which undergoes change. Hence according to Plato the real world cannot be perceived. He lived about two hundred years later than Buddha who lived in 600 BC.

Plato's student Aristotle took a different view, he thought Universals are observable and are concepts borne and shared by Particulars (Marc & Reeve, 2021). In his "Metaphysics" Aristotle says these Universals are made of matter, shape, and substance. The changes they undergo are due to their attempt to achieve their potential. Thus according to Aristotle the real world can be known. It is believed that his ideas paved the way for the development of modern science which strives to know the world.

We have discussed Scottish philosopher David Hume's (1711 – 1776 CE) scepticism in Chapter 7 on Causality. He was of the view that reality cannot be known and believed that knowledge could be gained mainly by experience. Immanuel Kant (1724 – 1804) the German philosopher wrote his best known work "Critique of Pure Reason" as a response to Hume's scepticism. He was of the view that objects of experience are mere appearance and therefore nature of phenomena cannot be gauged by experience alone. He attempted to find a way through the impasse created by the conflict between empiricism and rationalism. He said objects of our senses must conform to the forms of intuition and therefore we can have a-priori knowledge of the objects of our senses. As this a-priori knowledge is gained in the mind prior to the intervention of experience by pure intuition other thinkers called it "transcendental idealism" ("Critique of Pure Reason", Trans. P Guyer, A Wood 1999).

We have mentioned the German philosopher Arthur Schopenhauer (1788 – 1860) in Chapter 6 on Causality. He was influenced by Kant. His famous book "World as Will and Representation" (Trans. Haldane and Kemp, 2020) attempts to show the phenomenal world as a product of blind noumenal will. Here noumenal means "thing in itself", not caused by any other outside factor. Schopenhauer was one of the earliest Western thinkers who showed appreciation of Indian philosophy. He seems to be in agreement with concepts such as "No-self" and the notion of world as appearance.

Thus we see that from the earliest times of Plato to the times of Schopenhauer in Western philosophy there had been difference of opinion about the reality of the phenomenal world. Same could be said about Eastern philosophy as seen in India from the time of the Vedas in the 2nd Mileneum BC to the times of Nāgārjuna (2nd Century CE), Mahāyāna (1st Century CE) Asaṅga and Vasubandhu (5th Century CE). These Indian philosophies may have influenced the 18th Century Western philosophers.

Chapter 9

Controversies related to Matter

Subject of Matter is related to Reality which was discussed in the previous chapter. The relationship between subject and object was discussed and whether the object in that relationship is matter that we consider here would be a question that naturally arises in the discussion of matter. Again the question whether a material world exists apart from the experienced world arises. In this chapter we will not go into these questions but will consider the material world and matter as described in the Buddhist texts and other contemporary religions and philosophies.

In the "nama-rupa" complex "nama" is mind and "rupa" is matter. The analysis of the mind have been discussed in Chapter 3 on Mind. The "rupa" is primarily analysed into "apo, thejo, vayo, and patavi" (water, fire, air, earth). In the Abhidhamma these four maha buthas are further analysed. Y. Karunadasa has discussed these Abhidhammic analyses in his book "Buddhist analysis of Matter" (1967).

Aristotle had described matter as formed of five components; earth, water, air, fire and aether ("Metaphysics" Trans. Ross). Several philosophies both in the West and the East had expressed similar ideas and have spoken about these substances as the constituents of matter. This is understandable as what is seen and felt in the environment obviously are these elements.

"Rupa" in Buddhism is defined as matter that has the characteristic of "ruppana" which means it could be deformed, disturbed, knocked about, oppressed, and broken by the effect of cold, heat, flies, mosquittos etc. There are different views among the different schools of Buddhism regarding the nature of the "ruppana" or change these dhammas undergo. Early Theravādins identified three stages in this process; birth ("jati"), decay ("jara") dissolution ("bheda"). In keeping with this idea later Theravādins who composed the Abhidhamma also identified these three stages in the process of change that dhammas undergo due to the action of the above mentioned agents. However Sautrāntika had put forward their theory which had only two stages in this process. Material or mental factors appear and immediately disappear giving no time for decay. Thus in Sautrāntika the change is due to the disappearance of one dhamma and the appearance of another in its place (Karunadasa, 1967).

The Theravāda Abhidhamma analyses matter into their ultimate units which cannot be further divided. These atoms or elements have two important characteristics; one is they are impermanent and the other is they are in motion and seems to have energy. Abhidhammatta Sangha written by Sri Lankan monk Ven Anuruddha (8th – 12th Century) which is more like one of the explanatory commentaries on the Abhidhamma has described these particles in detail.

Buddha has not put forward an atomic theory as such but he has said the minutest particle of matter is in constant flux (Jayatilake, 1975). When a monk had asked him whether there was any substance which was eternal, stable, lasting and not subject to change Buddha has said there is no such matter. The significance of Buddha's view is that there is no character in matter that is permanent and therefore we cannot hope to find salvation by attachment to such matter. This, as a matter of fact, is a sermon on morals in relation to matter. Thus Buddhism gives a realistic description of physical nature of matter while focusing on the psychological implications, thereby pointing towards the moral aspect that one must attempt to derive from the definition.

In the Dhammadayada sutta of the Majjima Nikāya matter is classified with reference to time as past, present, and future, with reference to the individual as internal and external, and with reference to the nature of matter as gross and subtle, with reference to the value of matter as base and ethereal, and with reference to space as near and distant. Matter includes non-living as well as living and both organic and inorganic. This analysis could be considered a precursor of the Abhidhamma analysis of matter which is discussed below.

K.N. Jayathilake (1975) says according to Buddhist conceptions life is a by-product of matter. Whether one could speak of life as a by-product of matter is questionable when one considers "paticcasamuppāda" which says everything arises as conditioned phenomena. According to "paticcasamuppāda" "nama-rupa" (mentality-materiality) arises conditioned by consciousness. A complex phenomenon called "nama-rupa" arises with consciousness as condition. Here rupa is material. And life arises in a complex process where several factors and conditions are involved and matter is just one factor and moreover in life mind is a larger factor which is given greater importance in Buddhism. It may not be correct to say life is a by-product of matter.

According to DhammAsaṅgani in the Abhidhamma Piṭakaya matter is causally conditioned and is impermanent and subject to decay. It is morally neutral neither good nor evil. Matter can be perceived by the six sense organs. Because of its characteristics individuals can be sentimentally attached to it. Matter could undergo change due to external factors like heat, cold, atmospheric change such as wind, and also internal factors like hunger, thirst. It could undergo change due to stings and bites by bees and snakes etc. All matter could exist in the solid ("patavi"), liquid ("apo") and gaseous ("vayo") states according to temperature. According to Abhidhamma the conception of matter is that which undergoes change due to heat. This as we know is in agreement with modern science. These states of matter are not exclusive of each other and could exist as extension of one state into another. The characteristics of matter are therefore cohesiveness, mobility, extension and temperature and these are inseparable though distinguishable. Atoms differ from each other due to the presence of these characteristics in varying degrees.

Abhidhamma speaks about four great forces of matter and they are the above mentioned four characteristics. These forces except cohesiveness could be perceived by our sense organs. Cohesiveness could only be inferred. All material things whether organic or inorganic are derived from these four forces or energy. Life is a derivative of these four forces. The other characteristics of matter such as weight, growth, continuity, decay and impermanence are also derived from the four primary energies.

K N Jayathilaka (1975) is of the opinion that these theories of matter indicate that Buddhism subscribed to the existence of an external world independent of our sensory organs. We have discussed this issue in Chapter 8 on Reality and our discussion points to a different point of view, in the sense Buddha did not categoriclly say that the material world exists or does not exist independent of the mind. It is the four primary forces mentioned above which have caused the existence of that external world. What we perceive as colour, form, sound, smell, taste and touch are by-products of these four forces. All our physical volitional activity are due to operation of material function but accompanied by "citta" or mental activity. None of the Abhidhamma texts mention heart as the centre for mental activity though that was an idea prevalent at the time the Abhidhamma was being composed.

Atomic theory in India developed at the same time that Democritus (400 BC) in Greece was speaking about atoms. It is possible that Jainism was the first Indian philosophy to develop an atomic theory. However some thinkers believe it was the ancient Indian natural scientist Kanada who founded the Nyaya Vaishesika school of Hinduism, who first developed the atomic theory (Subash Kak, 2016). Words used to refer to the atom was "anu" and "paramānu" which are still in use. Anyhow three philosophies; Nyaya Vaisheshika, Jainism and Buddhism

(Theravāda Abhidhamma) developed their atomic theories more or less at the same time. At the same time there was opposition to the atomic theory cutting across the religious bases. Some Schools of Hinduism supported the atomic theory while others opposed. Same was true in relation to Schools of Buddhism. Theravādins were keen on their atomic theory while Madhyamaka and Yogakara raised objections. In Hinduism the Nyaya Vaisheshika supported the atomic theory while Vedantins opposed (C Sharma, 2000).

Thus it is seen that the atomic theory had developed in the different schools of Buddhism but there was no complete agreement among them. Above is a description of what is given in the Theravāda Abhidhamma. While agreeing in general with the Atomic theory of Buddhism Sautrāntika held that atoms had a dimension. However, Sarvāsthivādins did not agree with these ideas and said that atoms had no parts or extensions. Space was a conditioned matter according to Sarvāstivāda, but Theravādins refuted this idea (Jayatilake, 1975).

Idealists like Madhyamaka, Yogācāra argued that if an atom has dimension it is further divisible and if it has no dimension the atom does not exist. They said that matter therefore does not exist and the matter was a construct of the mind. Jayathilake (1975) says the mistake all these Schools did was to derive knowledge of the atom by means of rational speculation. In "Kālāma Sutta" Buddha had advised against reliance on reason as means of gaining knowledge.

Theravādins had even speculated that the atom is a complex structure and that it has smaller particles within it. Sarvasthivādins spoke about "dravya paramānu" and a more complex "sanghata paramānu". It is possible that Theravāda ideas on the atom may have been arrived at by using extra-sensory perception methods available to the Arahath.

The atomic theories of these Schools were similar in the main though there were differences in some aspects. All atomic theories had basic categories such as earth, water, air and fire. Buddhist theorists stuck to this basic system and said these were formed by the coming together of atoms. Other religions added other categories such as space, time, soul and thoughts to these basic categories.

Hinduism had a basic theory on matter that was more or less common to all its main Schools though there were differences in some aspects. According to this basic system all matter is based on three inert "gunas" (qualities); "sattva" (goodness), "rajas" (passion), and "ramas" (darkness). There are three states of the "gunas" that make up all matter; 1) "pradhana" (root matter) which are "guna" in unmixed unmanifested state, 2) "prakriti" (primal matter) which are "guna" in mixed unmanifested state, 3) "mahat-tatva" (matter of universal womb) which are "guna" in mixed manifested state. "Pradhana" has no consciousness or will to act on its own and has to be initially agitated by a primal desire to create. Manifest material elements range from most gross (physical) to most subtle. Manifested gross matter are the "pancha maha bhuta"; 1) Space/Ether, 2) air, 3) fire, 4) water and 5) earth. Manifested subtle elements are "ahankara" (ego) "buddhi" (intelligence) and "citta" (mind). It is seen that functions of the mind like intelligence which are considered non-material in Buddhism as could be ascertained from the "nama-rupa" division, are however taken to be material in Hinduism   (Sharma, 2000).

In the atomic theory of Jainism everything except soul and space was formed by atoms. Jain texts like "Pancastikāyasara", "Kalpa Sūtra" give an elaborate atomic theory. Each atom has one kind of taste, one kind of smell, one colour, and two kinds of touch. They could be in one of two states; subtle state in which the atom could fit into infinitesimally small space, and gross state in which the atom could fit into a finite space. Atomic theory of Jainism resembles modern atomic theories in that the atoms are in continuous motion, either in a straight line or when attracted by other atoms in a curved path. They also have something similar to positive and negative charges which give them binding force. Atoms are made of same basic substance and can combine to form the basic six aggregates; earth, water, shadow, sense objects, karmic matter, and unfit matter. Atoms can combine, react, vibrate, move and perform other actions all of which are deterministic. Atoms are infinite in number in the universe, and all of them are eternal. As discovered by omniscience, which the Jainists claim they have mastered, atoms are neither created nor destroyed (D Paul, 2002).

Ājīvikas had also developed a comprehensive atomic theory. Their theory is somewhat closer to the theory put forward by the Vaisheshika School of Hinduism. They said qualities of things are derived from aggregates of atoms. Nature of these atoms was predetermined by cosmic forces consisting of what are called "kāyas" of which there were seven; 1) "prithuvi-kaya" (earth), 2) "apo-kaya" (water) 3) "tejo-kaya" (fire) 4) "vayo-kaya" (air) 5) "sukha" (joy), 6) "dukkha" (sorrow), 7) "jīva" (life). These elements are neither created nor destroyed, do not multiply, have an existence of independence from other atoms, they are defined, indivisible, never growing or expanding, and they move and assemble to form the perceived. Coming together of these "kāyas" could take different forms; dense as in diamond or loose as in bamboo. Atoms cause "sukha", "dukkha", and life as determined by cosmic powers. These systems are predetermined and there is no free will for human beings to take their destiny into their hands (Basham, 1951). This is in keeping with the basic philosophy of Ājivika.

While there are differences of view on the theory of matter between different Schools of the same religion there are similarities between Schools of different religions. This indicates the degree to which there had been inter religious influence.

It is remarkable how close the atomic theories of some of these religions and philosophies that existed before the Christian era are to the modern theories. In modern physics matter and energy are interchangeable. There is continuous motion of atomic particles. In the atomic theory of Theravāda Buddhism also the atoms are in constant motion and there is force in these movements. The Theravāda theory spoke about the atom being complex in structure and and hence has constituents. In the Commentary to the "Vibhanga sutta" (Samyutta Nikāya) they had even given the size of an atom which is not very far from modern estimates (Jayatilake 1975).

Theravāda Abhidhamma analysis of matter have avoided all metaphysical speculation. It has also avoided the confusion of matter and mind complex and had treated them separately. In contrast Hinduism has included ego and intelligence as elements in its atomic theory. It is true that mind cannot exist without matter and matter also cannot exist without mind. However, whether phenomena like thought, intelligence and ego could be considered as matter is an issue that has not been resolved. In the Dhamma theory of the Theravāda Abhidhamma the mental and physical dhammas are considered separately. Mind arises dependent on body but neither are substantially or ontologically material phenomena. They are dependently arisen conditioned phenomena.

In modern physics the atomic theory is not fully resolved. Sub-atomic particles have been found and nucleus also has thirty particles and some more may be found in the future. Nature of the particles, whether they are point form or wave-like or string-like, is not resolved and remain as unproven theories just as it was in 400BC in India and Greece.

Chapter 10

Controversies related to the nature of the Universe

Controversies related to the Universe regarding its origin, whether or not it is eternal, finite or infinite, expanding and so on had arisen during Buddha's time and remain unresolved until the present time. There have been theories then as well as now. Early Indians and Greeks had put forward these theories. Anaximander (600 BC) a Greek philosopher had been the first to think of many worlds being present, appearing and disappearing. Later Democritus had spoken about innumerable atoms and an infinite void where worlds appeared and disappeared. Contemporary Indian thinkers prior to Buddha's time had also put forward cosmic theories larger in variety and number than what Greek thinkers proposed (Burnet, 1930).

Aristotelian view was that the Earth was in the centre and the other planets circled it in different orbits. He also thought the universe was finite in extent. This view was supported by the Christian church as it gave credence to the Biblical theory of creation of the earth and subsequently the sun, moon and stars. But there had been thinkers in the East, India, and Arab who were of the view that the Sun was in the centre and the planets revolved around it. For example Aryabhata (4th BCE) an ancient Indian Buddhist scientist and Avicenna an Arab scientist of the 1st Century CE had described planetary system with the Sun in the centre. However the credit for formulating a cosmic theory with the sun in the centre is given to Nicolas Copernicus (15th CE) a Polish by birth who had studied astronomy and medicine in Italy. Later Galileo Galilei (16th CE) a Italian by birth with better telescopes could confirm the heliocentric theory.

Herschel (18th CE) a German born British astronomer developed the concept of the universe which postulated that the unit of the universe was not the solar system but the galaxy consisting of millions of solar systems. And there are millions of such galaxies in the universe. These galaxies occur in clusters which may contain galaxies ranging in number from few to thousands. The solar system of the planet Earth is in the cluster of galaxies called the "Milky Way" which may have about twenty galaxies. Earlier it was thought there were about ten billion galaxies. There were empty spaces in the universe, earlier thought to be void of any planets. The Hubble Space Telescope, however, has found these spaces to be full of galaxies. Now space scientists say there could be at least 200 billion galaxies in the whole Universe (RT Lauer, 2021).

In early Buddhism four questions were raised regarding the Universe (Aggivacchagotta sutta, Majjima Nikāya). Whether or not the Universe is finite and whether or not the Universe is eternal were the questions. These belong to the ten unanswered questions ("thapaniya", "avyakata"). The Buddha had four ways of dealing with questions; 1) questions that could be answered unilaterally, 2) questions that need to be answered analytically, 3) questions that need to be answered by raising a counter question and 4) questions that need to be set aside. Buddha decided not to answer the four questions related to the universe. Buddha has said a discussion on any subject with a person who doesn't answer questions according to these four methods is a waste of time and a meaningless exercise. The first four of these ten questions deal with the nature of the universe;

Is the world eternal?

Is the world not eternal?

Is the world finite?

Is the world infinite?

We have discussed the issue regarding why these questions were unanswered in Chapter 4 on Knowledge and we have shown that these questions have been in existence from pre-Buddha times. Vasubandhu in Abhidhammakosa commenting on these questions says that the setting aside of these questions is itself an answer. Buddha has said such questions are not relevant to the realizing of the ultimate goal in Buddhism and therefore he doesn't want to answer them.

However though Buddha had not answered these specific questions Buddhism had developed an elaborate cosmic theory. The planets in space were called "akasa loka". The Commentaries to the "Vissuddimagga" describe a thousand-fold Universe with suns and moons that revolve shining and shedding light in space. In another passage in the same text the Universe is described as comprising of three stages. Following are the three stages;

Thousand-fold Minor World-System ("sasshi culanika loka-dhatu")

Twice-a-thousand Middling World System ("divasasshi majjhimika loka-dhatu")

Major World System. ("maha loka-dhatu")

The first of these three stages is the smallest unit and consists of few thousands of planets and these may be inhabited by various types of life forms. These units may correspond to galaxies. The second stage refers to collections of these units which may be similar to clusters of galaxies. The third stage is the whole of the Universe. "Sankarruppati Sutta" in the Majjima Nikāya also make reference to these units of planets, galaxies and also clusters of galaxies. This sutta also describes three tiers of worlds, one with thousands of worlds, a second with millions and a third with billions. These systems have a close resemblance to the modern views on the cosmos particularly the galaxy system.

Cosmology of Buddhism does not give a fixed number regarding the totality of planets. This is probably because two of the unanswered questions were regarding the finitude of the universe. Further Buddhism did not commit on the question whether or not the universe is eternal. This question was also unanswered.

However in Buddhism the "world" is samsara, the wider world of conditioned experience and samsara has no beginning. It arises according to the laws of "paticcasamuppāda" which does not give a first cause. Though the process begins with ignorance, ignorance is not the first cause, ignorance is also conditioned. Buddha in Aṅguttara Nikāya says "First beginning of ignorance is not known....".

Samsara could be ended by attaining Nibbāna. However in Buddhsm samsara is considered neither eternal nor non-eternal. If it is eternal Nibbāna cannot be attained. If it is not eternal everybody would attain Nibbāna without a moral commitment and effort. This is one way of answering the question whether or not the Universe is eternal where instead of the mere physical aspect of the Universe the Buddhist view of the world as a mind and matter complex is taken into consideration (Jayatilake, 1975).

It may be interesting to look at the point of view of Mahāyāna which gives more prominence to the aspect of mind. Mahāyāna considers the Universe as consisting of several "Buddha-fields" ("Buddhaksetra") with a Buddha residing in each and teaching the countless beings. This concept is very much similar to the theory of the universe in Hinduism (see below) and may be considered as evidence that Mahāyāna was heavily influenced by Hinduism. Three types of Buddha-fields are to be found distributed throughout the ten regions of space. These are; pure ("visuddha"), impure ("avisuddha") and mixed ("miraka"). "Sukhavati" is the best known of the pure. "Saha" is the most important of the impure fields, it is located in the South region and it is where Earth our planet is located. It is the field of the Buddha "Sākyamuni (Sāsanaratana, 1952).

In the Vedic tradition "Loka" was not just a place but a position of religious and psychological interest with special value of function. It further mentions a concept of "Tri-Loka" or Three-worlds consisting of Earth, Atmosphere and Heaven making up the Universe. This concept had influenced most of the Indian religions particularly the Hindu philosophy (Theos, 1999).

Hindu texts describe innumerable Universes existing all at the same time moving around like atoms each with its own Brahma, Vishnu and Shiva. Every Universe is covered by seven layers; earth, water, fire, air, sky, energy and false ego. Presence of ego which is a mental phenomenon as part of the Universe shows the tendency of all Indian religions to look at the Universe not merely as a physical phenomenon but one associated with religious and psychological dimensions. This tendency originated in the Vedic tradition as shown above.

Jainism also speaks about three types of Lokas. These include 1) heavens, 2) the realm of the humans, animals and plants and 3) the realm of hell. The three types of Lokas have several units. The Universe was uncreated and eternal which works according to natural laws. Jainism has also produced treatises on Sun, Moon and Earth (Dundas, 2002).

Chapter 11

Controversies related to Creation

The question regarding the beginning of the Universe had been occupying the mind of scientists and philosophers from ancient times to the modern. The creation myths that originated in ancient civilizations like Babylonian, Egyptian, Chinese and Indian have been analyzed and five main concepts have been arrived at (Long CH, 1963).

1) The myth that the god created the world and life on it out of nothing. This view had directly influenced three of the Abrahamic religions, Judaism, Christianity and Islam.

2) Creation from chaos. Creating order from disorder. There had been elements in disorder floating about and order had been created out of this chaos.

3) World Parent theory. There had been a parent or two parents together out of which the world has split and evolved with life.

4) Emergence theory. The present world has emerged from a previous world which would have been the womb of the present universe.

5) Earth diver theory. There had been a supreme being who had send an animal, probably a bird, who had dived into the primal waters to find bits of sand and mud to build the habitable land.

Most of the religions and also theorists have borrowed from the above ideas to formulate their theories on the beginning of the Universe and life on it. The Greek Creation Myth, for instance, put forward by poets Homer and Hesiod seems to have been influenced by the Chaos theory. Hesiod has proposed that out of the chaos and vastness of the space the first goddess Gaea (Earth) was born and she created Uranus (Heaven) who became her husband and they produced many lessor gods. The division between Heaven and Earth occurred when one of their sons, Cronus, out of jealousy attacked his father Uranus. Zeus the one who became the chief god was born from Cronus and his wife Rhea (Mark, 2018).

Buddhism did not believe that the Universe was created by a personal god. In fact it has not spoken about the beginning of the Universe. This is in keeping with its view that the world is not just a physical place but is the phenomenon of conditioned experience and moreover world and samsara in this sense are one and the same. Samsara had no beginning as such and could be ended by the attaining of Nibbāna. Thus Buddhist view on the beginning of the Universe cannot be categorized under any of the five myths mentioned above.

However, Buddha had given a comprehensive theory on the origin of life (not the Universe) in the Aggañña Suttanta of the Dhiga Nikāya. In this Suttanta the main purpose of the Buddha had been to refute the Vedic caste system and its basis; the theory that humans were born out of Brahma's body and the people who belonged to various castes were born from various parts of the body of Brahma. Buddha described how life arose in the world to show that humans were not born out of Brahma's body and that everybody was equal and there was no superior caste as Brahmins claim.

In the Aggañña Suttanta Buddha starts with the dissolution of the world. This is to show that there is no beginning to the world and life. As the world dissolves beings leave the world and go to the heavenly sphere with radiant gods, called the "Abhassara". Buddha does not call those who leave the world and go to live in the heavenly sphere human but he calls them beings. These beings remain in the heavenly sphere for a long time. Now there is darkness and there is no sun, moon or stars. But there are the beings, mind-made, self-luminous and traversing the space. And then there is water and later savoury earth spreads over the water. Then one being who is greedy tastes the savoury earth and craving was born. Others follow and they eat lumps of savoury earth. Then their self-luminosity vanishes and the sun and moon appears and day and night are discernible. Those beings continued to live feeding on the savoury earth. Some of them became good in complexion while others did not. Those who had good complexion felt superior to others and this superior feeling conditioned the disappearance of the savoury earth.

Now a fungus appeared and the beings fed on the fungus, then the complexion improved in some of the beings. Those with better complexion felt proud. This feeling of pride conditioned the disappearance of the fungus. A creeper appeared and the process repeated, this time the better complexioned beings feeling despise towards those with bad complexion. This process continued with appearance of rice and feeding on rice causing the development of the sex organs and passion. With fever as condition the male and female joined in sexual activity.

Buddha goes on to illustrate how craving affected human beings to acquire material wealth and how differences of people in society occurred and how four different castes were created. He says whoever is a monk among those four castes he is highest among them in terms of the moral. Buddhist theory on the origin of life is in keeping with the "paticcasamuppāda". Further the moral dimension which is the basis of every Buddhist doctrine is clearly present. There was no creator god and the cyclic nature of the process is apparent. Buddha starts the description with the end of the process, the dissolution of the world. Arising and dissolution of the world occur continuously as a cyclic process. The "Sattasurya sutta" of the Aṅguttara Nikāya describes how the dissolution of the world occur due to the arising of seven suns.

Jainism also has an elaborate theory on the origin of the world and life in it. They consider universe as uncreated and that it had existed since infinity with neither beginning nor end. Jains do not believe the world was created. It had existed always and continue to exist, it may change from one form to another. Cosmic natural laws govern it and no creator is involved. Most of these ideas agree with modern science. And there is a similarity with Buddhist theory on the origin of the world except that there is a soul involved with the world (Dundas, 2002).

RgVeda is the oldest of the Vedas and may have been started in 1500BC. It has a famous hymn on creation called Nasadiya Suktha also called Hymn of Creation which is given below (Trans. Basham, 1954);

1. Then even non-existence was not there, nor existence,
   There was no air then, nor the space beyond it.
   What covered it? Where was it? In whose keeping?
   Was there then cosmic fluid, in depths unfathomed?

2. Then there was neither death nor immortality
   nor was there then the torch of night and day.
   The One breathed windlessly and self-sustaining.
   There was that One then, and there was no other.

3. At first there was only darkness wrapped in darkness.
   All this was only unillumined cosmic water.
   That One which came to be, enclosed in nothing,
   arose at last, born of the power of knowledge.

4. In the beginning desire descended on it -
   that was the primal seed, born of the mind.
   The sages who have searched their hearts with wisdom
   know that which is, is kin to that which is not.

5. And they have stretched their cord across the void,
   and know what was above, and what below.

Seminal powers made fertile mighty forces.
Below was strength, and over it was impulse.

6. But, after all, who knows, and who can say
Whence it all came, and how creation happened?
the gods themselves are later than creation,
so who knows truly whence it has arisen?

7. Whence all creation had its origin,
the creator, whether he fashioned it or whether he did not,

the creator, who surveys it all from highest heaven,
he knows - or maybe even he does not know

What it says at the end is that nobody knows the origin, even the creator may not know his own origin though he created the world. There had been darkness and cosmic water. Then desire had descended on it. This is a very significant saying. It may have influenced Buddhist thinking on the origin of the world. Though Buddhism does not talk about a creator it talks about darkness and water, and then about defilements that had a role to play in the origin of humans, just as desire had in the RgVeda.

RgVeda talks about a Cosmic Man, "Purusha", a divine emanation of God, an individuation of consciousness, the personal aspect of God. Purusha is divided to create all of the physical universe, men, animals, and plants. Three fourths of the Purusha "ascended high and only one fourth took birth again here". We see only one fourth of reality.

Other Vedic texts, "Manu Dharma Shastral" for example, describe the creation of heaven and earth, the soul and individual creatures. "Manu" the son of the first being performed "tapas" and very difficult austerities to create ten great sages who then created seven other "Manus, who are the progenitors of the human race (Subamoy Das, 2019).

Here an omnipotent God is the creator which is unacceptable to Buddhism. Omniscience, omnipotence and omnipresence are powers that Buddha disclaimed. Buddhism accepts several planes of existence including heaven and hell but these spheres are not created. Further according to the theistic philosophies the world and its inhabitants could be regressed backwards into a single absolute and permanent entity, which is God, which concept Buddha had refuted unequivocally.

None of the different Schools of Buddhism had subscribed to the theory of creation of the Universe by a personal god. Even Mahāyāna and its branches which had been influenced by Hinduism to a good extent had not accepted the creator god theory. The concept of reality and perception of the world in Mahāyāna is different from that in Hinduism. Both its major branches, Madhayamaka and Yogācāra hold that world is a construct of the mind. Thus Mahāyāna obviously cannot agree with the concept of a personal god who created the world.

The modern scientific view on the origin of life seems to be that life originated from matter. There had been several theories. Few of them are given below:

Extraterrestrial origin – This theory postulates that seeds of life exist in planetary bodies in outer space – the so called panspermia theory. These could be carried to Earth by impact-expelled rocks. These seeds of life could form simple organisms like bacteria which could evolve into complex life forms (Ritcher, 1865, Wickramasinghe, 2011).

Spontaneous origin – Non-living matter could form into prebiotic molecules which could develop into more complex structures and acquire the ability to replicate themselves. These structures may have given rise to RNA and later to DNA which is the core structure for generating life.

Biochemical Evolution – This theory was put forward first by Russian scientist O.I. Oparin (1923) and later endorsed by

British scientist J.B.S. Haldane (1928). It suggests that common gases like nitrogen, hydrogen, oxygen, carbon dioxide combined to form simple organic compounds and these formed more complex structures under the conditions that prevailed on the primitive Earth with a "primordial soup" being present in the great mass of water.

According to these theories water was of prime importance. Everything happened in water. In non-theistic religions like Buddhism and Jainism also water was involved in the theories on the origin of life. Further, from simple structures more complex ones were formed according to the Buddhist theory as was the case in the scientific theories.

Chapter 12

Controversies related to God

From the very beginning Man has been bewildered by the mystery of the world around him, the wondrous sights in the sky, mysterious natural events like rain, lightening, cyclones, mysterious diseases and other natural evil. He was also puzzled by his own existence and wondered why he was present on earth and who put him there and for what purpose. He thought some supreme invisible power was responsible for all this and he started pleading and praying for clemency from the evils of nature. He also started to speculate and formulate theories to explain these issues. The concept of god may have originated in this manner.

Due to these speculations and theorizing several types of religions originated and these had theories about god. Some of the religions had god as the creator of the world and life and the Supreme Being responsible for everything including the origin of that religion. Some religions had one god and others had several, each responsible for a specific function or phenomenon; hence there were mono-theistic (Abrahamic religions) and pantheistic religions (Hinduism, Greek mythology). Other religions like Buddhism spoke about the existence of gods but they were separate beings who had no role to play in the origin or destiny of man or the world. Buddhism mentions several types of beings in existence in the different planes of existence and the sphere of gods is one of them.

As Buddhism does not propose that the world was created by a personal omnipotent, omniscient god it is atheistic. The attempt by Mahāyānists as described in the Mahāyāna text Saddharmapunderika Sūthra to make a transcendental, larger than life, omniscient being out of the historical human being that was Buddha, led to the development of the view that according to Mahāyāna Buddha was god. This distortion was so strong that Buddha was almost made an avatar of Vishnu by the Brahmins (Kalupahana, 1995).

Before we look at the reasons why Buddha rejected all types of theism we must have an understanding of the different types of theism that were in vogue during Buddha's time. In pre-Vedic period (3500 – 2000 BC) three stages could be recognized in the development of the concept of god. In the first stage man is central and the god who created him is peripheral but could interfere in man's activities. God has definite form, has human qualities like greed, love, hatred etc. In the second stage there is a purer conception of god, He is the refuge of the whole universe. In the third stage the theory shifts from human created conceptions to truth centred concepts. God is infinite spiritual reality.

Vedic literature reflects all these three stages in varying degree. God evolves in stages into super natural, transcendental, highest, absolute, and finally into spiritual infinite (Nirguna Brahman) in the Vedanta or Upanishads. This description of the evolution proceeds in the form of deliberate questions and analysis rather than an authoritative description. A debate about the religion and philosophy, the personal god and impersonal reality runs together. The approach is inclusive, not exclusive and there are no loose ends to be sorted out. Conception of God leads to conception of absolute Reality (Brahman). Brahman is the personal God, Creator and Lord of the universe. In Vedic tradition God is not an extra-cosmic creator who creates the world out of nothing. Salvation is by prayer to god and sacrificial ritual (Gavin D Flood, 1996).

Makhali Gosala's religion which was known as Ājivika was also theistic and was popular in the 6th Century BC during King Bindusara's reign. In Gosala's religion morals have no role in the destiny of humans. Everybody will attain salvation not through personal effort but by the grace of god in a process of evolution. Whether one does good or evil eventually one will end up attaining salvation like a ball of thread which when flung unravels on the ground until the end of the thread is reached. God is impartial and treats everybody equally. Human being is relieved of responsibility of his actions and is destined to reach salvation in spite of his actions. In this sense Gosala's concept of god compares well with that of other forms of theism where the concept of god involves an omnipotent, omniscient supreme being who has the power to pardon sinners. Further it is consistent in the sense that its strict determinism requires an omnipotent, omniscient god to supervise the world (Basham, 1951).

In Jainism there is no creator god. But everybody has the potential to become god. When humans get rid of all karma he is born in Moksha as a god who has infinite knowledge, supreme bliss and eternal life. In Jainism there is no single god, there are innumerable gods and the number is increasing as more and more reach that state (Dundas, 2002).

Buddha had said there were four types of religions which were false, and four others which were unsatisfactory though not exactly false. Two types of theistic religions were false according to Buddha; one was where individual salvation was not due to personal effort by doing morally good deeds but by the grace of god as in Vedic tradition. The other was where salvation was predestined by theistic evolution as in Ājivika. Buddha had two reasons for criticizing these theistic religions. If god determined everything including man's good and evil deeds and designed the whole world man is an instrument of god's will and god is responsible for man's evil deeds. This was known as the Puppet Argument (Jayatilake, 1975).

To escape this argument the theistic religions that proposed a predestined salvation by theistic evolution said that god had given man a free-will. However divine providence cannot be compatible with a free-will. If god provides for man's salvation man doesn't have to make an effort mentally and physically. Moral behaviour is not required. One has to give up theism or free-will one cannot have both. There cannot be an omnipotent and omniscient creator as well as human beings with free-will, the two are not compatible.

A second Buddhist argument against theism is based on evil that is rampant in the world. If Brahman is all powerful and could have designed the world anyway he wanted why did he create evil, misfortune and unhappiness? For what purpose has he made the world full of injustice, deceit, falsehood? Lord of creation is evil for he had made the world unjust when he could have made it just. All attempts by theists to explain evil have proved to be unsatisfactory. Most of these theories attempt to shroud evil in a mystery that is known only to god. God has his reasons for creating evil seems to be the best explanation (Jayatilake, 1975).

There are other arguments against the concept of god put forward by Theravādins. If ordinary parents cannot remain indifferent when their children suffer how could an omnipotent omniscient god keep aloof when the people he created are suffering? If that is possible then to say that god is extraordinarily kind is meaningless. If god is too great for man to comprehend then his abilities such as being able to design and create a complex world is also beyond comprehension by man. In that case if normal meanings are given to words like all-knowing, all-powerful and infinitely good the evidence is against the existence of god. And on the other hand if those normal meanings are not given to those words the concept of god is meaningless (Jayatilake, 1975).

It may be argued that theism has some good in it such as the feeling of security it gives the helpless people. This may be true but it could be seen that strong belief in god though useful could even cause wars in the name of god.

Though Buddhism is atheist it doesn't approve any type of atheism. Materialist atheism is not approved by Buddhism. Materialists in Buddha's time such as Ajitha Kesakambala believed that there was nothing called good morals and that fools and the wise all end up at death and there is nothing after that. The result and the end was the same whether one did good or evil. Buddha totally refuted such ideas and called them nihilist which was one extreme that Buddha avoided (Jayatilake, 1975).

A majority of modern scientists are atheists (Larson & Witham, 1968). A majority of members of societies of science at the highest level like the Royal Society which is the scientific society in Britain are atheists. A majority of recipients of the Nobel Prize for sciences are atheists.

Modern scientists have put forward several arguments against the theory of creation by a personal god (Dawkins, 2006). Few of them are given below;

Lack of explanation of evil – We have discussed this above.

Poor design – If an omniscient, omnipotent god had designed the universe he could have avoided the weaknesses in design that abound in the universe. If these appear to be weaknesses in the eyes of the humans that god has created, they should not have been committed by an all-knowing, all-powerful god.

Parsimony – Since natural theories adequately explain the development of religions and belief in god actual existence of such supernatural agents is superfluous.

Russell's Tea Pot – If somebody says there is a tea pot circling the earth in space, the burden of proof of this claim lies with the person who made the claim. Similarly the burden of proof that god exists must lie with the theists and not with the atheists. However nobody has proved that God exists.

Stephen Hawking the eminent physicist had deflected the question; Who created the universe to the question; Who created God.

Theists in response to the theory of evolution which is difficult to refute have proposed the Intelligent Design theory which postulates that an intelligent being or force has created the universe and had directed its evolution. They say the theory of natural selection is inadequate to explain the process of evolution of species. Atheist scientists have strongly criticized these theories. The problem of weaknesses in the design mentioned above is applicable to the Intelligent Design theory as well.

Though Buddhism does not subscribe to a theory of creator god Buddhism believes in the existence of gods. As mentioned earlier Buddha has said that there is a world of gods ("deva-loka") which is one of the five destinies that beings could be born in. These gods are not eternal and are subject to impermanence and karmic consequences. They are not omniscient or omnipotent. They are not above Buddha in knowledge or any other quality. They could be reborn in any of the five destinies. Buddha had also spoken about a "Maha Brahmma" who presides over all gods and who had invited Buddha to teach his Dhamma for the good of everybody. Maha Brahmma however is not the Brahma of Hinduism who is the creator (Jayatilake, 1975).

Chapter 13

Controversies related to Truth

Ancient philosophers had pondered over the question regarding truth, what is truth, and whether truth could be known, whether there is an absolute truth and so on. Greek philosophers Socrates, Plato and Aristotle were of the opinion that truth was the relationship between thoughts or statements on the one hand and things and objects on the other. Truth is arrived at when cognition corresponds with the object. Later these ideas were put together into what is known as the Correspondence Theory of Truth (Prior, 1969).

There are several such theories on truth in Western philosophy;

Coherence theory – When propositions in a coherent system lend mutual inferential support to each other such a system would be truth.

Pragmatic theory – This proposes that truth is only the expedient in our way of thinking.

Consensus theory – When there is agreement on some idea or object among a group the idea could be considered the truth.

What is the Buddhist theory of truth? Early Buddhist view is that a statement is true when it is in accordance with facts. This idea appears to have a close similarity with the Correspondence theory mentioned above. When a statement is not in accordance with fact it will be false (Jayatilake, 1975).

Similarly consistency and coherence in ideas and statements would mean that there is truth in them and on the other hand when there is inconsistency and incoherence in the ideas and statements those would be false. Here it appears that Buddhism has adopted the Coherence theory of truth. Buddha had used this method to prove that assertions by his opponents are not true.

If there are several theories regarding the nature of man all cannot be true, there has to be one true idea or statement. Here it is consistency that matters. However, all those theories could be wrong. If several religious leaders put forward several different theories about an issue could all be true? Obviously not. In the Sutta Nipatha (Kuddhaka Nikāya) it is said that consistency is a criterion for the establishment of truth (Premasiri, 2018).

When these theories of truth adopted by Buddhism are applied to the ideas and views of Materialists, Sceptics, Ājīvikas, Jains etc. it is seen that all those ideas of all those philosophies cannot be true. One has to carefully weigh the evidence to find out what ideas meet the criteria of the Correspondence Theory or the Coherence Theory that Buddhism recommends.

Buddhism has not recommended the Pragmatic theory as applicable under all circumstances. For instance it does not say that what is false if useful could be adopted because it is pragmatic to do so. However this policy on pragmatism may change under different circumstances. For instance ideas which are true and useful but are unpleasant could be adopted though such a policy seems to belong in the category of pragmatism (Jayatilake, 1975).

The above categorization refers to the possibility of two alternatives i.e. true or false. However there could be more alternatives. For instance if the two alternative theory is applied to the state of the mind of happiness, a person could be either happy or unhappy. But there could be other states of mind regarding happiness. A person could be partly happy and partly unhappy or neither happy nor unhappy. In order to deal with all these alternatives the four cornered logic or "chatuskoti" (tetralemma - Greek) was developed. The four alternatives may be given as follows; 1)Happy, 2) Unhappy, 3) Partly happy and partly unhappy 4) Neither happy nor unhappy.

However opponents of this method of logic point out that these four alternatives may not be exclusive of each other. For instance 3) above has within it both 1) and 2). Further, 4) is equivalent to 3).

In the Mūlamādhyamakakāriika Nāgārjuna also uses the four cornered logic to refute all possible alternatives that could arise with controversial issues like soul, nature of Thathāgatha etc.

Some have observed that negation of all four alternatives amount to silence regarding the issue in question for the words in the language in use cannot explain the problem. In other words it is inexplicable. When this inexplicability concerns the nature of Thathāgatha for instance the question arises whether the state of the Thathāgatha is transcendental. This aspect will be discussed in Chapter 18 on Nibbāna.

Truth features significantly in the Vedas. The Sanskrit word for truth is "satya". In the Vedic literature satya is a central theme. Another important concept in the Veda is "Rta" which means order, rule, nature, balance, harmony and that which is properly joined. "Rta" results from "Satya" as it regulates and enables the operation of the Universe. "Satya" is considered essential and without it universe and reality falls apart as it cannot function without the support of each other.

In RgVeda truthfulness is considered as a form of reverence for the divine. In the Brihadaranayaka Upanishad "Satya" is called the means to Brahman. "Satya" is also the Brahman. It also equates "Satya" to Dharma which is morality, ethics and law of righteousness. In Mahabharata it is said that the Righteous hold that forgiveness, truth, sincerity, and compassion are the foremost of all virtues (Hindery, 2004).

It is noted that according to Upanishads Truth is Brahman. Further in the Baghavad Gita Krishna represents Truth. Thus in the Vedas and Hinduism truth is given a divine state and made equivalent to Brahman.

The Two Truths concept is another distinguishing feature in Buddhism. This concept assumes importance on account of its relevance in the understanding of Buddha's teaching. The concept of two truths in Buddhism appears in the Sangiti sutta (Dīgha Nikāya). The two types of truths are the conventional truth ("sammuti") and the absolute truth ("paramatta"). For instance a human being may be recognized by the characteristic features of the species and the being is called human. This is the conventional truth about the human being. This human being is comprised of the five aggregates and this definition of the human being could be the absolute truth. Buddha said both these truths have their uses and one is not superior to the other when their usage and context in which they are used are considered. Here the conventional truth about the human being would be useful in social interaction and moral behaviour while the absolute truth would be useful when the impermanence and soullessness of the human being is contemplated.

Nāgārjuna also uses the two truth analysis to answer the question; if his theory of emptiness is correct would the Four Noble Truths be negated ("Mūlamadhyamaka-kārikā" Chapter 24). Nāgārjuna's answer to this question is that Buddha uses two truths concept in his preaching. The conventional truth helps in understanding the Dharma and the absolute truth helps in attaining freedom. In this sense his theory of emptiness is a conventional truth while the Four Noble Truths may be considered an absolute truth.

This concept of two truths is not found in the Vedic literature. However, Mimamsa (5th CE), one of the six orthodox schools of Hinduism, had criticized and refuted the two truths concept saying it is idealistic. Eigth Century Mimamsa philosopher Kumarasila Bhatta rejected the Two Truth Doctrine in his

"Shlokavarthika" (Debiprasad Chattopadhyaya 2001). Mimamsa came into being at a time when the idealist Schools of Buddhism, Madhyamaka and Yogācāra, were well established and their idealist interpretations of the two truths concept were known. Yogācāra interpretation was that all objects were constructs of the mind and therefore they compose the conventional truth while pure consciousness was the absolute truth. Madhyamaka interpretation was that the conventional truth was the illusory mode of appearance of objects which is not in agreement with their mode of existence. The absolute truth was the mode of appearance of objects that was in agreement with their mode of existence. The idealist tilt in these interpretations is not difficult to ascertain. This idea was put forward by Chandrakirti (6th CE) one of the theorists of Maddhyamaka who authored and was responsible for its development (Thakchoe, 2017).

The two major breakaway groups of Theravāda, the Sarvāstivāda and Sautrāntika, also had their interpretations of the two truths concept. The former said the whole of an object which is reducible is the conventional truth of the object and the irreducible particles, atoms, constitute the absolute truth. The latter held that the workability of phenomena decided whether they constitute the absolute truth or the conventional truth. If the phenomenon is workable it is the absolute truth and if it is not it is the conventional truth. The influence of the Sarvāsthivādin's atomic theory and their Abhidharmic approach are evident in their interpretation of the two truths theory. Sautrāntika did not subscribe to the Abhidharma project and their analysis of Dhamma consisted of the "mahabutha" and "citta" and not any further. Thus their theory of the two truths concept is based on the workability of phenomena (Warder, 2000).

Jainism also had proposed a two truth concept, according to them there could be mundane perspective which could be considered the conventional truth and ultimate perspective which is the absolute truth.

Chapter 14

Controversies related to Religious Rituals

It may be possible that man in early times practised rituals. He was bewildered and fearful of his environment which to him appeared to be full of evil. The various ailments and injuries that afflicted him also would have made him feel helpless. He would have wondered how and why he came into being and also what created him and his world. He may have looked for solace in the objects of wonder that were present in his environment like the sun, the moon, the stars, rocks and trees. He would have prayed to these objects and asked for help. He may have performed dances and made offerings of animals, flowers, incense etc. and asked for mercy and protection from evil.

Feeling of awe and wonder at the sight of wonderful, mysterious and gigantic phenomena could be an inherent feature. This character may be observed in the behaviour of chimpanzees, the closest ape to humans in the evolutionary process. The well-known "waterfall dance" of chimpanzees could be due to an evolutionary trait than accident. When chimpanzees approach a waterfall they seem to be awe-struck and start swaying back and forward in rhythmic movement as if overwhelmed by the feeling of awesomeness at the sound of the cascading water and the sight of the waterfall.

Such emotions may have been inherent in the human system as well and such strong emotions may have influenced the creation of objects of worship, rituals, religions and perhaps god. Ancient people believed in the magical abilities of rituals and many cultures used fire to worship their gods. Religious rituals have developed as a feature in all societies (Lindenfors & Svensson, 2021).

In the Vedic tradition rituals grew in complexity and became the central theme of the tradition. It is difficult to imagine Vedic culture without its ritual component. In early Vedas animal sacrifice was one of the main ritualistic features. Later Hinduism has adopted rituals as a main feature of their religious practice. Eighth Century Mimamsa philosopher Kumarila Bhatta was highly influential with his defence of the Vedic rituals (Debiprasad Chattopadhyaya, 2001). Mimamsa was a School of Hinduism that developed much later than Buddhism.

Rituals seem to provide the people with some psychological solace and hope against calamity. Rituals were supposed to fulfil the following benefits to people;

Rituals cast a magic spell that would protect the people from evil.

Remove sin and resolve karma

Rituals are an act of charity and service

Rituals are a duty to god

Rituals help to overcome suffering

Rituals are a means of exchanging gifts

Rituals would bring peace and happiness

Rituals would celebrate life and its events

One could see that rituals which could be a set of activities involving gestures, words, bodily movements, objects etc. have a long history and may have a Darwinian evolutionary origin. Subsequently religious rituals have developed with the advent of religions and have become an essential component of almost all religions. Religious rituals are usually performed with the expectation of benefits as mentioned above (Flood, 1996).

However rituals as part of religious practice have not been mentioned in early Buddhism. The four major Buddhist Nikāyas, Dīgha, Majjima, Aṅguttara and Samyutta do not mention rituals as a component of religious practice. Buddha had not asked his followers to perform any rituals, worship, chanting, offering, sacrifices etc.

There is no mention of rituals that lead to Nirvāna in early Buddhist texts, either in the Tipiṭakaya or in the Chinese Agama. These are the texts considered as the source material for early Buddhism which is believed to be closest to what the Buddha preached.

However, it is important to consider, first of all, the significance of rituals in the religious context. In religions which have an omnipotent god or some other kind of saviour, worship and praying are encouraged and sometimes compulsory for devout practitioners of those religions. The worshiper is made to believe that salvation is possible by the intervention of god or similar force in answer to the prayers. Further the practitioner of these religions are required to have unwavering faith and are expected not to question the ability of the god to deliver despite apparent failures in that regard. This is nothing but blind faith that one is expected to have in god, deity or similar being. It is claimed that when one prays one is rewarded by the grace of god but there is no evidence to support this claim. In theistic religions the final goal is union with god in a transcendental realm beyond the sphere of this world for which god's grace is required. Thus the basis of religious rituals is the belief in a supernatural being who helps one to achieve the final goal which makes the philosophical basis of such a religion a transcendental theory.

In Theravāda Buddhism, however, the final goal is Nibbāna which could be achieved only by one's own effort. According to

Theravāda Buddhism Nibbāna cannot be achieved by prayers, worship and similar rituals for there is no supernatural being who could respond and help the practitioner of rituals. In Mahāyāna, on the other hand, the transcendental features in the form of Bodhisathva and the "Thrikaya" concept bring in the need for the practice of rituals.

In Theravada the word used is Bodhisatta while it is Bodhisathva in Mahāyāna. The word has different meanings in Pāli and Sanskrit reflecting the difference in Theravāda and Mahāyāna interpretations of the concept. In Pāli Texts "Bodhi" meant wisdom and "satta"meant goodness. In the Sanskrit texts Bodhisathva means a strong person who does good deeds for everybody. Bodhisathva in Mahāyāna has to perform rituals in his journey to the final goal.

Further Mahāyāna proposes an alternate path to the final goal which is called "Bhakthi Marga" (Path of Faith) as opposed to "Ñāna Mārga" (Path of Wisdom) which is the only path advocated by Buddha. "Bhakthi Marga" is based on rituals and is a concept found in "Bhagavadgita" a major Hindu text. Mahāyānists believed that rituals would help in finding union with "Dharmakāya" one of the "Thrikāyas" or three manifestations of Buddha which is comparable to the "Thrimūrthi" concept in Hinduism where Vishnu, Ishvara and Brahmma were the three manifestations of god. In contrast no union with any transcendental being is necessary to achieve Nirvāna that Buddha discovered. Thus rituals are compulsory in Mahāyāna for attaining the final goal which is transcendental like in other theistic religions. In this respect Mahāyāna seems to be closer to Hinduism than to Early Buddhism (Sasanārathana, 1952).

There is sufficient evidence to conclude that the Buddhism brought to Sri Lanka by Ven Mahinda was free of transcendental features due to the efforts of Ven Moggalliputtatissa at the Third Dhamma Sangāyanāwa which was held under the auspices of King Dharmasoka just before his son went on his mission to Sri Lanka (Kalupahana, 2008). Therefore it may be surmised that the Buddhism practiced in Sri Lanka since then until about the 5th Century was free of transcendental features which as mentioned above is the basis of rituals in religion.

Mahāyāna was the dominant religion in Sri Lanka from the 5th Century to the 10th. During this period it succeeded in getting some of its important tenets introduced into Buddhism in Sri Lanka, chief among which was transcendentalism and its offspring the rituals. When Mahāyāna declined in India so it did in Sri Lanka too. Yet the damage had been done and its ill effects such as yanthra, manthra, yaga, puja etc., which arrived in the wake of rituals, remain. Natha and Saman deviyo whom Sri Lankan Buddhists worship are adaptations of Bodhisathvas named Avalokethisvara and Samanthabadda respectively.

The building of stupa had started soon after the demise of the Buddha by the younger generation of monks. They were saddened by the loss of their beloved teacher and they started building stupa in his memory. But veneration of these stupa may not have been in practice at that time and may have been introduced later due to the influence of other religions and the development of Mahāyāna which was more amenable to accepting tenets of Hinduism as suggested above. Though relics were placed in the stupa they may not have been objects of worship (Marasinghe, 2015).

Kevaddha Sutta (Dīgha Nkaya) mentions four persons who are worthy of being respected by building stupa for the purpose of enshrining their relics. These four are; Buddha, Pacceka Buddha, a disciple of Buddha, and Chakkawathi king. Obviously such stupas are not meant for veneration and worship but for respect which Buddha encouraged. Further such respect is not given in expectation of any benefit which is the case with rituals.

As mentioned earlier Buddhist discourses do not mention rituals yet some Commentaries written later speak about rituals. For example the Commentary on the Dhammapada, the Dhammapadattakatha (attributed to Buddhagosa) says Buddha in a previous birth as the brahmana Saṅkha cleared away the grass in the compound of a chetiya containing the relics of a Paccekabuddha and offered flowers, and the merit of this act was reaped when he became Buddha. While the Buddhagosa's Commentary of the Dhammapada seems to recommend rituals the Dhammapada itself gives hardly any value to the practice of rituals (Adikaram, 1946).

"Sumangalavilasini" the Commentary on Dīgha Nikāya authored by Buddhagosa describes how Buddha's relics which usually remain in one mass, as has happened in the case of previous Buddhas, had separated into several pieces to enable them to be deposited in stupas far and wide for purposes of worshiping by many people. Further "Sammohavinodani" the Commentary on the "Vibhanga" of the Abhidhamma, authored by Buddhagosa says the belief that the presence of a relic is equivalent to the presence of Buddha was deep rooted in the minds of Sinhalese Buddhists. Though the Commentaries seem to encourage the practice of rituals the corresponding Texts do not mention rituals to be of any value. This deviation has to be considered together with the moral ethics that Buddha preached which in contrast do not give any value to rituals. For instance the five precepts ("panchaseela") do not recommend worship of the Buddha, neither do the eight or ten precepts ("Ata or Dasa sil"). The Nikāyas do not mention worshiping of Buddha by his disciples though greeting and respect that they pay to their teacher are mentioned.

Later Buddhist philosophers like Moggallaputtatissa, Nāgārjuna, Asaṅga, Vasubandhu, and others have not spoken about rituals nor practiced them. In their writings they start with a verse to pay their respect to Buddha but have not used language that could be construed as veneration or worship that derive benefits in return.

Chapter 15

Controversies related to Emptyness ("Śūnyatā")

The word "śunya" means empty. Feeling of emptiness could mean boredom or depression. In Buddhism the word has a deeper meaning pertaining to existence. Buddha had used the word śūnya in his discourses and there is a discourse titled "Cūlasuññata sutta" (Majjhima Nikāya) which explains Buddha's idea of suññatā. In this discourse Buddha says he dwells in the dwelling of emptiness. The question here is whether Buddha equated the state of Nibbāna with the state of emptiness which some thinkers have said to be probable. This may not be correct for what the Buddha means by emptiness may be lack of self and substantiality in the world and life. Buddha had described in detail the final stage of Nibbāna in the Sāmaññaphala sutta (Dīgha Nikāya) and he makes no reference to a state of emptiness in relation to Nibbāna. What he describes in the Cūlasuññata-sutta is the insubstantiality of life, the emptiness of everything that is dispositionally conditioned. In this Sutta Buddha advises his disciples not to focus on people and society but to focus on the forest and then on the earth for the former was full of sense pleasures but the latter is not so. He wants the monks to concentrate on objects which are empty of self and substantiality which will help them to "descend into undistorted pure emptiness". Buddha does not refer to Nibbāna in Cūlasuññata-sutta just as much as he does not refer to emptiness in the Sāmaññaphala-sutta which describes the path to Nibbāna. The word "suñña" also appears in "Mahāsuññata-sutta" (Majjhima-Nikāya"), "Suttanipāta" and in "Kaccāyanagotta-sutta" (Saṃyutta Nikāya). In these discourses also Buddha had used the word suñña to mean the insubstantiality of the material world. The word Nibbāna does not appear in any of these discourses. Moreover the word "suñña" does not appear in the descriptions and explanations of Nibbāna in the Sutta Piṭaka.

Vedic literature does not speak about "śūnyatā" in the same sense that Buddha spoke about it or Mahāyāna later theorized about it. In the Nāsadīya-sūtra of the ṚgVeda which carries a poem on creation, which we have mentioned earlier in the Chapter 11 on Creation, it is said that at the beginning there was neither existence nor non-existence, and no sun or moon, in fact it could mean that there was nothing. Apart from this reference to nothingness there is no deep idea on a theory of emptiness in the Veda that pertains to existence.

However there were Western philosophers who were impressed by the theories coming out of the East particularly the Yogācāra and Madhyamaka ideas on "śūnyatā". Thousand five hundred years after these theories were developed by Eastern philosophers like Asaṅga (4th CE), Western philosophers like Fredric Nietzsche (19th CE), Martin Heidegger (19th CE) influenced by these theories developed their ideas about nihilism, being and existence.

Nāgārjuna also used the word "śūnya" in the same sense as the Buddha. During Nāgārjuna's time, in the end of the 1st CE substantialist ideas had been adopted by Sarvāstivāda school of Buddhism. The concept of "svabhāva", an essence that is permanently present in all Dhammas, was put forward by Sarvāstivāda. This was in response to the questions raised by detractors of Buddhism; if there is no self or substance in the Dhammas who would be responsible for karma and who is reborn?

Sautrāntika school of Buddhism had, in opposition to the "svabhāva" concept, proposed their nihilistic concepts. They were of the opinion that there was no phase of existence as such in the arising and disappearance of Dhammas. They arise and soon disappear without existing. This idea was thought to be nihilist. Nāgārjuna in his Mūlamadhyamakakārikā was intent on disproving these theories as well as refuting several other views. These matters will be discussed further in Chapter 25.

Nāgārjuna has clearly shown in his closing verse in the "Mūlamadhayamakakārikā" and also by making reference to the "Kaccāyanagotta-sutta" (which describes "paṭiccasamuppāda") that the basis of his treatise is the "paṭiccasamuppāda". The latter Sutta espouses the importance of adhering to the middle path avoiding the extremes of existence and non-existence and then goes on to describe the "paṭiccasamuppāda".

A.Tilakaratne (2001) is of the opinion that Nāgārjuna in the "Kārikā" has indicated that the middle path, the pratītyasamutpāda and "śūnyatā", all three convey the same truth. Nāgārjuna says that in the manner that all Dharmas are subject to "pratītyasamutpanna" (dependently arisen) they are also subject to "śūnya".

Some thinkers, however, hold that Nāgārjuna's idea of "Śūnyatā" is transcendental truth (TRV Murti, 1955). They say the final reality is "śūnyatā" and "śūnyatā" is part of reality. This may not be correct for what Nāgārjuna did was to use "śūnyatā" as a means of refuting all views and not propound a new theory. "Śūnyatā" theory of Nāgārjuna does not add anything new to reality (Kalupahana, 2008). Ven.Nāgārjuna has said in the "Kārikā" itself that if anybody attempts to adopt "śūnyatā" as a view he is suffering from an incurable disease.

D.J.Kalupahana(2008) also is of the opinion that Nāgārjuna's enterprise was to prove the fallibility of the substantialist and nihilist views that had entered into Buddhism as well as to refute all other such views that were not in conformity with Buddha's teachings.

In the Cūlasuññata-sutta (Majjhima Nikāya) Buddha preaches on the method to "descend into undistorted pure emptiness" and he also says he "dwells in the dwelling of emptiness". Nāgārjuna however, does not talk about emptiness as a state into which one could descend into or dwell in. Hence the question arises whether they were talking about the same thing. However if Buddha's idea of "descending into" and "dwell in" means that he is advising monks to take up the middle path and avoid extremes and if middle path is similar to emptiness as Nāgārjuna has suggested there is no disparity between what Buddha preached in "Cūlasuññata-sutta" and what Nāgārjuna said in "Kārikā". Nāgārjuna is only expanding on what Buddha had said.

As mentioned earlier Nāgārjuna's ideas about emptiness had developed into an idealist school of Buddhism, Madhyamaka, which spread first in South India and then in China and Tibet. A.Tilakaratne (2001) identifies four stages in the development of this school. These stages are as follows; 1) Nāgārjuna(1st – 2nd CE) and his close pupils write the early texts on the "śūnyatāvāda", 2) Two monks Buddhapālita (5th – 6th CE) and Bhāvaviveka (6th CE) write commentaries on the "Kārikā", 3) Ven. Candrakīrti (7th CE) writes "Prasannapadā" and supports the views of Buddhapālita, 4) Two monks Śāntrakṣitha and Kamalaśīla begin the project to develop concepts with the intention of bringing together Madhayamaka and Yogācāra philosophies.

Controversies related to Emptyness ("Śūnyatā")

Two of the pupils of Ven. Nāgārjuna who wrote commentaries on the latter's works were Ven.Āryadeva and Ven. Nāgabodhi. Ven Āryadeva had accepted Bodhisattva concept and his main treatise was "Catuṣṣataka" which had attempted to refute the views of several philosophies of that time such as "Saṅkhya", "Vaiśeṣika", Jain and Theism. The other pupil Nāgabodhi also wrote commentaries on Prajñāpāramitā texts and helped to develop a link between Madhyamaka philosophy and Prajñāpāramitā sūtra which are Mahāyāna texts.

In the second stage of development of the Madhayamaka philosophy the writing of commentaries by Buddhapālita (470 – 540 CE) and Bhāvaviveka (500 – 570 CE) was the important activity. Buddhapālita attempted to reject the criticism aimed against the "Kārikā" and develop what is known as "Prāsaṅgika" sect of the Madhayamaka School. Bhāvaviveka developed another sect called "Svātantrika" again by writing commentaries on the "Kārikā". His position was that "Prāsaṅgika" methods of Buddhapālita was inadequate because mere refutation of views of others is not good enough and that "Kārikā" has to be strengthened by strengthening its own views and for this purpose he adopted methods of logic that were being developed by thinkers like Dignāga and Dharmakīrti (see Chapter 26 on these two philosophers).

In the third stage of development of Madhayamaka philosophy Ven.Candrakīrti's commentary titled "Prasannapadā" was written and it supported Ven.Buddhapālita's "Prāsaṅgika" method. This commentary includes a lengthy study of the first verse of the first chapter of "Kārikā" which says, "Indeed no existents whatsoever are evident anywhere that are arisen from itself, from another, from both, or from non-cause". In this lengthy analysis Candrakīrti criticizes Bhāvaviveka's "Svātantrika" method. Further he endorses Buddhapālita's

"Prāsaṅgika" method of refuting all ideas critical of "Kārikā" as the best method of appraisal of "Kārikā". "Prāsaṅgika" ideas have developed as a separate sect of the "Madhyamaka" school in Tibet and Mongolia (A Tilakaratne, 2001).

Development of Madhyamaka philosophy outside India was mainly in China and Tibet. Ven Kumārajīva was instrumental in taking the Madhayamaka philosophy to these two countries.

What is important and crucial in these discussions is to see whether Ven. Nāgārjuna's intention was to start a separate school of thought based on the concept of emptiness that had been mentioned in Early Buddhism. Are the thinkers and philosophers listed above who developed the new schools of Buddhism correct in what they did and are their actions justified? The opinion on this matter is varied.

In finding an answer to this question what is most important is to see whether "Mūlamādhymikakārikā" propounds a new philosophy. It can be seen that in the 27 Chapters of this treatise an examination of all fundamental doctrines of Early Buddhism such as perception, aggregates, dhātu etc. has been carried out. According to A.Tilakaratne (2001) there is no association between the different analyses and there is no attempt to put forward a coherent theory for the development of a new philosophy. However D.J.Kalupahana (2008) thinks there is some continuity in the analyses given in the different chapters though he also is of the view that Nāgārjuna's intention was not to formulate a new philosophy profound enough to develop into a new School of Buddhism.

What is quite clear is that Nāgārjuna in "Kārikā" attempts to refute the extremist substantialist views, both eternalist and nihilist, that had crept into Buddhism in relation to these doctrines due to the activities of different schools of Buddhism like Pudgalavāda, Sarvāstivāda and Sautrāntika. What he does is to take up the contradictions in these views and show the emptiness of the views. He also refutes the four-cornered "tetralemma" or "catuṣkoṭi" logic that had been used by the substantialists to augment their theories. His main idea is that no one should be attached to views which are void of any character that make them worthy of being attached to. Buddha in the Brahmajāla-sutta (Dīgha Nikāya) shows that views could be a significant constraint on the path to Nibbāna.

Kalupahana (2008) says the first twenty verses of the "Kārikā" contain Nāgārjuna's assumptions about the criticism of his views, particularly those about emptiness, by the opponents. The rest of the verses which amount to about 480 attempt to reverse the arguments against him. Kalupahana says what emerges out of this refutation is Buddha's concept of emptiness based on "paṭicca-samuppāda".

Further Kalupahana is of the opinion that Candrakīrti completely distorted the intentions of Nāgārjuna in the "Kārikā" and attempted to portray him as a Mahāyānist. Candrakīrti in his "Prasannapadā" claims that Nagārjuna had asserted that "pratītya-smutpāda" itself is empty. Thus he supports a theory, which had its roots in the works of Nāgārjuna's close pupils mentioned above, that everything is empty meaning that nothing including the mind exists.

Nāgārjuna's main intention in the "Kārikā" has been to rescue Buddha's teachings which were being adulterated by eternalist and nihilist views. He tries to show that all views including those of Buddha such as "Pratītya-samutpāda" and Nirvāṇa are empty of any character that makes them worthy of being attached to with egoistic emotion. Candrakīrti and others had misinterpreted his thesis and had distorted the arguments to make it appear that Nāgārjuna had claimed Nirvāṇa is equivalent to emptiness.

Yogācārins criticized the Madhyamaka theory calling it nihilism. Yogācāra has put forward an idealist philosophy which says everything exists in the mind. Madhyamaka goes beyond that and says even the mind does not exist. Nāgārjuna, however, may not have meant any of that. It is his pupils and later philosophers like Buddhapālita and Candrakīrti who were responsible for the creation of a separate School of Buddhism based on former's views.

Yogācāra had their own view on emptiness. Asaṅga who is supposed to be the founder of Yogācāra, in his "Abhidharmasamuccaya", says emptiness is the non-existence of the self and the existence of the no-self. The non-existence of duality is indeed the existence of non-existence, this is the definition of emptiness. It is neither existence nor non-existence, neither different nor identical.

Early Buddhist schools such as Mahāsāṅgika and also Sthavira schools except Pudgalavādins held that all Dharmas were empty. Sarvāstivādins based their idea of emptiness on "pratītyasamutpāda". Early Theravāda Abhidhamma text "Paṭisambhidāmagga" speaks about the emptiness of the five aggregates. Prajñāpāramitā Sūtras of Mahāyāna also say all entities including Dhammas are empty of self. Kathāvatthu authored by Moggalīputtatissa and included in the Tipiṭaka argues against the idea that emptiness is conditioned.

It could be seen that from early times to the present there had been, in the main, two views on emptiness. One is that emptiness means the absence of self or anything substantial in all phenomena. The other view is that emptiness is an ultimate reality which may be equivalent to Nibbāna. The former view is held by Theravādins and their breakaway groups. The Madhyamaka schools subscribe to the latter view. In China and Tibet the basic and pervasive philosophy of Buddhism seems to be the "śūnyatāvāda" which was initiated by the pupils of Nāgārjuna and later developed into a religious philosophy by monks like Buddhapālita and Candrakīrti. This division has been persistent right up to the present times as could be seen in countries where Theravāda is practiced i.e. mainly in Sri Lanka, Thailand, Myanmar and Cambodia while an amalgamation of Yogācāra and Madhyamaka is practiced in China. In Tibet further modifications have taken place resulting in Tantrayāna. "Śūnyatāvāda" features strongly in the religious philosophies in China and Tibet. These religious philosophies will be discussed in a later chapter.

Chapter 16

Controversies related to the Path of Enlightenment

"Ariyaṭṭhaṅgikamagga" is the Theravāda path to enlightenment or Nibbāna. Buddha has said that an intelligent and committed person can follow this eightfold path unaided and by his own effort reach the final goal of Nibbāna. "Sāmaññaphala-sutta" of the Dīgha Nikāya gives a comprehensive description of the path and also the mental state of the person who had reached the final goal.

Clearly it is a process of first cleansing and preparing of the mind and then an intensive training to concentrate the mind in order to prevent entry of perceptions that would lead to formation of "saṅkara" and consciousness and finally to suffering. When the mind is free of all influx it could spew out the defilements "Loba, Dvesha, Moha" which is the state of Nibbāna. In the process of concentration the individual would pass through several stages of higher knowledge; "Sohān", "Sakurdāgāmi", "Anāgāmi" and finally "Arahath".

Thus Nibbāna in Theravāda Buddhism is a higher form of knowledge obtained through wisdom. Therefore the method is known as the "Ñāna Mārga" or Path of Wisdom. The Buddha had not recommended any other method. The discourses do not mention any other path. Buddha had not spoken about a method where there could be accumulation of merit while going through "samsara" and by virtue of this merit attain Nibbāna.

Though the Noble Eight-fold path or "Ariyaṭṭhaṅgikamagga" is accepted as the recommended path as mentioned in the Samannpahala sutta in several other suttas in the Sutta-Piṭakaya slightly different methods with alternative sequence of stages and different numbers of stages are given. The following suttas show such differences;

Tevijja sutta (Dīgha-Nikāya)– 10 stages

Cula-Hattipadopāma sutta (Majjima-Nikāya) – 12 stages

Mahā-Assapura-sutta (Majjima-Nikāya)– 16 stages

Sekha-sutta (Samyutta-Nikāya) – 9 stages

Let us look at these discourses which describe the path to enlightenment. In the Tevijja-sutta (Dīgha-Nikāya) two Brahmins Vasetha and Bharadvaja who have different views on the path to find Brahma, the creator god, ask Buddha to tell them the right path to Brahma. Buddha after saying that the Brahmins versed in the Three Vedas do not know the path to Brahma for they are immersed in household desire, explains the life of the recluse who has given up household desires and how the recluse gets rid of the five hindrances and finds Brahma. Here it appears that the path described by Buddha does not end up in the state of Thathgatha. Some are of the view that the path described in the Tevijja-sutta ends up in the state of "Brahma Vihara". The word "vihara" means dwell. There are four "Brahma Viharas" in Buddhism and they are "metta, karuna, mudita, upekka". Here what Buddha refers to as Brahma is a god who features in Buddhist discourses as a chief god but not the creator god found in Hinduism.

The "Cūla-Hattipadopāma-sutta" (Majjima-Nikāya) is another sutta where Buddha talks about the path to Nibbāna. Ven. Mahinda selected this sutta for his first sermon to the people of Sri Lanka. In this sutta Buddha employs the simile of the elephant foot print to explain the process gone through by the Buddha to attain enlightenment. When one sees a large foot print of an elephant in a forest one must not come to the conclusion that the foot print belongs to a large elephant. Only when the foot prints, tusk scrapings and breaking of branches at a high level and the large elephant itself are seen could one come to that conclusion. Buddha refers to the stages gone through in the path to enlightenment and says they are the four foot prints of an Arahath.

While staying in Assapura Buddha delivers the "Assapura-sutta" (Majjima-Nikāya) in which he advices monks how to achieve mindfulness, cleanse the mind and body, get rid of the five hindrances and arrive at four "jhanas".

Sekha-sutta (Samyutta-Nikāya) describes how to discern between a learner and an adept and in the process elaborates on the method of attaining enlightenment.

Anyway all these methods describe more or less the same method of attaining enlightenment which involves first a process of purification of body and mind and then intense concentration to spew out the defilements mainly "Loba, Dvesha, Moha" and attain the state of wisdom which is Nibbāna. Ariyaṭṭhaṅgikamagga which is widely accepted as the method that corresponds closely with the process described in the "Sāmaññaphala-sutta" (Majjima-Nikāya) has the following eight steps; 1) "sammā ditti" (right view), 2) "sammā saṅkappa" (right concept), 3) "sammā vāchā" (right speech), 4) "sammā kammantha (right action), 5) "sammā ājiva" (right livelihood), 6) "sammā vāyā" (right effort), 7) "sammā sati" (right attentiveness) and 8) "sammā samādi" (right concentration).

Note that it starts with right view and also right concept so that one gains a good understanding of the nature of life, as enunciated in the "anicca, dukha, anatta". Then there is virtuous living with correct speech, physical action and livelihood. The virtuous life is followed by right effort where there is no laziness and one is ready to make a great effort. This stage is followed by achievement of attentiveness and then concentration. The "Ariyaṭṭhaṅgikamagga" is aimed at giving the practitioner a correct view of life and then with a great effort to cleanse the mind of impurities and finally to intensely concentrate in order to stop all influx of perception, get rid of defilements, "loba, dvesha, moha" and thereby achieve the wisdom of Nibbāna.

In addition to the above the "Visuddimagga" written by Buddhagosa and included in the Sutta-Piṭakaya describes a method comprising several stages of purification. Whether such purification leads to Nibbāna is a matter of conjecture. It initially says that when taking the path of liberation the presence of others could be a hindrance. But later it paradoxically says presence of others such as corpse and teachers would be helpful. The presence of corpse would help in the realization of impermanence and unattractiveness of human body. Teachers may help in giving constructive criticism and instruction on the method of meditation etc.

"Visuddimagga" means the path of purification. The text gives a path of purification consisting of seven stages as follows;

Purification of conduct ("sīla visuddi")

Purification of mind ("citta visuddi")

Purification of view ("ditti visuddi")

Purification of overcoming of doubt ("kankara vittārana visuddi)

Purification of knowledge and vision of what is path and not path

Purification by knowledge and vision of the Course of Practice

Purification by knowledge and vision

Ven. Buddhagosa had come to Sri Lanka mainly to translate the commentaries of the Tipiṭaka from Sinhalese into Pāli presumably for the benefit of Indian scholars. His famous work titled "Visuddimagga" apparently describes a method of purification which leads to enlightenment. Buddha's "Ariyaṭṭhaṅgikamagga" has purification of the mind as a component of the path to enlightenment which has to be followed by intense concentration and insight meditation. Path of Purification in "Visuddimagga" talks about purification by knowledge and vision. Whether these steps correspond to the final steps in the "Ariyaṭṭhaṅgikamagga" where wisdom plays an important role is debatable. Insight meditation, without which attainment of Nibbāna is not possible, may be an exercise that goes beyond purification. The word purification may not define the change that occurs in the mind of a practitioner of insight meditation in the final stages of enlightenment. This is borne out by the fact that Buddhagosa in recommending this method says he does not want to attain Nibbāna but would wait to hear preaching by the next Buddha, Meithriya.

However, another alternative method has been introduced into Theravāda Buddhism, which was not mentioned in Early Buddhism, and this has happened due to the influence of Mahāyāna which was the dominant religion from the 5th CE to the 10th CE. "Bhakthi Marga" was the new method that was introduced into Theravāda as a means of attaining Nibbāna. The concept of "bhakthi", which means faith had not been a feature of early Buddhism. This is a significant and gross deviation from the method preached by Buddha that appears in Early Buddhism. "Bhakti Marga" is a concept that is found in Hinduism and it involves total devotion towards a personal deity as part of the means of attaining "Moksha". In Early Buddhism no personal devotion towards Buddha is required for attaining enlightenment. Instead of "bhakthi" what practitioners of Buddhism demonstrate towards Buddha, Dhamma and Sanga is "saddhā".

The word "bhakti" is mentioned in the "Shvetashvatara" Upanishad which meant devotion and love in any activity. The word had no religious significance in the Veda. Later "Bhakthi

Marga" or "Bhakthi Yoga" was developed in the Bhagavadgita as a means of attaining "Moksha". Three methods of attaining "Moksha" is mentioned in the Bhagavadgita; "Bhakthi Yoga" "Jnana Yoga" and "Karma Yoga". Yoga means union and here it refers to the union of Atman and Brahman. As Hinduism is pantheistic and there are several deities, the personal god to whom devotion is offered in the practice of "Bhakthi Marga" varies with the devotee and could be any one of the following gods; Ganesha, Krishna, Rādhā, Rāmā, Vishnu etc. In "Bhakti Marga" the practice of rituals, which included reciting of devotional poems and songs, was believed to help in the attaining of this union. Anyway Hinduism also had "Jnana Marga" as a means of attaining "Moksha" which is based on meditation that brings forth wisdom and the final goal. However, Buddha had rejected "Bhakthi Marga" as a means of attaining Nibbāna (Sasanārathana, 1952).

Hinduism was a strong force and had started to influence Mahāyāna quite significantly. Several Hindu ideas and concepts had invaded into Mahāyāna and "Bhakthi Marga" was one of them. Some of the early Mahāyāna texts like "Sadharmapundarika-Sūtra" mention "Bhakthi Marga".

Mahāyāna was a dominant religion in Sri Lanka too when it was strong in India. Several Mahāyāna features were introduced into the practice of Theravāda in Sri Lanka. "Bhakthi Marga" was one of them. Introduction of Mahāyāna into Sri Lanka was undertaken intentionally and forcefully. These matters shall be discussed in Chapter 31.

At present lay practitioners of Buddhism as well as the Sanga seem to believe in the ability of "Bhakthi Marga" to take the practitioner on the path to Nibbāna. They perform all kinds of rituals that include worshipping of statues, stupas and shrines with offering of flowers and incense, recital of "gatha" etc. in the belief that such practice would enable them to accumulate merit which would finally help them to attain Nibbāna.

In Hinduism the final goal of "Moksha" includes all comforts that could be enjoyed in lay life. The union of Atman and Brahman entails such a state of permanent existence. This idea of a union between the seeker of enlightenment and an ultimate reality too was introduced into Mahāyāna. For this purpose the "thrikaya" concept was constructed and the Buddhahood was divided into three different manifestations; 1)"Nirmānakāya", 2) "Sambogakāya" and 3) "Dharmakāya". This "thrikaya" concept is directly borrowed from Hinduism and the division of Buddhahood into "thrikāya" in Mahāyāna is similar to the division in Hinduism which has the following three manifestation of Vshnu; Brahma state, Ishvara state and Mūrthi state. "Dharmakāya" is equivalent to Brahma state, "Sambogakāya" to Ishvara state and "Nirmānakāya" to Murthi state. Mahāyānists adopted a concept where the final goal is union between the person who attains the final goal and "Dharmakāya" which is one of the manifestations of the Buddhahood and which is equivalent to Brahma state in Hinduism. This is in total contradistinction to the final goal described in Theravāda and Early Buddhism. There is no division of the Buddhahood into "kāyas" and there is no union between Buddha and the are discussed in detail in Chapter 18 on Nibbāna.

In Early Buddhism the Satipattāna-sutta (Majjima-Nikāya) describes the fourfold method of establishment of mindfulness. At the beginning of the discourse Buddha says this is the path with one goal for the overcoming of sorrow and ceasing of suffering, for the attainment of right method for the realization of freedom. The fourfold establishment of mindfulness consists of 1) reflect on the body, 2) reflect on the feelings, 3) reflect on thought and 4) reflect on ideas. Here the reflection is on the body and the mind. When reflecting on the body all its unattractiveness, its impermanence, death etc. are focused upon. This enables the practitioner to get rid of the emotional attchment to his own physical body. When reflecting on the mind three of its functions connected with influx of feelings, thought and ideas are focused upon. These are the influxes that need to be got rid of. Buddha describes in detail how these influxes could be got rid of by the realization of their true nature. This is the method of insight meditation described in Early Buddhism which is an essential component of the "Ariyaṭṭhaṅgikamagga".

Breakaway Schools of Theravāda also developed alternate methods of attaining Nibbāna. For example, Sarvāstivāda developed a path to enlightenment consisting of five stages. These were later adopted by Mahāyāna into their method of enlightenment. These were mentioned in the Abhidhamma of the Sarvāstivāda and also in Vasubandhu's Abhidhammacosa. The five stages are as follows;

"Moksa-bhāgiya – state leading to morality and four foundations of mindfulness.

"Nirveda-bhāgiya" – state leading to penetration and realization of Four Noble Truths and its sixteen aspects.

"Darsana-mārga" – state leading to insight and according to Vasubandhu it leads to noble truths and helps to get rid of 88 afflictions.

"Bhāvanā-mārga" – path of cultivation of meditation leading to the ridding of ten further "kleshas".

Asaiksa-mārga – path of no more learning or consummation and state of total freedom (Dhammajoti 2009).

Yogācāra bhumi-sāstra (4th Century), an important Mahāyāna text, discusses several meditation methods including, different kinds of samadi, development of insight ("vipassanā"), tranquility ("samādi"), the four foundations of mindfulness, the five hindrances, four "dhyānas" and the classic Buddhist meditation methods focusing on the unattractiveness of the human body, impermanence, suffering and death. The four foundations of mindfulness in Mahāyāna are similar to those described in Early Buddhism which are mentioned above ("Sathipattāna-sutta"). Mahāyāna also describes the possibility of the visualization of Buddha while focusing one's mind on the Buddha and even listening to his preaching, live as it were. Thus there seems to be mysticism involved in the meditation methods of Mahāyāna. In contrast meditation in Early Buddhism was an empirical exercise involving intense concentration and there was no mysticism.

In Mahāyāna the path to enlightenment is based on the path of a Bodhisattva. The concept of Bodhisattva will be discussed in detail in Chapter 17, here the path that a Bodhisattva undertakes to attain enlightenment will be discussed. In Mahāyāna everyone is encouraged to take the Bodhisattva vow which is a promise to work for the enlightenment of all sentient beings by following Bodhisattva path. The latter could be discussed in terms of the Six Perfections or in terms of the Five Paths and Ten "Bhumis". Perfections are "Pāramitās" which are described in the Praññāpāramitās- Sūtras, Saddharmapundarika-Sūtra and many other Mahāyāna Sūtras. The Six "Pāramitāss" are the means by which an aspirant could attain enlightenment for the benefit of all. The Six "Pāramitās" are as follows;

"Dhāna Pāramitās" (giving of alms)

"Sīla Pāramitās" (development of virtue)

"Ksānthi Pāramitās" (development of Pāramitās Pāramitās)

"Vīrya paramitā" (development of effort)

"Dhyāna paramitā" (meditation)

"Praññā paramitā" (development of wisdom)

In the alternative description of the Bodhisattva Path there are Five Paths and Ten Bhumis. The Five Paths are the same described under the path adopted by Sarvāstivāda, mentioned above, which has been borrowed by Mahāyāna. The Bodhisattva Bhumis are subcategories of the Five Paths. They are as follows;

The very Joyous – enjoyment due to beginning of the path.

The Stainless – free of defilements

The Luminous – illuminating due to freedom from defilements

The Radiant – wisdom begins to shine

The Difficult to Cultivate

The Manifest

The Gone a-far

The Immovable

Good Intelligence

Cloud of Doctrine – benefits everybody like a cloud that gives rain to everybody

To understand the degree of influence that Hinduism had on Mahāyāna one must closely study the path of enlightenment in Hinduism. "Moksha" is the final goal in Hinduism and the method of attaining it is linked to the caste system which is based on the occupation of the individual. Bhagavadgita has described three methods of attaining "Moksha"; 1) "Karma-mārga", 2) "Dhyāna-marga" and 3) "Bhakthi-mārga". The individual is not totally free to choose the method. The God had decided on the nature of the work that people do and four groups are accordingly identified; The Brahmins who are priests, the "Kshasthriya" who are warriors or kings, "Vaisya" who are commoners and "Sudra" who are workers. By doing one's duty unemotionally as determined by the hierarchical and social order one would be serving God and could hope to find "Moksha". This is "Karma-marga". In the "Dhyāna mārga" one engages in yoga practice and through meditation could reach "Moksha". In "Bhakthi-mārga" the practitioner demonstrates devotional love towards a chosen deity and by ritual and singing of devotional songs etc. attain "Moksha".

"Moksha" is attained by the union between Atman and Brahman. The latter is not an ordinary god, it is the essence that is present everywhere in the Universe. Upanishads say Brahman is the Universe. Atman is the soul of the person that travels through "samsara" cycle. Atman is the representation of Brahman that is present within every person. "Moksha" is attained by breaching the cycle of "samsara" by getting rid of ignorance and desire and achieving the union between Atman and Brahman by practicing one of the three Margas to "Moksha" (Gavin Flood, 1996).

Thus similarities and dissimilarities could be seen between the methods and paths to enlightenment of the various religions and their different Schools. In this regard Early Buddhism avoided metaphysical phenomena like permanent soul and union between the seeker of freedom and god or a manifestation of the Buddha such as "Dharmakāya". Later Buddhist philosophies were to some degree forced to accept other doctrines from other religions which were politically more powerful.

Chapter 17

Controversies related to the concept of Bodhisatta

The term Bodhisatta (Pāli) was used by Buddha to refer to himself that existed prior to enlightenment. He had said "in the days before my enlightenment when I was Bodhisatta" (Dvedhavitākka-sutta, Majjima-Nikāya). The word Bodhisatta therefore meant a person who was aspiring to be a Buddha. The early suttas and Chinese Agamas use this word to mean a person who was working towards Buddhahood.

The word "bodhi" means enlightenment and "satta" means ambition. The Pāli word "Bodhisatta" had been used in "Majjima" and "Samyutta" Nikāyas which were written in the 4th to 5th Century BC. The Sanskrit word "Bodhisathva" was used in discourses much later in the 3rd to 6th Century CE. While the Pāli word had been translated into Sanskrit word several new meanings also had been given to it. Though Buddha had a simple definition for the term Bodhisatta later Schools including Theravāda had given the term more complicated meanings and definitions. For example Bodhivamsa-sutta (Khuddaka-Nikāya) which is a Theravāda discourse describes the life stories of twenty five Bodhisattas with their names and also the names given to them after they attain Buddhahood. It also mentions ten "paramitās" and eight conditions that Bodhisatta has to follow in his path to enlightenment. Thus the concept was developed that a person who aspires to be a Buddha must take a vow in front of a living Buddha. The idea that he could postpone the entry into Nibbāna for the benefit of other aspirants to Buddhahood was also developed in these Schools of Buddhism. Sārvasthivādins also put forward their concept of Bodhisathva which was similar to the above description in many ways (Sasanārathana, 1952).

Gautama Buddha, when he was an aspirant to become Bodhisathva is said to have taken a vow in front of Buddha Dipankara and then spent many "kalpa" (aeons) before he could become Buddha. These stories are mentioned in later Theravāda texts such as Nidhānakathā and Bodhivamsa included in the Khuddaka Nikāya but not in the main Suttas of Early Buddhism which suggests that these later additions may have resulted due to influence of Mahāyāna and Hinduism.

The Bodhisathva concept in Mahāyāna is a complex theory. Not only has it been developed into a major concept, this development has transformed the path to Nibbāna into something totally different from what was preached by Buddha. In Mahāyāna the final goal is not Arahath but Buddhahood and anybody who aspires to Buddhahood has to go through the stage of Bodhisathva. Mahāyāna evolved around this idea of Bodhisattva. In Early Buddhism on the other hand the word Bodhisatta was descriptive and had no special significance. According to Theravāda a person who is aspiring to attain Nibbāna which would give him the status of Arahath was not referred to as Bodhisatta obviously because he was not going to be a Buddha (Sasanārathana, 1952).

Though it is not certain when Bodhisathva concept had come into being it is believed that it may have started in the 2nd Century CE and spread throughout the Bharatha until the 7th CE. During this period this concept had spread to Sri Lanka as well and remained there until the 16th CE.

At the beginning Mahāyāna did not have this concept. The main reasons for the origin of this concept were the development of "Bhakthi-Marga" (Path of Faith) and "Viññānavāda" (Idealism). "Bhakthi-Marga" had been mentioned in the Bhagavadgita a major text in Hinduism. It was later introduced into Mahāyāna and became its main method of attaining enlightenment. When "Bhakthi-Marga", which gives primacy to devotion towards deity as the means of attaining the final goal, is adopted as a strong feature of a religion it will be difficult to prevent the intrusion of ritualistic practice from other religions. Mahāyāna was weak as a doctrine and Hinduism was in ascendency and consequently the former was more or less forced to accept tenets and practices of Hinduism. As a result Buddha came to be treated as a deity who had reached the highest state. To reach that state one need to be a Bodhisathva.

The spread of Mahāyāna and the development of Bodhisathva concept happened more or less together. In the 1st Century CE Buddhism, particularly Theravāda, had declined as the Maurya Dynasty had lost its power. Hinduism was growing in influence. As a result Mahāyāna, heavily infiltrated by Hindu concepts and practices, could displace Theravāda. From about the 2nd CE till about the 7th CE Mahāyāna and the Bodhisathva concept spread in the region but came to Sri Lanka rather late in the 5th CE. However, Bodhisathva ideas remained in Sri Lanka till about the 12th CE. Even after the disappearance of Mahāyāna in Sri Lanka the Bodhisathva concept continued to influence the society, culture, literature, art and craft of the country for a long period (Sasanārathana, 1952).

"Viññānavada" (Idealism) or Yogācāra, a branch of Mahāyāna was more suited to accept the metaphysical concept of Bodhisathva. It had adopted transcendental ideas and Buddha was made into a transcendental phenomenon which elevated him beyond the realm of this world with god-like features and eternal existence. Bodhisathvas also were endowed with similar features though at a lower level and made into beings who deserved to be venerated and worshipped. Astasāhāsrika-praññāparamitā Sūtra, one of the earliest Mahāyāna texts, describes three stages that a Bodhisathva goes through in his journey towards enlightenment; first stage is settling into the vehicle, second is reaching the irreversible stage and third is the one-more-birth stage.

After Mahāyāna matured and broke up into its major branches Madhyamaka and Yogācāra, these Schools put forward different models for Bodhisathva. Madhyamaka had the Ekayana theory which said that instead of having several paths there should be one path. Yogācāra had a different model consisting of three lineages; 1) Arahath, 2) Pratyeka-Buddha, 3) Samyak-Sambuddha.

The journey of the Bodhisathva as described in Mahāyāna seems to be arduous and complex. First he has to take a vow and be endorsed by a living Buddha as suitable to undertake the journey. Then he is required to develop the mental state called "Bodhicitta" consisting of compassion and wisdom with an undertaking to strive to help everybody to reach the state of Bodhisathva which reflects the philosophy of Mahāyāna, The Great Vehicle. In order to develop "Bodhicitta" the aspirant to Bodhisathva status has to practice the following rituals: "Vandanā, Pujā, Saranāgamana, Pāpadesana, Punyānumodanā, Adyesana and Atmabhvada"

After developing "Bodhicitta", according to most Mahāyāna texts, the Bodhisathva has to go through ten "Bhumis" ("Dasa-Bhumi") before they could attain Buddhahood. Some later Theravāda texts mention ten "paramittās" that the aspirant to Nibbāna must fulfil. However Sāmaññaphala sutta or any other Early Buddhist sutta that describes the path to enlightenment do not mention these ten "paramitas". Further the ten "Bhumis" that feature in Mahāyāna has no similarity to these ten "paramitas" of later Theravāda. One of the Mahāyāna "Bhumis" contain six "paramitas" but these too are different from those in the later Theravāda tradition.

It is seen that the path to Buddhahood in Mahāyāna is via Bodisatva and the method comprises mainly of rituals in keeping with the "Bhakthi-marga" it espouses. The attaining of "Bodhicitta" involves rituals and the passage through the ten "Bhumis" also is full of the practice of various rituals.

In Mahāyāna there are innumerable number of Bodhisathvas but only a few were identified by name. Among them there were eight who were known as "Bodhisathva Mahāsthāna Prāpthi Thrilokyavijay" and their names are as follows;1) Avaloketīsvara, 2) Akashagarba, 3) Vajragarba, 4) Kshithigarba, 5) Sarvanivārana Vishkamhi, 6) Maithraya, 7) Samanthabadra and 8)Manjusri. These Bodhisathvas are deified and are worshipped by Mahāyānists. They each have a "mudra" (gesture with fingers), "saṅketha" (symbol) and a vehicle (usually an animal). These ideas are adopted from Hinduism which has similar features in relation to its deities (Sasanārathana, 1952).

Bodhisathva concept was brought to Srilanka when Mahāyāna came here and people who came to believe and practice Mahāyāna started to worship the Bodhisathvas as well. Bodhisathva "Avaloketīsvara" was treated as the chief among Bodhisathvas. "Manjusri" also was one of the leading Bodhisathvas. What is significant about these deities is that in Sri Lanka some of them have been converted to Buddhist gods and are being venerated in Buddhist temples and kovils. "Avalokethisvara came to be known as "Natha deviyo" and "Samanthabadra" was "Saman deviyo". They have kovils dedicated in their names and these kovils are to be found within the premises of Buddhist temples.

It is seen that several features which were not present in the Buddhism that was brought to Sri Lanka by Ven. Mahinda had been introduced into the practice of Buddhism in Sri Lanka due to the influence of Mahāyāna. Of these the "Bhakthi-marga" is critical because that changed a basic tenet of Buddhism taught by Buddha. There was no "Bhakthi-marga" in early Buddhism, Buddha had relied totally on the "Ñana-mārga" (Path of Wisdom). The other important concept that has been introduced into Buddhism in Sri Lanka is the Bodhisathva concept with all its implications. It gives credence to the "Bhakthi-mārga" and the practice of rituals and also lead to new interpretations regarding the path to enlightenment, the Arahath concept and Buddhahood. These aspects will be discussed in Chapter 23.

Chapter 18

Controversies related to Nibbāna

The word Nibbāna (Pāli) or Nirvāna (Sanskrit) does not appear in the Veda or Upanishad. It appears in the Bhagavadgita as a synonym for "Moksha". It is probable that Bhagavadgita had borrowed the word from Buddhism and the word was used first in Buddhism (Collins Steven, 1998). The word means "blow out" like a fire. In all the religions where the word is used; Buddhism, Hinduism, Jainism and Sikhism, it carries the meaning that when Nibbāna is attained there is release from samsara and suffering. But the nature of the state reached after gaining such freedom differs in these religions and also the method of achieving it is quite different. This point of view is applicable to all religions that offer an avenue for gaining freedom from the human predicament.

In the Sāmaññaphala-sutta (Majjima Nikāya) Buddha describes his mental state attained in the final stage of attaining Nibbāna. It is a form of superior knowledge that he gains. He could very clearly see his mind like a crystal clear pond. After spewing out all defilements, he knows "this is suffering", "this is the arising of suffering", "this is the way leading to the ceasing of suffering", "these are the influxes", "this is the arising of influxes", "this is the ceasing of influxes", "this is the way leading to the ceasing of influxes". Buddha says that one who knows this, is released from the influx of sense pleasures and influx of becoming and ignorance. In the one who is released there is knowledge that "I have been released", "there will be no more birth" "the higher life has been lived", "done has been what has to be done". Buddha goes on to say that there is no more superior fruit of recluse-ship than this. This knowledge is not a propositional knowledge but a realization or a conviction (Tilakaratne, 1993).

Buddha achieved this state by living a life of virtue, cleansing the mind and developing commitment and effort to train and concentrate the mind to spew out the defilements "loba, dvesha, moha" and stop influx of sense pleasures and thereby stopping the influx of becoming which leads to birth, suffering and death. There was no ritual or devotion to a deity or any external factor involved.

Buddha had attained Nibbāna during his life time and this state would remain though his "panchaskanda" or five aggregates would continue to exist in the normal way except that he will have complete control over influxes of sense desires. This state of Nibbāna is known as "Sopadhishesa-Nibbāna" (Nibbāna with remainder) as the five aggregates are still in existence. The state reached after the demise or "Parinibbāna of the Buddha is called "Anupadhishesa-Nibbāna" (Nibbāna without remainder). Whether anything exists after the demise of the Buddha in order to be in the state of "Anupadhishesa-Nibbāna" is a question that will be discussed later in this Chapter. The feelings of the person who is in "Sopadhishesa-Nibbāna" have been described by the Buddha and also Arahaths and all of them have said they experience joy and peace as mentioned in Thera and Theri Gatha. The usual needs for existence like hunger, thirst etc. are felt by the person who has attained Nibbāna but there is no attachment to such needs and food and drink and other needs would be partaken without greed or aversion.

In other religions there usually is an external factor involved in the process of attaining the final goal. In Hinduism there is Atman which is the soul and there is the Brahman which is the ultimate reality and the final goal is union of these two. In the Abrahamic religions the final goal is achieved by the grace of God and the person enters the God's Kingdom. In these religions the external factor is transcendental in the sense it is beyond the realm of this world and also the external factor cannot be explained in the words of the languages that human beings use (Tilakaratne, 1993).

The word transcend means to surpass the normal and transcendental in the religious sense means the phenomenon is beyond the realm of this world and therefore cannot be explained. Some thinkers like R Otto (1923) consider that transcendentalism is an essential feature of religions (Tilakaratne, 1993). This mystic element is necessary to generate faith and devotion in religious practice. However according to Early Buddhism faith and devotion were not required to attain the final goal Nibbāna.

All religions have a final goal for salvation of human beings for they accept that humans are in an unsatisfactory predicament and in need of assistance. God was the answer to this problem in many theistic religions. However Buddha had a different view as he could not accept a metaphysical idea of a God. He based his theory on empiricism and what he could learn by experience. He said external factors cannot help human beings and they have to help themselves. The final goal in Buddhism therefore had to be something that is not beyond the realm of this world and something that could be explained in clear terms.

However there are different points of view held by ancient as well as modern thinkers on this matter. These differences of view have arisen due to the question; what happens after death to a person who has attained Nibbāna. This is one of the ten questions that Buddha set aside which according to some could be explained on the basis of Buddha's own preaching (Tilakaratne, 1993).

This question is raised in the Aggivacchagotta-sutta (Majjima Nikāya). Vacchagotta asks the Buddha "where does a monk who is so released in thought arise". Buddha's reply had been "arises is not appropriate". Then Vaccha had said "in that case one does not arise" and Buddha's reply had been "does not arise is not appropriate". Vaccha had said "in that case one both arises and does not arise" and when the answer had been the same Vaccha had said "in that case one neither arises nor does not arise" and Buddha's reply had been similar. Buddha's opinion had been that all those four alternatives are not appropriate in relation to a person who has attained Nibbāna.

On hearing Buddha's opinion Vaccha had said he is confused. Buddha then had spoken about a fire that is burning on grass and sticks and asked Vaccha once the grass and sticks are burnt over what would happen to the fire. When Vaccha had said if there is no more grass and sticks the fire is extinguished Buddha had asked whether anybody could say where the fire has gone. Vaccha in reply had said the question is not appropriate because the fire was extinguished due to non-availability of fuel. Buddha had said that similarly when explaining the nature of Arahath it could be said that the five aggregates (panchaskanda; "rupa, vedanā, saññā, saṅkāra, viññāna) by which he could be explained have been abandoned and the root cut off and therefore terms like "arises" are not appropriate.

This explanation appears to be applicable to the status reached after the demise of the person who has attained Nibbāna. On the other hand with regard to the enlightened person who is still alive there does not appear to be any controversy in Early Buddhism. His mental state is free of influxes of sense pleasure and he is not subject to suffering. He is also endowed with the ability of extra-sensory perception such as retro-cognion and clairvoyance.

However Buddha's explanation regarding the nature of the enlightened person after death has been construed as an indication of ineffability. As mentioned above ineffability is considered a feature of transcendentalism in the religious sense. For instance God is not explainable in the words we normally use and therefore God is transcendent. Some thinkers and commentators have interpreted Buddha's explanation as an acceptance that the phenomenon cannot be explained and therefore Nibbāna is a transcendental phenomenon. K.N. Jayatilleke (1975) says "There is no doubt that Nirvāna is a transcendent reality beyond space, time and causation..".

However, a theory of transcendentalism would entail a permanent and substantial existence. In Early Buddhism Nibbāna is not considered a permanent and substantial state. Buddha's answer to the question whether Arahath exists after death, does not exist, both exists and does not exist, neither exists nor does not exist, had been that where Arahath is concerned these questions do not arise. This shows that Buddha does not subscribe to the idea that Nibbāna is an eternal and substantial state.

The other question that arises is whether Nibbāna is annihilationism. Buddha in his answer to Vaccha had said that in Nibbāna the five aggregates have been cut like a stem from its root. This implies that Nibbāna may be a theory that suggests annihilation as the final goal. Further Buddha has said there is no more birth in Nibbāna but had not given a positive answer to the question what happens after death. But Buddha had countered this argument by saying that a person who has attained Nibbāna cannot be measured and his consciousness cannot be traced even by the most powerful and intelligent god. He cannot be measured by his five aggregates. He is said to be 'deep, immeasurable, and unfathomable like the great ocean'. Such a person would not continue to exist after death as a normal human being or to cease to exist in an annihilation theory (Jayatilake, 1975).

However Mahāyāna which came into being in the 1st Century CE had transformed the concept of Nibbāna into a transcendental theory. In order to do this it had to make Buddhahood an eternal being. They also made Buddhahood the final goal which meant that Arahath is not the final goal but only a transient stage in the path to the final goal. The trend to convert Buddha into a transcendental being had probably started in the "Lokotharavada" branch of Mahāsāṅgika School. One of their texts "Mahavasthuwa" was dedicated for this task. Buddha and his life incidents were made to appear mystic and transcendental in nature in these texts (Sasanārathana, 1952).

According to Mahāyāna the Theravāda path to Nibbāna does not lead to the final goal but only covers part of the journey and a further distance remains to be completed. Those who follow the Theravāda path, after completing it, would have to get on to the Mahāyāna path in order to reach the final goal which is Buddhahood. This means the state of Arahath which was the final goal in the Theravāda path is not the final enlightenment in Mahāyāna. One must proceed further to reach that status.

There may have been vague ideas of transcendentalism in some early Buddhist discourses such as "Mahāpadāna sutta" of the Dhiga Nikāya and "Acchariyabuthadhamma sutta" of Majjima Nikāya. These vague ideas may have been influential in the origin and evolution of transcendental theories in the Mahāsāṅgika School. Sārvasthivadins also seems to have been influenced by these ideas and based on them they had produced a text called "Lalithavisthara" which was later gladly taken over by Mahāyāna. This text attempted to make Buddha a transcendental being and to deify him. "Mahāsāṅgika" sect, the first breakaway group, had said that the state of Arahath reached in Theravāda is inferior to Buddha and that Buddha has supreme powers. It seems to propose that Buddhahood is the final goal that all aspirants to enlightenment must aim at (Akira Hirakawa, 1993).

According to Mahāyāna "kleshavarana" only, which means removing obstruction to the spewing out of defilements, will not bring about the attainment of Buddhahood. In addition "ñayāvarana", which means getting rid of the obstruction that hinder the gaining of omniscience, has also to be done. This cannot be done by the eightfold path proposed by Hinayana which will bring about only the removal of "kleshavarana". In order to achieve "ñayāvarana" one has to follow the Bodhisathva path. Buddha in the "Tevijja-Vacchagotta-sutta" (Majjima Nikāya) had said he does not have the powers of omniscience, thus the need for "ñayāvarana" or removal of obstructions to the gaining of omniscience may not arise.

Yogācāra school of Mahāyāna was of the opinion that there are two types of Nirvāna. What is gained by the Theravāda method of enlightenment was called "Pratisthitha Nirvāna" which means the status is localized. Thus it is not the final enlightenment. The final stage of Buddhahood is called "Apratisthitha Nirvāna" which means it is non- localized, and therefore it is the highest form of Nirvāna. What is significant here is that in the non-localized status the Buddha can return to samsara to help sentient beings to attain Nirvāna. Some are of the opinion that this idea is in agreement with the non-dualistic doctrine of Mahāyāna (Akira Hirakawa, 1993). This doctrine proposes that there is no differentiation between "samsara" and "Nirvāna". In Theravāda however, there is no possible way of equating Nirvāna with Samsara.

Non-dualism of Mahāyāna contends that there is no difference between "Samsara"and "Nirvāna". This theory is comparable to the non-dualist theory of the Vedanta and also Hinduism which holds that Atman and Brahman are one and the same. Mahāyāna may have borrowed this theory from Hinduism. The Atman/Brahman concept of Hinduism may conform to its theory on Self. In Buddhism however there is no Self. Mahāyāna seems to be agreeable even to compromise on this vital doctrine of "No-self" in order to accommodate Hindu intrusion. Obviously there has to be a difference between the dweller in "Samsara" and the person who is freed from fetters of "Samsara". In Theravāda there is no suggestion of a non-dualistic interpretation of "Samsara" and "Nirvāna" (Bikkhu Bodhi, 1994). Mahāyāna cannot adopt a non-dualistic theory on these two widely different phenomena without resorting to borrowing from Hinduism.

Sārvasthivadins also had their view on Nirvāna. Their Abhidhamma analysed Nirvāna as "nirodha" (extinction) gained through knowledge. They said Nirvāna was defined by their "Svabhāva" concept implying that there was a substantial element in Nirvāna. They said Nirvāna was a real existent ("dravyasat"). These substantialist and eternalist ideas of

Sārvāstivāda have obviously contributed to the development and growth of Mahāyāna. Puggalavādins who also subscribed to substantialist views held that Nirvāna is gained by elimination of defilements and they claimed that there is real existent in Nirvāna (Akira Hirakawa, 1993).

Sautrāntika debated this point saying that there is no real existent in Nirvāna and that it is only a designation where there is non-existence succeeding existence, which seems to be in keeping with their annihilationism. For the Sautrāntika the concept of Nirvāna meant getting rid of latent defilements. Yet their idea of "non-existence succeeding existence" is not in agreement with the Early Buddhist idea of "neither existence, nor non-existence" in its definition of Nibbāna.

Nāgārjuna had examined Nibbāna in his "Mūlamadhyamaka-kārika" (Chapter 25). In verse 25.3 of Chapter Twenty five of his "Mūlamadhyamaka-kārika" he says of Nibbāna "Non-relinquished, not-reached, non-annihilated, non-eternal, non-ceased and non-arisen – that is called freedom". This gives more or less the positive side of Nibbāna. Also it refutes the argument that Nibbāna is annihilation. Similarly he shows that Nibbāna is not eternal either (Kalupahana, 2008). However he attempts to show that Nibbāna is empty of all that is attributed and endowed to it. This he does with most of the subjects he examines in this text. One may construe two possible meanings to his arguments. One is that he actually meant that Nibbāna and "Śūnyathava" are one and the same. The other is that he was trying to refute the misconceptions that had arisen with regard to the nature of Nibbāna. This matter is further discussed in Chapter 22.

Chapter 19

Controversies related to Gauthama Buddha

No written records of Buddha's life that could be traced to the period of his life or one or two centuries later are available. The earliest written reference to him is to be found on the stone pillars that carry King Dharmasoka's edicts of 3rd Century BC.

The earliest text that deals with the life of the Buddha is the "Buddhacarita" written by Asvagosha in the 1st CE. "Lalithavisthara" a compilation by Sārvastivāda/Mahāyāna in the 3rd CE is the next oldest text that gives a description of the life of Buddha. "Mahavastu" is another major biography of Buddha written by "Lokotharavāda", a branch of Mahāsāngika School, in the 4th CE. Buddhagosa also had composed a biography of the Buddha titled "Nidhānakatā" in the 5th CE.

Most of these texts describe in different degrees mystic and miraculous events in connection with Buddha's previous lives where he is referred to as Bodhisathva, his early life, renunciation, his life as a recluse, enlightenment, his life as a Buddha and his "Parinirvāna". Even the early Pāli texts like Mahāpadāna sutta (Dhiga Nikāya) and Acchāryabhuta sutta (Majjima Nikāya) though not biographies include similar mystic events related to the life of the Buddha such as the Bodhisatta's descent from "Thauthisa" into his mother's womb.

The four major suttas of the Pāli Nikāya and the Chinese Agamas do not attribute miraculous powers to Buddha. Early Buddhist texts do not say that Buddha possessed omniscience or try to deify him in any other way. Retrocognition, clairvoyance and the ability to see the future karmic consequence of other people which Buddha possessed are not considered as miraculous powers but higher knowledge that

Buddha had acquired by cleansing the mind of defilements, and deep concentration of the mind.

However Mahāyāna texts and also some later Hinayana suttas like "Mahāvastu" have mentioned omniscience as an attribute of Buddha and also spoken about other god-like features that Buddha possessed. In "Mahāvastu" it is said that Buddha had a painless birth and does not need sleep, food or drink and has the ability to suppress karma and live as long as a kalpa if he wishes. These texts and also the "Jātaka kathā" describe hundreds of previous lives of Buddha both as Bodhisathva in these stories and is depicted as a person who is striving to reach Buddhahood and is performing meritorious deeds and "Pāramitās" for that purpose and meeting with other Buddhas. He finally meets Deepankara Buddha and makes a vow to become a Buddha and receives the latter's blessings.

However there is no mention of any of this in the early Buddhist texts. Buddha is depicted as a normal human being though a few miraculous incidents in his early life are included in these texts. These incidents may have crept in as later additions to the texts which were written down several centuries after Buddha's demise. However inclusion of these incidents though minor may have influenced the later biographers to exaggerate and create fantastic and mystical stories around the life of Buddha in order to make him a transcendental phenomenon and make him god-like.

As mentioned earlier the need to make a larger than life being out of the historical Buddha had been observed among the younger monks soon after Buddha's demise. They may have been saddened by the loss of their beloved teacher and would have wanted to create an image of the Buddha they thought would appeal to the laity. They may have been influenced by other religions which engage in such practices in relation to their leaders. This may have been the origin of transcendentalism in Buddhism.

Jāthaka Kathā is a large collection of stories that deal with the previous births of the Buddha both as human and also in animal form. The collection is included in the Sutta Piṭaka under the Kuddhaka Nikāya. These stories had been written for the sole purpose of bringing forth the altruism of the Bodhisathva. He performs great acts of merit helping others to solve their problems even at the risk of his own life. Accumulation of all this merit, it is believed, would enable him to reach Buddhahood. Obviously this is a deviation from the preaching of the Buddha and is closer to Mahāyāna concept of Bodhisathva.

An effort to strengthen the concept of Bodhisathva could be observed in the Nidānakathā of Buddhagosa which is an introduction to the Commentaries on the Jāthaka stories. It has three sections; the first deals with the life of Bodhisathva Sumedha (the Bodhisattva who was going to be the Gautama Buddha), the second with the period from the birth of Siddhārtha to the enlightenment and the third the post-enlightenment period. The text focuses mainly on the supernatural powers and miraculous occurrences in the life of the Bodhisathva and the Buddha. Buddhagosa's motive for such distortions while living under the roof of Mahāvihara the chief centre of Theravāda would be discussed in Chapter 27 and 28.

Early Buddhist texts do not give much information about Buddha's childhood nor any description of his previous lives as a Bodhisathva. For instance the Ariyapariyasena sutta (Majjima Nikāya) deals with the reason for his renunciation of princely life. The explanation given is that Siddhārtha realized how impure the household life was compared to the life of a Sramana. However, in the later discourses such as the Buddhavamsa the reason given is that he saw an old person, a sick person, a dead body and a monk and he realized that life was full of suffering and decided to give up lay life and go in search of a solution to the problem of suffering.

There are different accounts about how Buddha came to decide that the best way to find enlightenment was to avoid extreme practices like self-indulgence and self-mortification and to follow the middle path of insight meditation. According to the Ariyapariyesana sutta (Majjima Nikāya) he had first practiced extreme self-mortification in the company of five ascetics. Realizing the futility of this method he had studied meditation under Alara Kalama and then Uddaka Rasaputhra. He had gained a certain degree of higher knowledge from these two teachers and realizing that these methods are inadequate to achieve what he was pursuing he had developed his own method and had been successful in attaining Nibbāna.

In contrast "Buddhavamsa" (Kuddhaka Nikāya) which describes the life of twenty four Buddhas who preceded Gautama Buddha, attempts to show that Siddhārtha as a young child had possessed mystical and super natural powers. It says that Sramana Siddhārtha while meditating had remembered how as a child he gained entry into the state of "jhana" while seated in a field where his father was conducting a harvesting ceremony and that the memory of this incident made him realize that "jhana" method was the best suited to attain Nibbāna.

The nature of Buddhahood is described in the "Sāmaññaphala sutta" (Dīgha Nikāya). It says in the final stage Buddha gained three types of superior knowledge; the ability to see previous births, the ability to foresee karmic consequences of other people and the ability to get rid of the three major defilements; "Raga, Dvesha, Moha" (greed, aversion and ignorance). The later texts, which tend to introduce a mystic element into the life of Buddha and his Dhamma, give a description of Mara sending his three daughters named "Tannha, Arati, Raga" (greed, aversion, desire) to tempt Buddha and prevent him attaining Nibbāna. Buddha by his extra-ordinary powers overcomes these obstacles and proceeds to attain Nibbāna.

After attaining Nibbāna Buddha was hesitant about teaching his Dhamma to others. According to Ariyapariyasena sutta (Majjima Nikāya) he was invited by Brahma to preach the Dhamma. However the parallel discourse in the Chinese Agama does not mention this incident though several of the later texts describe it in detail. This initial reluctance of the Buddha to teach his Dhamma is construed by some thinkers as further evidence of the ineffability of his Dhamma and its transcendent character (Nagao, 1992). However this latter view is based on the factual correctness of the metaphysical being Brahma inviting the Buddha to teach his Dhamma.

In the attempt to disseminate his Dhamma Buddha had travelled mainly by foot in the Gangetic basin in the states of Bihar and Uttar Pradesh teaching and developing a large group of Sangha. In the last twenty years of his life he had lived mainly at Sravasthi. The Mahāparinibbāna Sutta (Dīgha Nikāya) describes his final years of life. The Sutta begins with an account of Buddha's advice to King Ajāthasattu who was planning to go to war against the Vajji kingdom. Buddha had told the King that Vajjis would prosper as long as they did seven things including the manner in which they should conduct their meetings. Buddha had included these seven principles in his advice to the Sanga on how they should conduct themselves.

When the Buddha in his old age was falling ill Ven. Ananda had asked the Buddha to appoint a leader to succeed him. Buddha had disagreed and said that the Sanga must live as islands to themselves and seek refuge in the Dhamma.

Buddha had continued to travel and teach even in his last days. His last meal had been served by a person named Cunda and Buddha had fallen violently ill. However, Buddha had told Cunda that the meal had nothing to do with his illness and that Cunda would accrue merit for serving the last meal to a Buddha. The constitution of this last meal is a debated issue, Theravādins say it contained pork while Mahāyānists say it was a mushroom. Mahāyānists are believed to be vegetarians and this may be the reason why they refused to accept that the last meal had pork in it.

Buddha before his "PariNirvāna" had spoken about the impermanence of the physical body and advised his disciples to be guided by the Dhamma and Vinaya. His last words had been "All 'sankāra' decay. Strive for the goal with diligence". Buddha had entered his final meditation and reached the four "jhanas" and had been in the fourth "jhana" at the time of death.

Chapter 20

Controversies related to "PariNirvāna"

Buddha's "PariNirvāna" denotes the final attainment of Nibbāna without leaving any residue and the end of "samsara". The five aggregates which had existed as the Buddha in "Sopadisesha-Nirvāna" are dissolved without leaving a residue and Buddha now enters the state called "Anupadisesha-Nirvāna". We have discussed the nature of this state in detail in Chapter 18 on Nibbāna.

The MahapariNibbāna-sutta (Dīgha Nikāya) is the Theravāda text that describes the final few months of Buddha's life. It has four parts. First part deals with the discussion Buddha had with the Chief Minister of King Ajāthasatha which explains to the monks the seven conditions that lead to non-decline (avoidance of decadence) taking the Vajjis as an example. The King had sent the minister to ask for advice from Buddha on his plan to invade the Vajji Kingdom. The second part describes how Buddha spent the three months of the rainy season. He preaches to the monks about the fact that Dhamma is their refuge and to always adhere to the Dhamma and the Vinaya. When Ananda suggests that a leader to succeed Buddha has to be appointed Buddha says that the Dhamma has to be his successor. The third part gives a detailed account of Buddha's illness he contracted after partaking of a meal consisting of pork and his death. The fourth part deals with how Buddha's relics were distributed and stupas were built.

The description of the final stages of Buddha's death is in keeping with the Theravāda philosophy. Buddha had chosen to lie down under a tree, which is a very familiar place for him and had started to meditate. He had gone through the four "jhanas" in a process similar to what he underwent in the final stages of Nibbāna. He had reached the fourth "jhana", then gone back to the first and returned to the fourth before he passed away. This was routine meditation for Buddha who often practiced it and he has said that was how he kept the "Mara" at bay meaning the defilements.

In contrast the "PariNirvāna-Sūtra" of Mahāyāna does not give a description of the events related to the death of the Buddha except the last meal and the illness, instead it attempts to portray Buddha as a being who is not subject to the natural phenomenon of death. The text makes use of the event of Buddha's death to propagate Mahāyāna theories like the eternal Self of the Buddha and the "Buddhagarba/ Buddhadhatu" concept. "Buddhagarba" which means the Buddha-nature, is supposed to be present in everybody but concealed by ignorance and defilements.

According to "PariNirvāna-Sūtra" of Mahāyāna, the Buddha has taught that "pariNirvāna" is the realm of the Eternal, the Self, Bliss and Pure. "Thathāgatha garba" is depicted as the "Atman" or eternal self. This idea is also to be found in "Thathgatha-garba Sūtra" as well as "Lankavatara Sūtra". These texts say that Buddha had advised the monks not to meditate on the idea of non-self, non-eternal, sorrow, and impure but to meditatively cultivate the idea that Nirvāna is Eternal, has Self, and is Bliss and Pure. Mahāyāna seems to say the exact opposite of what Early Buddhism recommended in its lessons on meditation (vide "Mahasatipattana sutta", Dīgha Nikāya).

"PariNirvāna-Sūtra" of Mahāyāna had probably been written in the 4th CE in Andra Pradesh, South India and later found its way to the North-West, Central Asia and East Asia. It has had a great impact in East Asia and helped the spread of Mahāyāna in these areas (Hodge, 2004).

Chapter 21

Controversies related to Arahath

The term 'Arahath' had been in use in the pre-Buddhist times to denote a saintly person with miraculous powers. The word is used in Rgveda with the same meaning. In Early Buddhism Arahath means a person who has attained Nibbāna and as mentioned earlier the person who has attained Nibbāna has no miraculous powers (Warder, 2000).

In Early Buddhism and also in Theravāda, Arahath and Buddha are qualitatively more or less equal except that Buddha is supposed to have some characters which are not present in the Arahath. The main difference is in the fact that it was Buddha who discovered the path to Nibbāna and taking that path had attained Nibbāna while the Arahath has followed the path and reached Nibbāna.

However, as mentioned earlier, according to Mahāyāna Arahath is not the final goal but Buddhahood is the final goal. Arahath is inferior to Buddha and aspirants to Nibbāna are discouraged from entering the path leading to Arahath. They must instead follow the Bodhisathva path. Even if they reach the status of Arahath they will have to enter the Bodhisathva path and then strive to reach Buddhahood.

Though Mahāyānists have claimed that Arahath is inferior in quality compared to Buddha they have not explained in clear terms what exactly the difference is. Mahāyānists have said Arahath has achieved "kleshavarana" but not "ñayāvarana" which has to be achieved to reach Buddhahood. "Kleshavarana" means uncovering of obstacles that prevent the getting rid of defilements. "Ñayāvarana" means the uncovering of obstacles that prevent achieving omniscience. Thus the difference between Arahat and Buddha in Mahāyāna seems to be that Buddha possesses omniscience and the Arahath does not. According to Early Buddhism, however, omniscience is not sine quo non to attain Nibbāna.

In the Thevijja-vacchagotta-sutta (Majjima Nikāya) Buddha has clearly stated that he has no claims to omniscience. Further in the "Brahmmajala-sutta" (Dīgha Nikāya) he has criticized those who claim omniscience, such as Makhali Gossala.

Mahāsaṅgika School and several of its branches held that Arahat is inferior and fallible. Surprisingly Sārvstivāda which was a Sthaviravada school that belonged with the Theravāda, also agreed with the idea that Arahath was inferior (Bharua, 2008). Such gross deviations were testamentary of the growing trend exhibited by these Schools of Buddhism to be more receptive towards Mahāyāna theories. The latter School too has borrowed from the former.

Mahāyāna had a hierarchical arrangement for the stages of attainment in the pursuit to Buddhahood. The highest was the "Samyaksambuddha", second was "Sahasatta", third was "Pratyekabuddha" and lastly Arahat. However Bodhisathva may be considered higher than Arahath for the latter has to be a Bodhisathva before he could attain Buddhahood (AK Warder, 2000).

Sravaka is the monk who aspires to Arahathship in Theravāda and Bodhisathva is the parallel state in Mahāyāna. The question may be asked what is the qualitative difference between the two. The Bodhisathva follows "Bhakthi-marga" with devotion to the Buddha whom he met in his long sojourn in Samsara and to whom he made the vow and who gave him blessings. Sravaka follows a path shown by Buddha which is "ñāna-marga" (Path of Wisdom). There is another important difference, Bodhisattva has to help the sentient beings to attain enlightenment, while the Sravaka has to help himself as there is no one else or external agent which could take him to Nibbāna.

This altruistic nature of the Bodhisattva seems to be the difference between Bodhisattva and Sravaka.

Chapter 22

Controversy related to Ven. Nāgārjuna

Ven Nāgārjuna was one of the greatest Buddhist philosophers after Buddha. He was also called the Second Buddha. He was born in Andra Pradesh, South India to a Brahmin family and is believed to have lived in the latter part of 1st CE and early part of 2nd CE. He had entered Buddhist priesthood in early life. In his carrier he had advised both Theravāda and Mahāyāna schools.

His most important work titled "Mūlamadhyamaka-kārika" had attracted much interest and criticism. The work had been interpreted by his disciples as propounding a theory of "śūnyatha" or emptiness. It proposes that all phenomena in the world when analysed end up in emptiness. This theory – if it is a theory which is denied by its author – appears to be tending towards idealism as it questions the reality of the physical world and it appears to say that nothing exists. Based on this theory a new School of Buddhism called Madhayamaka had been formed which came to be one of the main branches of Mahāyāna.

Further in this work Nāgārjuna attempts to meet his critics who were trying to misinterpret his views. Several very important doctrinal concepts which were being distorted by metaphysicians were examined by Nāgārjuna in this text. These included the concept of Condition and an analysis of the four types of Conditions which are important in "Paticcasamuppāda" (dependent coorigination), the Buddhist concept of time in order to refute the "kshana theory", the faculty of the eye to show the unreliability of human perception and the theory of realism, the agregates ("panchaskanda") to show the absence of a self, the psychology of lust, "dhukka" to explain in Buddha's words the causation of suffering, "Sañkara" to show its role in life and how it could be prevented from progressing into suffering by its appeasement (Kalupahana, 2008).

These aspects have been dealt with in Chapter 15 on "Śūnyathava". In this Chapter the question whether Ven. Nāgārjuna belongs in the Mahāyāna sect or Theravāda sect or neither would be discussed.

One way of doing this is to examine his writings and see whether any of his ideas correspond to or support Mahāyānist theories. However there are so many writings which are attributed to him and some of these conform with Early Buddhism while others tend towards Mahāyāna. Further exactly what writings could be attributed to him is controversial. There is disagreement among modern commentators about the authorship of works attributed to Nāgārjuna. For instance the biographical writings in the Chinese language on Nāgārjuna make reference to several texts which are supposed to contain lakhs of verses. On the other hand according to Tharanatha the 16th Century Tibetan scholar and another 18th Century Tibetan historian Buston Rin-chen-grub Nāgārjuna has written much less (Tilakaratne, 1993). Tharanatha has said the number is five and Buston has said it is six. Christian Lindtner (1982) estimates the number to be thirteen. DJ Kalupahana (2008) also gives a lower figure. Several texts attributed to Nāgārjuna are Mahayanist in content.

Tharanatha is an advocate of Shentong view of Emptiness (Hopkins, 2007). He has written a commentary on the Heart Sūthra ("Praññāparamithā-hardaya sūthra") which is an important Mahāyāna text. Thus he could be considered as a commentator who supported the views of Mahāyāna. Yet he has not included in his list of Nāgārjuna's writings, the obviously Mahāyānist writings which are supposed to have been written by Nāgārjuna. Therefore one would be justified in considering that Tharanatha had been fair in his judgment and his estimate would be closer to the correct number.

In this regard it is important to find out which texts out of these large numbers would conform to the core philosophy of Nāgārjuna. His ideas about Buddha's philosophy is substantially contained in the "Mūlamadhyamaka-karikā" which attempts to show that the various views on the subjects considered in the "Karikā" are empty and therefore one should not be egoistically attached to them. This attitude is in keeping with Buddha's opinion that one must not be attached to views for such attachment would lead to conceit which is an obstacle on the path to freedom. Though Nāgārjuna's disciples and commentator Chandrakirti had misconstrued and converted it into an idealistic Mahāyāna concept and developed a new philosophy based on it Nāgārjuna in the "Karikā" itself had said that "śūnyathava" should not be taken as a philosophy. We have discussed this in Chapter 15 on "Śūnyathava".

Nāgārjuna's writings mentioned by Tharanatha and Buston are as follows; 1) "Mūlamadhyamaka-karikā ", 2) "Śūnyatha sapthathi" ,3) "Yukthi sasthika", 4) "Vigrhā vyavarthani", 5) "Vaidyalya sasthra", 6) "Vyavahara siddi".

Of these six texts three; "Mūlamadhyamaka-karikā ", "Śūnyatha sapthathi" and "Yukthi sasthika" delve into the subject of emptiness in relation to such concepts as being, non-being, samsara, Nirvāna etc. in an attempt to show that all these concepts are "śūnya". "Yukthi sasthika" has sixty verses and they cover the subjects mentioned above. These texts deal with more or less similar subjects though "Mūlamadhyamaka-karikā" is more comprehensive and unique in method.

"Vigrhāvyavarthani" according to Kalupahana (2008) is a response to the resurgence of Brahmanism that was intent on strengthening the concept of Brahma as the ultimate reality. And "Suhrllekha" (Letter to a friend) was an account on

Buddhist morals written in verse meant to be a letter to a friend who is believed to be the Satavahana King.

These are the important texts that most of the critics agree as authentic Nāgārjuna work. These do not discuss any of the more important Mahāyāna concepts like Bodhisathva, eternal Buddha, "Buddhagarba", "Bhakthi marga", "Thrikaya" etc. The question arises whether this was because he agreed with these ideas or he was unaware of them. Therefore the question regarding what Mahāyāna concepts had been developed and were available to Nāgārjuna has to be considered. At the time Nāgārjuna started his career as a Buddhist philosopher in late 1st CE Mahāyāna texts were beginning to make their appearance.

The work on the "Sadharmapundarika sūthra" (Lotus Sūthra) which set out the philosophy of Mahāyāna was probably started before Nāgārjuna came into the picture but was completed during his time (Kalupahana, 2008). Kalupahana has said Nāgārjuna would not have been aware of the doctrines developed in the Lotus sūthra. Hajime Nakamura (1980) however differs on this matter and says Nāgārjuna would have had access to the Mahāyāna texts. Nakamura was a professor of philosophy in the University of Tokyo and considered an expert on Indian philosophy. In his work titled Indian Buddhism (1980) he refers to Nāgārjuna as Mahayanist.

Nāgārjuna is supposed to have been intent on refuting the substantialist views of Sarvāsthavāda (3rd BC) and also nihilist views of Sautrāntika (1st CE) that were present in his time. Strong nihilist views were put forward by Sautrāntika which developed in opposition to Sarvāsthavāda in the 1st CE. He was also critical of Brahmanism which was in ascendency during that time. If Nāgārjuna was trying to defend Buddha's Dhamma with his writings why did he not see the Mahayanist views and its possible emergence as a threat to Early Buddhism is a pertinent question. He has not written anything critical of

Mahāyāna, whereas he has attacked Sarvāsthavāda and Sautrāntika and also Brhamanism.

Nāgārjuna adheres to early Buddhist scripture when he deals with important subjects like causality where he bases his discussion on the Four Noble Truths and "Paticcasamuppāda". If we take into consideration the above mentioned texts as authentic Nāgārjuna work, it appears that he keeps himself within the limits of Early Buddhism. If on the other hand all the thirteen texts that Christian Lindtner (2003) lists are also included under the authorship of Nāgārjuna then it seems that Nāgārjuna is Mahayanist for some of these works are distinctly Mahayanist.

Thus there is no clear answer and the controversy regarding whether or not Nāgārjuna is Mahayanist seems to be an unsettled question.

Chapter 23

Important differences between Theravāda and Mahāyāna

Theravāda means the views of the elder monks. These monks were the disciples of Buddha who were more interested in the propagation of the Dhamma while the younger monks were keen on doing things to perpetuate the memory of the Buddha. It was elder monks who organized the First Dhamma Saṅgāyanāva and took steps to preserve the Dhamma by arranging groups of monks who would learn the suttas and be responsible for the oral tradition of carrying the suttas from generation to generation. Even after the First Dhamma Saṅgāyanāva the dissentient views remained and hundred years later it was necessary to convene the Second Council. The Second Dhamma Saṅgāyanāva resulted in the major rupture in the Saṅga community and the younger monks broke away and formed their own School which was called the Mahāsāṅgika. The School in which the elder monks continued came to be known as Theravāda.

Mahāyāna developed in the 1st Century CE borrowing doctrines from Mahāsāṅgika and Sarvāsthavāda and also influenced by Hinduism. It had the core ideas of the younger monks who broke away from the main stream of the Sanga and these ideas were carrying elements of transcendentalism and metaphysical notions. In these ideas the historical Buddha was elevated to a bigger than life phenomenon. Mahāyāna converted Buddhahood into an eternal state and it was also to be the final goal in the path to enlightenment and Arahath was considered as below the level of the final goal which was Buddha (Sasanārathana, 1952).

Important differences between Theravāda and Mahāyāna

What was their purpose in making such radical changes in the core Buddhist doctrines, one may ask. Obviously they wanted to make Buddha a transcendental being. In Theravāda the answer to the question whether Buddha exists after "PariNirvāna", is that the question does not arise. This idea did not suit the Mahayanist idea of transcendentalism. If Buddha is transcendent he has to be eternal. Thus they had to change the concept of Buddha and also Arahath. Buddha was made into an eternal phenomenon and Arahath was demoted to an inferior state. In Theravāda the Buddha and Arahath are qualitatively equal and Arahath has reached the final goal. Not so in Mahāyāna, Arahath has to go further in the path to Nibbāna and would have to enter the Bodhisathva stream for this purpose. Thus Arahath stream is discouraged and the Bodhisathva stream is offered in its place.

Consequently Mahāyānists had to change the path to Nibbāna as well. Ariyaṭṭhaṅgikamagga was not good enough. It only helps to achieve "kleshāvarana" which means getting rid of the obstacles to the process of spewing out the defilements. The obstacles to the process of gaining omniscience also has to be got rid of and this process is called "ñayāvarana". Thus omniscience is also factored in as a character of Buddhahood. However as mentioned earlier Buddha had disclaimed omniscience as one of his abilities in the Thevijja-vacchagotta-sutta (Majjima Nikāya). In order to achieve "ñayāvarana" one has to follow the Bodhisathva path.

Bodhisathva path mainly consists of the "Bhakti-Marga". Bodhisathva concept has been brought in mainly to accommodate the "Bhakthi-Marga" which is borrowed from Hinduism. This shows that Mahāyāna was weak and could not stand on its own strength and was easily influenced or forced to accept tenets of more powerful religions.

Mahāyāna, as mentioned above, may have originated due to the presence of transcendental elements among the Saṅga. These may have been present even when Buddha was living. In order to give a philosophical basis for these notions Mahāyāna theories would have been formulated. The main transcendental idea was that Buddha was beyond the realm of this world. Eternalism, omniscience, ineffability, were the characters that needed to be factored in into such a phenomenon.

When this was done obviously the concepts of Buddhahood, Arahat, Ariyaṭṭhaṅgikamagga, had to be changed. Further Mahāyāna had to change their strategy when it came to contending with the "Trilakhana". The three characters that define existence in Early Buddhism, "Anicca, Dukkha, Anatta" are not mentioned in the Mahāyāna texts. Silence was their chosen strategy in this instance.

Further, "Bakthi-Marga" (Path of Faith), borrowed from Hinduism, was given equal status to "Ñāna-Mārga" (Path of Wisdom) which was the Buddha's most important creation. As a result Compassion took centre stage displacing Wisdom which was the highest virtue in Early Buddhism. Bodhisathva has to develop compassion to all sentient beings in order to attain Buddhahood. This is controversial because one could be compassionate to the maximum but that will not get rid of ignorance. Without getting rid of ignorance of the Four Noble Truths one cannot attain Nibbāna. Only Wisdom can get rid of Ignorance.

"Bakthi-Mārga" entails faith in deities and Mahāyāna had to invent a pantheon of deities for this purpose. These ideas are obviously borrowed from Hinduism. Early Buddhism did not encourage the practitioner to have faith in deities. The advent of rituals in Buddhism could be attributed to the introduction of faith as a virtue to be acquired by the practitioner. As mentioned above "Bakthi- Mārga" is a concept originally found in Bagavadgita, the most important Hindu scripture.

"Skill in Means" or "Upāyakaushalya" is another virtue that was probably borrowed from Hinduism by Mahāyāna. "Skill in Means" has to be developed by the aspirant to Buddhahood.

This in fact is the highest virtue in Mahāyāna, higher than even Wisdom. "Skill in Means" refer to strategies, interventions and tricks that may be employed by a Bodhisathva to help another aspirant to progress along the path to Nibbāna. Mythological stories may be used for this purpose. "Skill in Means" was first described in the "Saddharmapundarika sūthra" (Lotus sūthra) one of the early Mahāyāna sūthras which spelt out the philosophy of Mahāyāna and described its main tenets (Sasanārathana, 1952).

Thus in Mahāyāna there is a huge role for an external agent to play in the process of working towards Nibbāna. It is impossible for the practitioner to achieve the final goal without someone else's assistance. This is contradictory if Nibbāna entails purification of the mind. Nobody can purify another person's mind. One has to do it by oneself. This most visible contradiction in Mahāyāna has not been solved by its great theoreticians like Asaṅga.

Another obvious contradiction is the Oath that Bodhisattva has to take which requires the latter not to seek enlightenment until All Beings are ready for Enlightenment. Apart from the fact that no one else can purify another's mind the task of making all beings ready for enlightenment is so huge that it is almost impossible and would take so long that Bodhisattva will have to spend several "kalpas" to achieve his goal. Paradoxically this is exactly what Mahāyāna wants the Bodhisattva to do. He has to spend many "kalpas" going through samsara helping all sentient beings to be ready for Nirvāna.

"Thrikaya" concept of Mahāyāna seems to be another borrowing from Hinduism and possibly Jainism. This describes three manifestations of Buddha which are in total contradistinction with the historical Gautama Buddha who was born, lived and died a normal human being. The three levels of manifestations are "Nirmanakāya" which is the physical body which lives among the people, the "Dharmakāya" which is the truth body or where the Dhamma is located and

"Sambogakāya" which is the blissful state of the Buddha. "Astasashrika-prañāparamitā-sūthra" spoke about these "Kāyas" before any other Mahāyāna sūthra. However it mentioned only the "Nirmanakāya" and the "Dharmakāya". Later "Sambogakāya" was added by the Yogacārins to make it "trikāya" (Sasanārathana, 1952).

The "Dharmakāya" of the "Trikāya" concept is comparable to the "Brahmapadārtha" in Hinduism, all the adjectives used for the latter are also applied to the former except the idea of Self, while the latter has Self the former does not.

Ishavara state in Hinduism is comparable to the Sambogakāya in the Trikāya of Mahāyāna. In Hinduism Brahmapadārtha assumes the Ishvara state for the purpose of preaching. Similarly in Mahāyāna "Dharmakāya" takes the form of "Sambogakāya" for the purpose of preaching.

"Murthi" state in Hinduism is comparable to the "Nirmanakāya" in Mahāyāna. Vishnu in order to satisfy the devotees takes various forms of "Murthi". Similarly Buddha takes the form of "Nirmanakāya" and come down to earth to look into the Dharmic needs of the people.

Famous Indian scholar Radakrishnan says "The Dharmakāya answers to the personal absolute, the Brahman of the Upanishads. ... when we pass to the Nirmanakāya we get the several manifestations of this one activity in to avatārs or incarnations". We are reminded of the many avatār of Vishnu (Sasanārathana, 1952).

Mahāyānists did not believe that Buddhas are born in this world of humans, they reside in other worlds and when it is necessary they manifest in "Nirmanakāya" among people and preach to them. There is no limit to these manifestations, they could assume any form to suit the occasion in order to meet the needs of the people in their effort to attain Nibbāna. These Buddhas for instance may take the form of Brahma or Ven.Sariputta or

Ven.Subuthi. Lankavathara sūthra says the Buddha cannot preach while being in the human form, he has to assume one of the "Nirmanakāyas". According to Mahāyāna the Gautama Buddha is also a manifestation of "Nirmanakāya". But there is sufficient evidence to believe that Buddha lived and died as a normal human being and all these metaphysical ideas cannot apply to the historical Buddha.

"Dasa-bhumi" is yet another Mahāyāna tenet that is not found in Theravāda. A Bodhisathva has to follow these ten stages before he could reach the final goal. In these spheres the Bodhisattva acquires several virtues. At the end of the process the Bodhisathva finds union with "Dharmakāya" which is the final goal. This union resembles the union between Atman and Brahman found in Hinduism.

The "Dasa-bhumi" are as follows;

1) "Pramuditha", 2) "Wimala", 3) "Prabākāri", 4) "Arvinmati", 5) "Sudrarjaya", 6) "Abhimuki", 7) "Durangama", 8) "Achala", 9) "Sādumathi", 10) "Dharma-mega".

To give a description of just one of the above stages we shall take the first one "Pramuditha". The Bodhisathva when going through this stage find extreme happiness and realizes that just by getting rid of decay and death one cannot attain the final goal, for such attainments are impermanent and only by finding "Dharmakāya" could one attain the final goal. Further the Bodhisathva realizes that he cannot achieve it without helping everybody else also to progress along the path. Bodhisathva has to develop several virtues while in this stage like worshiping all Buddhas, acquiring wisdom, making everybody happy, helping everybody to attain Buddhahood etc. (Sasanārathana, 1952).

A system of ten perfections ("paramitā") have been described in the later Theravāda sutta Bodhivamsa (Kuddhaka Nikāya) that need to be completed by a Bodhisatta to attain Nibbāna. However, these "paramitās" are different from those in the

"Dasa bhumi" of Mahāyāna. The ten perfections in Bodhivamsa are as follows; "Dhana, Sīla, Naiskarma, Praññā, Vīrya, Kshanthi, Sathya, Adhistana, Maithri, Upeksha".

Mahāyāna also has described six main "paramitās" and four other "paramitās" as well which assist the six main ones. All these "paramitās" are to be fulfilled while the Bodhisathva is in the seventh stage of "Dasa Bhumi" which is "Durangama" mentioned above. The first six "paramitās" are as follows; "dana, seela, kshanthi, vīrya, dyana, praññā". The other four "paramitās" are "upayakaushalya, pranidāna, bala, ñana".

If we take one important "paramita", the sixth called "praññā" and compare it with Wisdom achieved by practicing the two final stages in the Ariyaṭṭhaṅgikamagga of Early Buddhism, "samma-sathi"and "samma-samadi" we could see whether there is any difference in what is meant by "praññā" or Wisdom in Early Buddhism and Mahāyāna.

In Early Buddhism the Wisdom achieved in the final stage of the Ariyaṭṭhaṅgikamagga is a superior knowledge. One who has attained Nibbāna has the knowledge that defilements have been got rid of and there are no influx of sense pleasures. In the one who is thus released there is knowledge that "I have been released", "there will be no more birth" "the higher life has been lived", "done has been what has to be done". Buddha goes on to say that there is no more superior fruit of recluse-ship than this (Sāmaññaphala Sutta, Dīgha Nikāya).

In Mahāyāna when the "Dyana paramitā" is completed the sixth "paramitā", "Praññā paramitā", is achieved. By this means Bodhisathva gets rid of the defilement ignorance. He also realizes that the whole world is totally empty (śūnya) and this knowledge is also called "śūnya-ñāna". However, this happens in the seventh of the "Dasa-bhumi" which means the Bodhisathva has to go through three more "bhumis" to reach the final goal. However in Early Buddhism Wisdom is what is achieved in the final stage of the Ariyaṭṭhaṅgikamagga.

Let us now look at the final stage of the "Dasa-bhumi" which is called "Dharma-mega" which means dharma clouds. In this stage the Bodhisathva has reached the final goal and he is omnipotent, has risen above the sphere of the sentient beings and finally unites with Dharmakāya of the Buddha. This is obviously totally different from the Nibbāna in Early Buddhism (Sasanārathana, 1952).

What was the reason for Mahāyāna to evolve in this manner? As mentioned earlier transcendental ideas had been present among the Sanga even during Buddha's life time. After his demise there had been a breakaway group called Mahāsaṅgika which cultivated the transcendental ideas. Further divisions occurred within Theravāda and several schools were formed such as Puggalavāda, Sarvāsthavāda and Sautrāntika which developed eternalist, nihilist and substantialist concepts. Mahāyāna borrowed some of these ideas and converted Buddha into an eternal, omnipotent, omniscient phenomenon. For this purpose they had to change the final goal into Buddhahood, degrade the status of Arahath, and change the method of attaining the final goal by introducing the Bodhisathva concept. There may have been a social need also for this because there was no system in Early Buddhism for external assistance to achieve the final goal and also there was no rituals for the devotee to practice and pray for solace.

There may have been influence and pressure from Hinduism forcing Mahāyāna to accept some of their tenets and concepts. The "Bhakthi-mārga", and "Trikāya" are two such concepts. Further "Upayakaushalya" which is considered as more important than Wisdom has been borrowed from the Vedas.

Chapter 24

Controversies related to Idealism in Buddhism

Idealism in philosophy would mean that the physical reality of the material world is a construct of the mind and is related to ideas. German philosopher Arthur Schopenhauer (18th CE) had said the world cannot be known. Emanuel Kant (18th CE) another German philosopher said that modes of representation of the material world are not features that existed within itself but characters that existed in the human mind that perceives the world. What this means is things that are independent of the mind are unknowable and reality exists in the mind.

Buddha in his preaching had given prominence to the mind and consciousness. He has paid special attention to the process of perception and emphasized the fact that what is perceived may not be the real object but something created by the process involving Saṅkara" or disposition. Buddha has also said that the world exists in one's mind. In the discourse titled "Loka" (Samyutta Nikāya) the world is described as what is perceived by the sense organs with the implication that there is no reality independent of the human mind. Further Buddha in the "Sabbam sutta" (Everything) (Samyutta Nikāya) explains what he means by Everything, he says what is perceived by the five sense organs and the mind constitutes everything and there is nothing else. Whether Buddha was preaching an idealist Dhamma would be discussed below.

However all these ideas that were present in Early Buddhism together with the transcendental ideas that had been developed in Mahāyāna had paved the way for the development of an idealist philosophy within Mahāyāna which was called Yogācāra or "Viññānavāda". This was one of the main branches of Mahāyāna and came into being in the 4th Century

CE. The word "Viññāna" means consciousness and "Viññānavāda" denotes the doctrine which contends that the world exists in the consciousness. Those who considered the Yoga precepts as the basis of this school called it Yogācāra.

Idealism in Yogācāra proposes that physical reality of the external world exists in relation to the consciousness. It says the external world is a mere expression of the functioning of the consciousness. While being in the sphere of Mahāyāna and apart from the influence it had from Early Buddhist thought on consciousness and the valueless predicament of the world, Yogācāra in its formative process has drawn from Sautrāntika also. One of its founders Ven. Asaṅga had been with Sautrāntika before he ventured into the new philosophy (Sasanārathana, 1952).

Several Mahāyāna sūthras such as the Lankavathara have put forward clear idealist thinking. Lankavathara sūthra may have been composed in the 2nd or 3rd Century CE and it may have been responding to Madhyamaka thinking about the concept of "śūnyathava". Madhayamaka philosophy had made its appearance before the compilation of Lankavathara sūthra.

The realization that the "Śūnyathavada" of Madhyamaka was espousing a nihilist theory, in that it sees an emptiness in all phenomena of the world, had probably been the stimulus that prompted the Yogacarins to formulate their philosophy of idealism. Does the Yogācāra idealism totally repudiate the idea of emptiness? There could be a subtle relationship between the two ideas, emptiness could be a form of idealism. If everything is empty of substance and self-existence the question arises what is it that we perceive. What we perceive may be existing only in the mind. However, in Madhyamaka even the mind may be non-existent. Yogācāra may have wanted to refute this nihilist idea and espouse their own theory of idealism which does not deny the existence of the mind.

Within the Yogācāra itself, when considered as a religious philosophy, dissenting viewpoints could be seen. For instance the three terms "mano", "citta", "Viññāna" are considered as synonymous by some of the leading figures of Yogācāra while others think these terms have different meanings. In Early Buddhism these terms were given slightly different meanings based on function. Further different thinkers have given Yogācāra different names. "Lankavathara sūthra" refers to it as "Cittamatra" while Vasubandhu has called it "Viññānapthimathra" (Sasanrathana, 1953).

The position that Yogācāra took with regard to "Śūnyathavada" was that although all phenomena may be empty of substance the consciousness that perceives these phenomena exist as an entity. In contrast Madhyamaka was of the opinion that even the consciousness is subject to the principle of emptiness. This of course is not the opinion of Nāgārjuna though he is credited with the authorship of Madhyamaka theory. However these interpretations have been developed after Nāgārjuna's treatise on "śūnyathava", the "Mūlamadhyamaka-kārika" was published.

The problem Yogācāra faced was it had to come up with a new analysis of "viññāna" or consciousness for it envisages the existence of all phenomena as illusions of consciousness. The new analysis it came up with proposes that consciousness has eight components. Six of these components are associated with the six agents or "salayathana" which consist of the five sense organs and the mind. The seventh is the defiled mind or defiled consciousness ("klista manasa" or "klista viññāna"). The eighth is the "Alaya-viññānaya". This analysis appears as a metaphysical theory in the Lankavathara sūthra with the eight types of consciousness occurring as separate entities (Kalupahana, 2008).

However in Vasubandhu's analysis (Vimsathika and Trimsathika) it appears as a description of the process of evolution of consciousness and there is no metaphysical connotation. The version found in the Lankavathara sūthra may have been subjected to Hindu and Vedantha influence.

In Vasubandhu's analysis "Alaya-Viññānaya" is the important component and actually the whole of it could be considered as a description of the evolution of the "Alaya-Viññānaya". In the "Samsaric" process the seeds of all karmas are deposited in the "Alaya-Viññānaya". It is the defiled mind that paves the way for the deposition of seeds of karma in the "Alaya-Viññānaya". Defilements associated with the Self e.g., Self-view, Self-love, Self-ignorance and Self-ego would facilitate the entry of karma into "Alaya-viññānanya".

Whether Vasubandhu had put forward an idealist theory has been questioned by some commentators (Kalupahana, 2008). It appears that his use of the word "viññānapthimathra" in reference to phenomena that is perceived by the sense organs has given rise to controversy just as much as the use of the word "śūnyathava" by Nāgārjuna had led to much controversy.

In Early Buddhism consciousness has been analysed based on the five sense organs and the mind. Each sense organ has a consciousness assigned to it for its function. "Chakku-Viññāna" is the consciousness connected to the eye. Similarly there are consciousness assigned to the function of hearing, smell, taste, touch, and functions of the mind like formation of views. There was no reference to any other consciousness.

Was there anything else in Early Buddhism apart from these six consciousness that could be even remotely related to consciousness which may justify the elaborate interpretations and new theories that Yogācārins developed and formulated? There doesn't seem to be in any of the Early Buddhist texts.

However as mentioned earlier the question whether Vasubandhu's "Alaya-Viññānaya" theory constitutes a philosophy that could be identified as idealism has to be considered. He discusses "Alaya-Viññānaya" in his treatise called "Trimsathika". In this work he carefully avoids making utterances that would categorize him as an idealist (Kalupahana, 2008). He does not make statements such as "all ideas arise dependent on consciousness". His intention was to analyse the evolution of consciousness which culminates in "Alaya-Viññānaya" or store-consciousness where seeds of all karmas are deposited and which finally would be responsible for rebirth.

If Vasubandhu's point of view is compared with that of the "Lankavathara-sūthra", which also describes the "Alaya-Viññānaya" concept, we find that the latter makes an unequivocal statement that objects of the world are manifestations of the mind and that consciousness is the only reality. Vasubandhu does not present similar points of view. Lankavathara is based on a conversation between Buddha and a Bodhisathva named "Mahamati" (Great-wisdom). According to this Sūthra Buddha is supposed to have said that the objective world is a manifestation of the mind.

In "Trimsathika" with the theory of "Alaya-Viññānaya" Vasubandhu attempts to show how the human mind develops concepts out of what it perceives. The concepts so formed of the object makes the latter substantial and incorruptible. Thus according to Vasubandhu such concepts are only "mere concepts" or in his words "viññāpthi-matra" lacking in substance and permanency.

It is said that the use of the word "vingnapthi-mathra" by Vasubandhu was latched on to by his commentator Sthiramathi and Vasubandhu was made into not only a metaphysical idealist but a leading theorist of Mahāyāna. The question whether Vasubandhu was Mahayanist could be examined by looking at his other major works. The "Trimsathika-vingnapthi-kārika" (The Thirty Verses on Conception) which deals with "Alaya-viññānaya" is included in the major treatise called "Viññānapthimatratasidhi" or "The Establishment of Mere Concept". This major work also includes the "Vimsatikakārika" (The Twenty Verses) in which he criticizes metaphysical views that reduce objects to particles. Then he refutes an absolute relationship between experience and concept that attempts to comprehend objects. The attempt to separate the object from the subject is mere conception. With these arguments what Vasubandhu attempts to do in "Vimsathika" is to show that concepts arise out of experience and the process is "mere conception" (Kalupahana, 2008).

Thus Vasubandhu in "Vimsathika" argues that perception is appearance only and in "Trimsika" he takes the argument further and deals with experience to show that "all this is mere conception".

Vasubandhu has authored a summarization of the Sārvasthavadin's Abhidharma and entitled it "Abhidharmakosa". In this work he criticizes some aspects of the Sārvasthivadin's Abhidharma from the point of view of Sautrāntika. Vasubandhu was born in Ghandara in the 4th Century BC and had been a follower of Sautrāntika. He had taught at Nalanda monastery in Bihar which was considered a Mahāyāna institution. Sautrāntika had a "beeja" (seeds) concept which proposed that seeds of karma are deposited in the consciousness. This concept had been borrowed by Lankavathara sūthra and based on it had developed the "Alaya-Viññānaya" idea. Whether Vasubandhu in adopting these ideas was propagating Mahāyāna philosophy is a matter of conjecture.

Vasubandhu had delved into logic also and had compiled a book on logic titled "Vada-vidi" (Method of Debate) which is considered very important in the context of beginning of Indian logic and also for paving the way for the emergence of eminent Buddhist logician Dignāga and others.

Vasubandhu's half-brother was Asaṅga the founder of Yogācāra and some believe that Vasubandhu was converted to Yogācāra by his half-brother. Vasubandu also wrote a treatise titled "The Sūthra on Generating the Resolve to become a Buddha" (Bodhisathva vow). In this text he discourses on the origin of the concept of Bodhisathva vow ("Bodhi-citta") and on each of the ten "Bhumis" through which the vow reaches fruition. The idea of the need for a Bodhisathva vow and the ten "Bhumis" and the six perfections for attaining Buddhahood, which we have described above, are clearly Mahāyāna concepts.

There doesn't seem to be any controversy about the authorship of these works. It is probable that Vasubandhu authored these books. Thus the question whether he belonged to the Mahāyāna school remains unresolved.

Several works are attributed to Asaṅga the half-brother of Vasubandhu some of which the authorship is uncertain. Of these the most important work is "Mahāyānasamgraha" which discourses the major tenets of Yogācāra in ten chapters. His "Abhidharma-samuccaya" is written in the general Abhidharma style of other Schools and according to Ven. Walpola Rahula (1978) in essence this work is closer to the Pāli Nikāyas than the Abhidharma of the Theravādins.

Asaṅga like his half-brother was born in Ghandhar (Peshawar in present-day Pakistan) in the 4th Century CE and like his half-brother had been a teacher at Nalanda monastery in modern day Bihar. Though it is uncertain whether Vasubandu's philosophy was oriented towards idealism and Mahāyāna there was no such uncertainty regarding the loyalties of Asaṅga, he was distinctly an idealist and a Mahayanist. An idealist basically holds that there is no reality in what is perceived and it is a creation of the human mind. A Mahayanist basically holds that Buddhahood is eternal and transcendental. Thus there is no doubt that Asaṅga was a Mhayanist and was the founder of the "Vingnavada" or Yogācāra sect.

Chapter 25

A comparison of "Puggalavāda", "Sarvāsthavāda" and "Sautrāntika"

About hundred years after the "pariNirvāna" of the Buddha various religious philosophies had started to question the theoretical basis of the Buddhist doctrines. One problematic issue was the "Anatta" or No-self theory of Early Buddhism. These opponents of Buddhism were busy organizing and systematizing their religious philosophies, doctrines and tenets. A need for similar work and effort was felt by the senior monks who were engaged in the study and propagation of the Buddha's Dhamma. The incessant questions that arose from within as well as without had to be met with satisfactory answers.

There was much discourse as well as discord among the leading Buddhist monks after the demise of the Buddha in the 4th Century BCE. This came to a head 100 years later due to the disagreement regarding the implications of the Anatta concept, which raised the question; if there is no Self or anything like it and there are only "Dhamma dathu" that are indivisible in the five skandhas how could rebirth, karma, and responsibility for one's actions etc be determined. Several theories were forwarded which attempted to conform to the main Suttas. At that time the Abidhamma was also being developed and these thoughts influenced that process too. These differences were too deep to be amicably resolved and several breakaway schools were formed. Apart from the differentiation into Theravāda and Mahāsāṅgika there was further separation from these main streams.

A major issue was the relationship between the Dhamma Theory of the Abhidhamma and the "Anatta" Theory. If every phenomenon is based on Dhammas and there was no Self apart from the five aggregates that compose the human form who or what is responsible for karmic consequence, rebirth and morality was the question that was difficult to solve. In such a situation there was difference of opinion and formation of groups taking up inflexible positions. Naturally such developments are bound to end up in breakaway and formation of new schools.

"Puggalavāda" (Personalist theory) was one of the earliest such schools which came into being in 280 BC. A monk named "Vathsiputhra" who belonged to Theravāda is the author of this theory. Later the school broke into two main sects; namely "Vathsiputhra" and "Sammitiya". The latter spread far and wide and for some time was the dominant school of Buddhism in several areas in India from the 2nd Century BC to the 10th Century CE, more than 1000 years, until Buddhism declined in that country. They were particularly popular during the time of Emperor Harshavadana in 600BC (Paul Williams, 2005).

"Puggalavāda" envisages that there is a "person" apart from the five aggregates, which is responsible for karmic consequence, rebirth and morality, which exists continuously as long as the samsaric process lasts. However they were believers of the "Anatta" (No-self) concept. This school came to be known as "Puggalavāda" and also as "Vathsaputhriya" after its founder.

"Puggalavādins" faced numerous questions from Theravādins regarding the nature of the "puggala". What is the relationship between "panchaskanda" and "puggala"? Are they different or same? Does it have an absolute and true existence? Is it external to the "panchaskanda"? These questions as could be seen arise out of Early Buddhist concepts and doctrines that govern existence and composition of human form.

In answer to these questions the "Puggalavādins" claimed that their theory is based on Buddha's preaching and pointed out that in the "Bara-Hara" sutta in the Samyutta-Nikāya Buddha had spoken about the burden (Bara) and also the bearer (Hara) of the burden. The burden here is the "panchaskanda" and bearer is the "Puggala". The response of the Theravādins to this idea was that "Puggalavādins" are confused about the manner of Buddha's preaching who used two methods to explain the Dhamma, direct and indirect ("nitatha" and "neiatha").

"Puggalavādins" maintained that the "puggala" is neither matter nor a mere concept, it exists parallel to the "panchaskanda" and is not the same as "panchaskanda" nor different. It is neither conditioned nor unconditioned. On further questioning they had said that the "puggala" or its relationship with "panchaskanda" was inexpressible, and cannot be described with the words in the language in use. "Puggalavādins" considered Nirvāna as a real entity, uncaused and therefore indestructible. The "Person" ("Puggala") and Nibbāna are neither same nor different. In "pariniravana" the "person" is unfathomable, it may be considered as non-existence for there is no physical body, faculty or thought and it could also be considered as existence for it has happiness (Sasanārathana, 1952).

Thus the definition of Nibbāna in "Puggalavāda" appears to be different compared to its definition in Early Buddhism and also Theravāda. Buddha was silent about the status after "parinirvāna". Further the status in Nibbāna, as mentioned in Chapter 18, is described as a superior knowledge on the nature of suffering, its cause and its cessation and also there is release from rebirth, decay and death.

Apart from "Puggalavāda" two other major schools that formed by separating from Theravāda were Sarvāstivāda which made its appearance in the 3rd Century BC and Sautrāntika which was a breakaway group of the latter and which came into being in the 1st Century AD. The importance of these two schools is the stand they took on several concepts such as existence, time, karma etc while remaining under the umbrella of Theravāda and the influence these different interpretations would have had on the future evolution of Buddhism.

These two schools of Buddhism did not adopt transcendental theories unlike Mahāsāṅgika sect which attempts to convert the historical Buddha into a larger than life image, hence their continuation in the stream of Theravāda. Yet their extreme views on some of the important tenets of Buddhism may have led to the growth of different schools such as Yogācāra etc. These views of the two schools, though they were centuries apart in origin, were often antagonistic but were rich in scholarly method and analysis. Thus certainly these different Schools of Buddhism, though some were divergent from Early Buddhism to a degree, where they had lost some of the essence of Buddhism, have enriched the quality of religious philosophy of Asia.

It appears that these two schools subscribe to the two different theories on existence that were in vogue during that time. One was that everything existed on a permanent basis and the other was that nothing existed, the former was eternalism and the latter nihilism which confronted Buddha too in his time and which Buddha refuted with his "Paticcasamuppadaya" or Theory of Coorigination. Sarvāsthavādins appeared to be supportive of the former view and they appeared to be very much concerned with the issues and queries raised by monks as well as other religious thinkers regarding the Dhamma Theory which at that time appeared to be difficult to resolve. To solve the above mentioned problem connected with the "anathma" theory they put forward the "svabhāva" concept which said there is something apart from "nama-rupa" complex which they called "svabhāva" that could explain rebirth, "karma" etc. This Dhamma called the "svabhāva" would be present not only in the present but also in the past and the future.

Katyayaniputra (150 BC) who is believed to be a theorist of Sarvāstivāda developed a Theory of Six Fold Causation in which the sixth asserts that cause is to be found in the effect. He was one of the first religious thinkers to have developed this theory (Dhammajoti, 2009). Theravāda however did not believe that the effect is to be found in the cause, the mango tree is not to be found in the mango seed. Sarvāsthivādins in response said the "mango-svabhāva" was present in the mango seed. Of course there were monks among the ranks of this school who did not agree with this concept and its explanation. This fundamental disagreement may have continued for several generations until in the 1st Century AD the breakaway group called the Sautrāntika was formed.

Sarvāsthivādins were keen debaters who placed greater importance on rational thinking than empiricist method. They gave lot of thought to the "anicca" theory particularly to the concept of existence. Conventionally in Buddhism existence is divisible into three stages; appearance, existence and disappearance ("utpada, vaya, tithassa angnathatha"). Sarvāsthivādins in their analysis of this process further divided the stage of existence into two and called them "sthithi" and "jara" so that there were four stages instead of three. With this division they introduced the theory of moments ("kshana vadaya") which defined the stage of "sthithi" (Karunadasa 1983).

Sarvāsthivādins rigorously propounded the theories of the Abhidhamma. Though they insisted they were guided by Buddha's discourses and like the Theravādins they had seven texts in the Abhidhamma their Abhidhamma differed to a great extent in content except in one text, "Dharmaskanda" which resembled "Vibanga" in Theravadin's Abhidhamma. One main difference in the analysis and definitions in the two versions is that in Theravāda there is only one unconditioned Dhamma which is Nibbāna while there are three unconditioned Dhammas in Sarvāstivāda; "akasha" "prathisankya niroda" and "aprathisankya niroda". "Akasha" doesn't mean the space between objects but the 'force' that bears all objects. "Prathisankya niroda" refers to the method of spewing out the defilements by a process of gaining wisdom while "aprathisankya niroda" means the removal of defilements by the gradual reduction of the causes of defilements. Thus they seem to subscribe to two methods of achieving the final goal.

Perhaps it is relevant at this juncture to recall that Mahāyāna has two methods of achieving the final goal; the "Ñāna Mārga" (Path of Wisdom) and "Bahkthi Mārga" (Path of Faith). These ideas have pervaded Theravāda too in Sri Lanka where Buddhists practice "Bhakthi Marga" (Dhammajoti, 2009).

Sarvāsthivādin's explanation of the idea of time was different to that of Theravāda. According to Theravāda the past is dead, therefore it does not exist and the future is not born and therefore it does not exist either and only the present exists in relation to time. Sarvāsthivādins took a different position, to them time was not just a concept but a Dhamma that exists throughout the past, present and the future and it is the field in which all Dhammas of the world travel.

Due to these new thinking on "svabhāva" which has existence in the past, present and the future and the introduction of the above mentioned new theory on existence - division into four stages - and the different explanation of time in which there is continuity of past, present and the future the Sarvāsthivādins came to be known as eternalists ("Utchedavadins") and also as substantialists though they insisted that they believed in the "anithya" and "anathma" theories (Akira Hirakawa, 1993).

Sarvāsthivādins had a different theory for Karma too. Buddha speaks about karma in the "Nibbedikapariyaya sutta" (Aṅguttara Nikāya) and he had not spoken about two types of Karma but Sarvāsthivādins have interpreted his words as conveying the idea of two types of Karma; one committed by the mind and the other by the body. On the contrary Buddha had said "chethana" (intention) was Karma and nothing else, irrespective of whether the Karma is committed by the mind or the body.

Sarvāsthivādins did not receive sponsorship from King Dharmasoka and after the Third Dhamma Saṅgāyanāva migrated to the North West of India and strongly established themselves in Kashmir and Gandhara region under the patronage of King Kanishka. Due to their extremist views and inflexible adherence to them the school broke up first into two groups which were known as Kashmir and Gandhar groups. Later these also fragmented into several minor groups.

Sautrāntika School came into being in the 1st Century AD as a result of the development of ideas in extreme opposition to those of Sarvāstivāda particularly on the concepts of existence and time. The term Sautrāntika means those who believe in "sūthra" only and not "sasthra". What is meant by "sasthra" here is Abhidhamma which was compiled after the "sūthra" and with lot of deductive interpretations of the "sūthra" which the Sautrāntikavadins said was unnecessary. This is not exactly true because they also engaged in studying and analysing the "sūthras" in depth which produced works similar to Abhidhamma of other Schools. Thus the Sautrāntika school of Buddhism has no Abhidhamma as such. The question arises whether the teachings of this school are closer to Early Buddhism because they claim it to be based on "sūthra".

Theravāda had recognized 82 ultimate Dhammas as described in its Abhidhamma. Sarvāstivāda describes 75 such Dhammas while Yogacarins mention 100 but Sautāntrica has only the "panchamaha butha" and "chitta" as their ultimate units. Thus there is no need for further analysis of matter and mind, all Dhammas are in the "panchamahabutha" and "chitta". They said "vedana" "sangna" and "chethana" were different forms of the "chitta" itself which cannot be further divided.

Sautrāntikavādins vehemently opposed the theory of time of the Sarvāstivāda. They questioned the possibility of four phenomena - "utpada" "sthithi" "jara" and "tithassa anganatha" - occurring in a "kshana" or moment. Their argument was that if all four stages occurred together they would nullify each other and if they occurred separately the "kshana" has to be divided into four. This showed their ability of thinking and rational argument. Their theory of existence was thus changed and there are only two stages; "jathi" and "vyaya" or birth and death which could be applied to all phenomena. There is no time for the phenomena to undergo change but would immediately disappear no sooner they appear. Further they said what is meant by change is appearance and disappearance and there is nothing in between that could undergo change. One could talk about change not in relation to one Dhamma but an entire system of Dhammas. This whole idea however is questionable for when a phenomenon occurs it has to exist even for a moment.

Explanation of perception of objects by sensory organs was not a problem for Theravādins as there were three stages in the existence of an object. There was time for "sañña" "saṅkara" and "Viññāna". It was not a problem for Sarvāsthivādins either as they had four stages in the process of existence. Sautrāntikavādins on the other hand had a problem about sensory perception (indra sanjanaya) because in their theory of existence objects arise and disappear and there is no time for perception. They had to use all their analytical ability to solve the problem. They said as the sensory organs perceive an object, immediately an image is formed in the "chitta". Comprehension (prathyaksha) of the object takes place indirectly in the mind on the basis of the image thus created and the presence of the object is not necessary. This theory is known as "aprathyaksha vādaya" where there is no need for the stages described in Theravāda; "sañña", "saṅkara" and "Viññāna". The absence of "saṅkara" which is an extremely important concept in Buddhism cannot be salutary to the Sautrāntikavādins (Akira Hirakawa, 1993). "Saṅkara" refers to the function of construction of concepts by the mind in relation to what is perceived by the sensory organs. Grasping which is a feature of the human being depends on what "saṅkara" constructs out of perceived things that are impermanent, without self and which lead to sorrow. This happens due to human ignorance of nature of the material world.

Sautrāntikavādins did not deny the existence of the external world independent of the mind. In this respect both Sautrāntika and Sarvāstivāda were similar in thinking to Theravāda. Yet the special place these theories gave to the mind may have led to the formulation of an idealism ("Viññāna vada") in Later Buddhism which propounded that the external world is a creation of the mind. The Yogācāra sect of Mahāyāna subscribes to a similar theory.

As the Sautrāntikavādins had said Dhammas do not change but appear and disappear they had to accept that the preceding Dhammas do not condition the causation of each Dhamma. This problem made it necessary that they give a new interpretation to the "paticcasamuppāda" theory of Early Buddhism as well. They had attempted to do so but not convincingly. They had to give new interpretation to the theory of karma too though they unlike Sarvāsthivāda accepted that karma is "chethana". Buddha had spoken about the prerequisites for the ripening or maturation of karma and the manifestation of its effect. Sautrāntika gave a new interpretation to this theory. Though they rejected determinism – the theory that everything is predetermined – they were tending towards it. Buddha did not believe in determinism. His theory of karma was not entirely based on determinism and he had described preconditions required for the maturation and final effect of karma.

Sautrāntikavāda had developed to such an extent that it could influence Mahavihara Theravādins in Sri Lanka. This had made Ven. Buddhagosa who came to Sri Lanka in the 5th Century AD and lived in Mahavihara to almost agree with the extreme viewpoint on existence of phenomena held by Sautrāntikavādins. He had used a language that hinted at permanency when he spoke about concepts like Nirvāna. Later he had said it was a "labelling technique" he adopted to refute Sautrāntika ideas of nihilism.

Early Buddhism had employed empiricism to arrive at its theories and doctrines. Sarvāsthivādins and to even a greater degree Sautrāntikavādins had employed rationalism and logic to build their theories. Buddha in his theory of knowledge had warned against excessive reliance on reason to gain knowledge. He relied mainly on personal experience (Sangarava sutta, Samyutta Nikāya).

According to Kalupahana (2007) Buddha had solved the problem of time, ie the differentiation of time to the past, the present and the future in relation to the theory of causality (paticcasamuppada) by inventing a new word; "paccuppanna" which joined the past and the present and which meant "that which has arisen moving toward" to replace the word "varthamana". The word "varthamana" therefore does not appear in the Pāli texts. Buddha did this to avoid the need to introduce an eternal substance to connect the cause and effect in relation to time. Both Sarvāsthavādins and Sautrāntika had disregarded Buddha's method and used the word "varthamana" which made way for substantialism (in Sarvāstivāda) and essentialism (in Sautrāntika). Substantialism of Sarvāstivāda is due to the theory of "svabhāva" they introduced to solve the problems that arose in relation to "anathma". Essentialism in Sautrāntika arises due to their idea that Dhammas have characteristics that do not change, they appear and disappear without undergoing change, which helped them to connect past with the present. Sautrāntikavada is also considered nihilist due to their theory on existence which said nothing exists between appearance and disappearance or birth and demise of Dhammas.

Buddha constructed "paticcasamuppāda" mainly to expound his middle path approach to the question of existence. During his time, as it was throughout history, there were thinkers who said everything existed on a permanent basis and others who said nothing existed. Centuries later this dispute resulted in the creation of these two schools of Buddhism. The debate continued for ages and several Buddhist philosophers down the line had attempted to solve it.

A comparison of "Puggalavāda", "Sarvāsthavāda" and "Sautrāntika

The work of Sarvāsthivādins and Sautantrkavādins continued causing disunity among the Saṅga. Brahamanism too raised its head with new strength partly due to the disunity among Buddhist Saṅga. In response Ven.Nāgārjuna (1st Century AD) attempted to deal with the problem in his "Mūlamadhyamaka-kārika".

It could be seen that these three Schools of Buddhism had attempted to provide a solution to the question of No-self and the consequent problem of accounting for the responsibility of karma, rebirth and morality. Puggalavādins had the "person", Sarvāstivāda had the "svabhāva" and Sautrāntika formulated a theory of seeds or "beeja" which carried the karma and could be responsible for continuity of Samsara and rebirth. We must remember that Early Buddhism and Theravāda was not entirely unencumbered by this question, they had an explanation for karmic consequence, they said a stream of consciousness was responsible for this.

Moggalliputtatissa (3rd Century BC) in the Third Dharma-Saṅgāyanāva, which he chaired, attempted a refutation of the theories of "Puggalavāda", entailing the Realist and the Transcendentalist. The other disciplinary matters dealt with may not be relevant to the present discussion. He preached the "Kattavatthu" at this convention which was included in the Tipiṭaka. The Third Dhamma Saṅgāyanāwa was held as King Dharmasoka wanted to get rid of all impurities that had crept into the Dhamma. With the King extending his sponsorship to Buddhism monks who had wrong view points had entered the Saṅga community with the intention of getting benefits.

The discourse takes the form of probing questions asked by Moggalliputtatissa sometimes taking the form of a cross examination and answers given by each of the three theorists; Realist, Transcendentalist and Personalist. The intention of Moggalliputtatissa is to show that these theories are flawed. Here we will consider the debate he has with the Personalist or "Puggalavādin".

Moggalliputtatissa puts forward two propositions to the Personalist. One is that there is a person who exists as an absolute truth and ultimate reality. Two is that there is an absolute truth and an ultimate reality in the world. The Personalist agrees with the first but in answer to the second says "one should not say so". In response Moggaliputtatissa says that without a conception of an absolute truth and an ultimate reality there cannot be a conception of a person who exists as an absolute truth and ultimate reality.

Further questions are asked regarding whether the "person" is identical or different from aggregates etc. The Personalist tries to prove his point by quoting Buddha where an existence of a person is mentioned. Moggalliputtatissa had responded by showing that in several discourses Buddha had spoken about the lack of a self in all phenomena in the world (Kathavatthu, Abhidhamma Piṭaka).

Chapter 26

Controversies related to Buddhist Logic

Logic deals with the methodology of reasoning and there could be two types of logic, formal and informal. The former has definitive systems involving symbolical analysis. Within formal logic mathematical logic represents mathematical aspects of arguments and philosophical logic deals with questions in knowledge, existence and such matters. Formal logic relies on deductive methods while informal logic uses inductive methods. Characteristic of deductive inferences is that the truth of their premises ensures the truth of their conclusions (S Haack, 1978).

Logic had been known to ancient philosophers like Aristotle (384 – 322 BCE) whose methods are still being used. In the Islamic world Ibn Sina (Avicenna) (980 – 1037 CE) developed a system of logic which replaced Aristotlian logic in the Islamic Arab. Aristotle had employed syllogism which is a method of inductive argument based on two propositions, one major and the other minor, asserted or assumed to be true.

Before discussing Buddhist logic it may be relevant to examine the logic expounded in Nyaya Sūtra, a Hindu text, composed by Akshapada Gothama which dealt with methods of reason and deduction (Fowler, 2002). The Nyaya thought could be traced back to Vedic traditions.

The Nyaya tradition had four distinct subjects; 1) "Tarka" (art of debate), 2) "Pramana" (means of valid knowledge), 3) "Avayava" (the system of syllogism) and 4) "Anya-mata-pariksha" (examination of views of others). Nyaya syllogism consists of five parts ; 1) "Pratijna" (the premise), 2) "Hetu" (the cause), 3) "Udaharana" (Example), 4) "Upanaya" (the application of that example) and 5) "Nigamana" (the conclusion). Given below is an example of a syllogism found in Nyaya Sūtra;

This hill is fiery (the premise)

Hill is on fire because there is smoke (the cause)

All that has smoke is on fire like an oven (the example)

The hill has smoke which is associated with fire (the application of the example)

Therefore the Hill is on fire (the conclusion)

If this syllogism is to be expressed according to Aristotlian logic it would take the following form;

Sign of fire belongs to all smoke (the major premise)

And smoke belongs to this hill (the minor premise)

Then fire belongs to this hill (the conclusion)

It could be seen that Aristotlian logic relies on deduction while Nyaya logic is based on reality as shown by the fact that an example is necessary. This is why Nyaya syllogism is considered to be important and cannot be dismissed as unnecessarily complicated with redundant items.

However Nyaya theorits considered not only the empirical but also testimony from reliable authority as sources of knowledge. This allowed the use of Vedic scriptures as a source of knowledge. We know that Buddha had said not to rely on scripture as a source of knowledge.

Buddha had not developed a specific system of logic though he had a well-developed art of debate. The earliest example of Buddhist logic may be found in Kattavatthu composed by Moggalliputtatissa (3rd Century BCE) which contains passages that shows that the art of debate would have been developed in his time. How the reality of Soul is negated demonstrates this possibility. However, methods of syllogism may not have been developed at that time. Taking an argument to its logical conclusion was an art that Moggalliputtatissa had apparently mastered.

After Moggalliputtatissa it was Nāgārjuna who employed logical argument and the art of debate mainly to show the fallacy of his opponent's views. In "Mūlamadhyamaka-kārika" the tetralemma or four cornered logic was used to negate all possibilities of interpretations of a view. In "Vigraha-vyavartani" Nāgārjuna employs a unique system of debate where nothing positive is proved but by applying test of relativity to the opponents positive theories they are defeated dialectically. Th Stcherbatsky (1932) says Nāgārjuna uses this method in "Vigraha-vyavartani" to refute four methods of proof used in the Nyaya School. And in "Vaidalya Sūtra" Nāgārjuna mentions 16 topics to be examined in the treatise written by Nyaya theorist Gothama. By applying the "critical axe" of relativity Nāgārjuna establishes that all 16 topics are relative and not absolute and therefore unreal. Everything is relative to some other thing and therefore they could be denied of ultimate reality when its dialectic nature is disclosed.

There were others who held different opinion on Nāgārjuna's intentions in writing the above mentioned texts. Indian scholar K.Bhattacharya (1978) says that Nāgārjuna by claiming that everything is 'void' does not deny or affirm anything, and only expresses the inexpressible, the Absolute. Kalupahana (2008) has a different viewpoint on Nāgārjuna. He says Nāgārjuna's intention in writing "Vigraha-vyavartani" was to respond to the resurgence of Brahamanical conception of Brahma. The fact that Nāgārjuna attacks the Nyaya theories gives credence to Kalupahana's opinion.

Nāgārjuna's thoughts remained in vogue for quite a long time and as a result Buddhist logic did not progress for centuries. In the 4th Century CE Asaṅga and Vasubandhu attempted to develop new ideas in the field of Buddhist logic and took up the challenge of studying Nyaya logic. Asaṅga developed a five membered syllogism and a set of rules in the art of debate. However these resemble Nyaya logic and are not original in construction (Th Stcherbatsky, 1978).

Vasubandhu wrote three treatises on logic. Of these the "Vada-vidhi" is important. It defines sense perception as a method of gaining knowledge and the knowledge comes from the object itself. This implies that the object is real. In this respect this definition is similar to Nyaya theory. These theories of Vasubandhu were criticized by his pupil Dignāga.

Dignāga was born in South India and had converted to Buddhim in the Puggalavāda sect. He had disagreed with his teacher on the core concept of a "puggala" that existed in addition to the five aggregates and had left the school and gone to the North probably looking for Vasubandhu who was a famous teacher at that time. He had studied under Vasubandhu and developed into a great teacher and a devoted propagator of Buddhism (Stcherbatsky, 1978).

While being a student he had produced two works of merit, one a summary of all the works of his teacher (Vasubandhu) titled "Abhidhammacosa-marma-pradeepa" and the other a summary of all the topics in the "Asta-shasrika-prangna-paramita sūthra" a Mahāyāna text. Rest of Dignāga's work was on logic. These consisted of short essays which were later compiled into one large text titled "Pramana-samuccaya" (A Digest of the Sources of Knowledge). In the first chapter of this text Dignāga says there are two methods of gaining knowledge; perception ("prathyaksha") and inference ("anumana"). Perception acquires information about particulars, while inference arrives at the knowledge of general attributes by a process of reason. Perception is a non-conceptual knowing of particular and is bound by causality while inference is achieved by reason and is conceptual. According to Dignāga perception or "prathyaksha" is personal and inexpressible and it does not depend on the existence of an external world. This system is different from that of Nyaya School which relies on comparison and analogy also for gaining information (Stcherbatsky, 1978).

Another Buddhist logician of repute is Dharmakirti. His teacher was a pupil of Dignāga. He had written a commentary on the great work of his teacher. Dharmakirti also mostly agrees with the epistemological viewpoint that knowledge could reliably be gained only by empirical means. This view is largely in agreement with the views of Buddha himself who clearly indicated that his means of knowledge was careful perception. Both Dignāga and Dharmakirti held that scripture is not a reliable source of knowledge (Stcherbatsky, 1978).

While Nāgārjuna took a dialectic stance based on relativity and espoused his theory of emptiness, Dignāga and Dharmakirti were of the opinion that what exists could be objects of empirical scrutiny and conceptual analysis. For some critics this viewpoint appeared to be going against the grain of the emptiness theory as the latter two philosophers are of the opinion that phenomena could be objects of empirical scrutiny which could mean they are not empty of substance or self. Others say one could come to this conclusion only if one gives a literary meaning to the word empty in Nāgārjuna's theory of emptiness. What he meant by emptiness is that all phenomena are empty of Self or anything like Self. He was on a mission to refute the eternalist and nihilist theories of Schools like Sarvāstivāda and Sautrāntika (Kalupahana, 2008).

Kalupahana (2008) is of the opinion that Dharmakirti had explained Dignāga as a metaphysical epistemologist and absolutist logician which made him a Mahayanist. Dignāga's assertion that perception as a source of knowledge is non-conceptual seems to have led to the misinterpretation by Dharmakirti that Dignāga is an absolutist logician making him a Mahayanist.

In the "Madupindika-sutta" (Majjima Nikāya) Buddha discourses on how perception occurs in relation to the five sense organs and the mind. If we take the visual aspect the process is described as follows; "Because of eye and material objects arises visual consciousness, the meeting of the three is sensory impingement, because of sensory impingement arises feeling, what one feels one perceives, one reasons about, one proliferates conceptually, what one proliferates conceptually due to that concepts assail him in regard to material shapes cognizable by the eye, belonging to the past, the future and the present". Ven. Katukurunde Ñanananda (2012) vividly describes this process as follows; "The vicious proliferating tendency of the Worldling's consciousness weaves for him a labyrinthine network of concepts… ". Thus the process of perception ends up in the formation of concepts though the process is empirical. This appears to be different from the viewpoint of Dignāga who held empirical knowledge is non-conceptual while knowledge gained by reason is conceptual. This matter, however, needs further elucidation (see below).

According to this Sutta (Mūlapariyaya) cognition process in relation to each of the sense organs ends with the formation of "obsessive perceptions and conceptions".

Note that perceptions and conceptions are mentioned separately. It is clear that the perceiver in this instance is an ordinary worldling, who as Ven Ñanananda(2012) says is ignorant of the Dhamma.

In this Sutta which is a discourse that gives a deep insight into the matter of concepts ("papanca"), Buddha describes the process of sense perception by four different types of perceivers; The Worldling who is ignorant of the Dhamma,

The Learner of the Dhamma, The Arahath, and Thathāgatha. The Worldling cognizes in two stages; Perception and then Conceiving. The Conceiving is the process of grasping of the twenty four concepts that Buddha enumerates. To take one of these twenty four concepts "the earth", the Worldling "conceives earth, conceives in earth, conceives from earth, conceives earth is mine". The Worldling grasps what is conceived as "this is mine, this I am and this is myself". Here the perception is perverted perception and not a perception of the true nature as it really is.

The Learner of the Dhamma has a different way of perception, he does not conceive it in the four ways Buddha has mentioned, he sees the object in its true nature that it is impermanent and subject to suffering. In the case of The Arahath and The Thathāgatha, in addition to perceiving the impermanence and suffering in relation to the object, they realize that "this is not mine, this I am not, this is not myself" (Mūlapariyaya sutta, Majjima Nikāya).

Thus Dignāga obviously is not dealing with perception by the ignorant Worldling but perception by a person who could be either a Learner or an Arahath. These two would not be susceptible to a "proliferation of concepts" out of what they perceive. Here perception may have to be non-conceptual and closer to the true nature of the object because concepts are abstract ideas and do not necessarily represent the true nature of the phenomenon for which an explanation has been provided by a concept.

Taking the above into consideration it could be said that Dignāga may not be an absolutist logician in the sense that the knowledge he was referring to is not about an absolute reality. Kalupahana (2008) in this regard says that Dignāga had not said perception as a source of knowledge is void of all or any and every form of conception but only certain types which are either Realist or Nominalist. Dignāga has discussed five types of concepts which could be interpreted as realist or nominalist.

Kalupahana says Dignāga's theory of the non-conceptual may not be absolute but relative to the two types of conceptions Realist and Nominalist.

Moreover Dignāga's reason for proposing two sources of knowledge is that the object of knowledge has two characteristics and nothing else i.e.; particular and the universal. The former could be known by non-conceptual perception and the latter by conceptual inference. When this is considered together with the possibility that Dignāga was not dealing with the gaining of knowledge by ordinary Worldling but probably by those who have learnt and practiced the Dhamma whose perception of the particular has to be non-conceptual and without proliferation of concepts, it becomes obvious that Dignāga was not an absolutist logician.

That brings us to the question; has Dharmakirti actually attempted to show that Dignāga was an absolutist logician and a metaphysical epistemologist. Also whether or not Dignāga was a Mahayanist.

AK Warder (1970) in his monumental work "Indian Buddhism" identifies Nāgārjuna and Vasubandhu (bracketed with Asaṅga) as Mahayanist and both Dignāga and Dharmakirti as loyalists of Sautrāntika. It appears that he has based his conclusions on extensive research into the writings of these philosophers. But the problem is as he himself admits these writings cannot with a reasonable degree of certainty be attributed to these philosophers except for a few texts. We have discussed this problem in regard to Nāgārjuna's and Vasubandhu's writings. Same could be said about the works of Dignāga and Dharmakirti.

Dignāga has written a summary of all the topics in "Astsashrika-praññāparamita sūthra" which clearly is a Mahāyāna text considered to be the oldest of the extant and it sets up the basis for the expansion and development of the "Prangnaparamita" series. It deals with the Bodhisathva system, how it should progress until the final goal is achieved. Here Dignāga's interest in Mahāyāna is clearly evident.

Dignāga had also written a summary of all the works of Vasubandhu titled "Abhidhammacosa-marima-pradeepa". Vasubandhu's "Abhidhammacosa-bashya" was a summary of the Sarvāsthivādin's Abhidhamma. This version of Abhidhamma has been adopted by Mahāyānists which may indicate that it suits Mahāyāna philosophy.

Dharmakirti lived in the 6th or the 7th Century CE and had worked at Nalanda monastry. His works are on the subject of epistemology and also Buddhist atomism. His largest work is titled "Pramanavartika-kārika" which is a commentary on Vasubandhu's "Pramana-samuccaya" and this commentary has largely influenced Yogācāra, Sautrāntika and Tibetan Buddhism. He agrees with Dignāga's views on epistemology. However he maintains that the Particular cognized by perception is real and the Universal arrived at by inference is not real. Some critics say Dharmakirti is Yogācāra loyalist, others say he belongs in the Sautrāntika School and yet others are of the opinion that he is a synchrony of the two sects (Tillemans, 2011).

However it is very difficult if not impossible to say that Dharmakirti has made a deliberate attempt to portray Dignāga as an absolutist logician and a metaphysical epistemologist given the fact that in the first place Dignāga's loyalty cannot be determined with any certainty. Moreover the loyalty of most of these great philosophers is conjectural to say the least.

Bhavaviveka (6th CE) was the first Buddhist logician to use 'formal syllogism'. He wrote a commentary to the "Mūlamadhayamika-kārika" in which he used syllogism to espouse Nāgārjuna's theory of emptiness. He drew from Dignāga's logic to develop his methods. Later "Svatanthrika" (not Sautrāntika) which was a branch of Madhyamaka School adopted these methods of logic. In Chapter 22 on Nāgārjuna we discuss the role played by Bhavaviveka in the development of the Madhayamaka school of Buddhism as a branch of Mahāyāna.

Jainism had developed a seven-valued logic to support their theory of pluralism. This system is referred to as Saptibhangavāda or Syadvāda first described by Bhadrabahu (5th Century BC). The seven predicates which are somewhat similar to the tetralemma used by Nagarajuna are as follows;

Arguably it exists

Arguably it does not exist

Arguably it exists, arguably it does not exist

Arguably it is non-assertible

Arguably it exists, arguably it is non-assertible

Arguably it does not exist, arguably it is non-assertible

Arguably it exists, arguably it does not exist, arguably it is non-assertible

Here basically there are three predicates; true, false and non-assertible. Four more values have been added by combining these three. It appears as if the system has only three alternatives but the presence of the word "arguably" makes the seven alternatives distinct from each other.

Jains had a philosophy based on pluralism or "Anekanthavāda" which was one of their main doctrines and which held that no view could claim to be the only true view and that phenomena may have several meanings and it is not possible to know all and every one of them due to human weakness. Jains used their logic to support this theory (Burch, 1964).

In Vedic tradition and later in Hinduism the four-valued logic was applied to negate the flaws or affirm the truth of views in all possible alternatives. It had been used in the Vasadiya-sūthra one of the oldest texts in the Vedic scripture. Later Hindu sages like Patanjali and scholars like Panini also had used the four valued system. These methods have been preserved up to the time of emergence of several Hindu schools such as Samkya, Mimamsa, Nyaya, Yoga, Vaishesika. These Schools of Hinduism also adopted the system of four-valued logic (Matilal, 1998).

Indian logic of ancient times was so sophisticated and advanced that scholar Max Mueller (1853) said that the origin of science of logic and grammar could be traced back to two ancient nations, Greece and India.

Chapter 27

Controversies related to Ven. Buddhagosa

Ven. Buddhagosa (5th CE) came to Sri Lanka from India mainly to translate the Commentaries of the Tipiṭaka that were written in Sinhalese to Pāli supposedly for the benefit of Indian scholars. He stayed at Mahavihara in Anuradhapura, the main Theravāda centre in Sri Lanka at that time. He wrote commentaries to the following canonical texts;

Name of the text	Name of the Commentary
Vinaya	
Vinaya Piṭaka	Samanthapasadika
Patimokkha	Kankhavitarani
Sutta	
Dhiga-Nikāya	Sumanagalavilasini
Majjima-Nikāya	Papancasudani
Samyutta-Nikāya	Sarttappakasini
Aṅguttara-Nikāya	Manorathapurani
Abhidhamma	
DhammAsaṅgani	Attasalini
Vibhanga	Sammohavinodani

Kattavattu

Puggalapannati

Dhatukatha		Pancappakaranathakata

Yamaka

Patthana

The following Commentaries in the Sutta Piṭaka are also attributed to Buddhagosa;

Khuddakapatha		Paramattajotika

Dhammapada		Dhammapadathakatha

Suttanipata		Paramatthajotika

Jataka			Jathakathakatha

It could be seen that Ven Buddhagosa had translated the Sinhalese commentaries of the most important texts of Theravāda Buddhism including the four major Nikāyas in the Sutta Piṭaka. Therefore a great responsibility lay on him to render an accurate representation of the discourses. A commentator's duty is to make the subjects discoursed clearer by explanations of matters that are difficult to understand in simple language. He should not add his own views or by the slightest degree alter the material content of the subjects.

The question must also be asked; what was the purpose of translating the Sinhalese commentaries to Pāli. The Sinhalese commentaries had been written for the benefit of the Sinhalese people who were keen students of the Dhamma. It was the intention of Ven Mahinda who brought the Dhamma to Sri Lanka that it should be learnt by the Sinhalese people. No doubt

Ven Mahinda would have encouraged the writing of Sinhalese commentaries and made available the facilities needed for the teaching of the Dhamma. Therefore these Sinhalese commentaries performed an essential religious requirement of the society.

From the point of view of teaching the Dhamma to the Sinhalese community there was no need for a translation of the Sinhalese commentaries into Pāli. It was of the utmost importance that these Sinhalese commentaries should have been preserved with care and commitment if Ven. Buddhagosa had any concern regarding the need for the learning of the Dhamma by the Sinhalese. If his mission was to make available a Pāli version of the Dhamma for the benefit of the Indian Buddhists and Buddhists of the world well and good. But he also had an obligation towards the Sinhalese. The least he could have done was to see that the Sinhalese commentaries were preserved. But according to Mahavamsa these were burnt!

Ven. Buddhagosa, who wrote "Visudhimagga", has been held in high esteem among Buddhist scholars and deservedly so for the yeomen service he did in writing voluminous texts on the Dhamma. But his successful attempt to create a larger than life image of the Buddha has distorted the Theravāda Buddhism in Sri Lanka to a significant degree. Buddha in his life time had eschewed a bigger than life image of himself and always resisted the entry of transcendental elements into the Dhamma. After his demise this policy was pursued by other great Buddhist philosophers like Ven, Nāgārjuna. However those elements had persisted and later developed as Mahāyāna as revealed by its most important text "Sadharmapundarika-sutta".

Ven Buddhagosa had lived in South India before coming to Sri Lanka and may have been influenced by Mahāyāna thought which were a strong presence in that part of India at that time. He may have accepted that Buddha was transcendental in nature. When he arrived in Sri Lanka and found that Theravāda in Mahavihara had no transcendental features particularly with regard to the life of Buddha and also there were no religious rituals he may have thought it was a critical void that needs to be filled and it would be an improvement that he could render to Buddhism.

Ven Buddhagosa's translations however differed to a significant degree from Early Buddhism and often contained additional material that attempted to make Buddha and his Dhamma transcendental phenomena. For example the description of the incident where Ven Ananda detects a wrinkle on Buddha's body differs significantly in the Commentary (Saratthappakasini, SamyuttaNikāya Attakatta) compared to the version in the Jara Sutta (Samyutta Nikāya). When Buddha is told about the wrinkle he says the 'panchaskandaya' is subject to decay and that one must not be attached to it and feel sorrow when it decays. This is the description given in the Jara Sutta which is in keeping with the non-transcendental view of the Buddha on his own life. The Commentary written by Buddhagosa however conveys a totally different viewpoint. It says that Ven Ananda made an error of judgment and there was no wrinkle on Buddha's body which was radiant and glowed in splendour as it was ageless and not subject to decay. This viewpoint attempts to change the nature of the historical Buddha into a transcendental phenomenon. Such gross amplification and deviation abounds in the Commentaries written by Buddhagosa compared to the Texts.

This, most importantly, reflects his lack of understanding of the significance of what is accepted as Early Buddhism, the fact that the four major Nikayas represented Early Buddhism and that they could be carrying Buddha's word as closely as possible. He could not appreciate the need to adhere to their content when translating the Sinhala Commentaries which were the result of the deligent work of Ven. Mahinda who brought to Sri Lanka a Buddhism that had been cleansed of impurities of the kind that had been subsequently introduced to it by Buddhagosa.

The Buddhism that was brought to Sri Lanka by Mahinda Thera 236 years after Buddha's "PariNirvāna" was cleansed of all metaphysical and transcendental elements in the Third Dhamma Saṅgāyanā conducted by Ven Moggaliputta-tissa who preached "Kathavatthu" on that occasion which removed all those impurities. "Kathavatthu" was considered important enough to be included in the TriPiṭaka. This is believed to be the version of Buddhism that was written down at Aluvihare. In the 5th Century AD however Ven Buddhagosa had tried and succeeded in introducing mystical elements to Buddhism. Advent of rituals which are not mentioned in Early Buddhism could largely be attributed to Ven Buddhagosa. Mystic elements, yanthra, manthra, yaga, exorcism etc. arrived in the wake of rituals. Mahāyāna which was the main religion in Sri Lanka during the period 5th to the 10th Century also contributed to the development of transcendentalism and mystic elements in Theravāda Buddhism some of which have remained to the present times.

During the period of Ven.Buddhagosa's stay in Sri Lanka Mahāyāna made a successful entry into the country and became the dominant religion that lasted from the 5th to the 10th Century. The former's influence may have contributed to the acceptance of Mahāyāna tenets by the people and also the monks. Ven.Buddhagosa, though he rendered a great service to Buddhism in translating the Sinhala Commentaries into Pāli, must take part of the blame for this gross betrayal of Buddhism.

"Visuddhimagga" (Path of Purification) was written by Buddhagosa to prove his competency to the Mahavihara monks before he was allowed to translate the Sinhalese commentaries. What he has written on Meditation is significantly different from what is found in the Suttas. Several writers had criticized this unwarranted deviation from the Buddha's Dhamma. Ven. Henepola Gunaratne (1992) says that Visuddhimagga had used some terms in reference to meditation which are not found in the Sutta such as "parikamma samādhi, upakara samādhi, appana samādhi". Further a technique called "kasinameditation" where "Jhana" is combined with mindfulness which is not found in the Sutta is included in the "Visuddhimagga". Bikkhu Sujatho (2005) says this is a distortion of the Sutta.

Kalupahana (2008) is of the opinion that a subtle attempt has been made by Buddhagosa to introduce ideas of other philosophies into Theravāda by mixing them with those in the Pāli suttas. In this regard he refers to several introductions of new material that are to be found in Visuddhimagga. Kalupahana in reference to Buddhagosa says "He was a great harmonizer who carefully blended old and new ideas without allowing any room for suspicion…". One of the additions that Buddhagosa makes is the "kshana-vada" which is an idea from Sautrāntika. Another is the fourfold definition of the major concepts in the suttas. According to Kalupahana Visuddhimagga is an encyclopaedic treatment of the path of purification where Buddhagosa relies on the suttas and the Commentaries that were available and the ideas he had acquired from Sarvāsthavāda, Sautrāntika, Madhyamaka, Yogācāra etc. Though Visuddhimagga is considered by some as the most comprehensive interpretational work on the Theravāda suttas it appears that it is a conglomerate of ideas drawn from several schools of Buddhism and is not loyal to the original works of Theravāda or Early Buddhism.

EW Adikaram (1946) also refers to several factual errors in the Vissuddhimagga. He also commends Buddhagosa for his scholarship. Several distortions with regard to the nature of the Buddha which tend to elevate him to a transcendental being are also mentioned by Adikaram. In the "Attasalini" which is a Commentary by Buddhagosa on the Abhidhamma he says that Buddha in formulating the seventh book of Abhidhamma, "Pathana", has demonstrated his power of omniscience. On the contrary Buddha in the "Thevijja-vatchagotta-sutta" (Majjima Nikāya) has clearly said that he does not possess omniscience.

Buddhagosa's activity at Mahavihara probably with the help of the monks therein had caused a significant constrain on the use and development of Sinhalese language at that time. G Usvattearatchi writing in The Island newspaper (20.05.2020) quoting GP Malalasekera (1928) says that as a result of Buddhagosa's work Sinhalese language was downgraded particularly in the intellectual use of that language and Pāli and Sanscrit were given pride of place instead. As a result no Sinhalese writing of consequence came out of Anuradhapura for the next seven centuries until Ven. Vedheya wrote "Sidat Sangarava"in the 13th CE. Deepawamsa and Mahawamsa which deal with the history of the Country were written in Pāli and Sanscrit. Before the arrival of Buddhagosa people and the elite used Sinhalese for all their work and Ven. Mahinda had provided for the teaching of Buddhism in Sinhalese. The Commentaries on the TriPiṭaka were written in Sinhalese with the blessings and assistance of Ven. Mahinda.

Chapter 28

Arahath Mahinda and Ven. Buddhagosa

This Chapter deals with the gross injustice Ven. Buddhagosa may have done to Arahath Mahinda, who stood for Theravāda Buddhism in its original form, as close to Buddha's preaching as possible, and also about the far reaching distortion he caused in the practice of the Dhamma in Sri Lanka. There are eminent scholars who are of the opinion that this was a well-planned gross betrayal (Marasinghe, 2015).

Arahath Mahinda created history in the 3rd Century BC when he not only brought Buddhism to Sri Lanka, but also catalysed the development of a rich civilization on the Island. This great achievement is unparalleled in the annals of Buddhism since the demise of the Buddha. Ven. Buddhagosa is held in high esteem among Sri Lankan Buddhists for translating the Sinhala Commentaries on the TriPiṭaka into Pāli in the 5th Century AD.

The huge enterprise undertaken by King Dharmasoka and his son Arahath Mahinda was to spread the Theravāda Dhamma cleansed of all impurities that had crept into it over time. The effort of Ven Buddhaghosa, in contrast, was to reintroduce some of these impurities back into Theravāda. These impurities had been removed at the Third Dhamma Saṅgāyanāva sponsored by King Dharmasoka, where Ven. Moggalliputtatissa preached the Kathāvatthu, which refutes and eliminates all these impurities. Kathāvatthu has been good enough to be included in the TriPiṭaka. By this means metaphysical and transcendental features were removed from the Dhamma before it was brought to Sri Lanka. Ven. Buddhagosa in his translation of the Sinhala Commentaries into Pāli has reintroduced these features into the Dhamma. His action had resulted in the introduction of ritual worship, and a larger than life image of the historical human being that Buddha was.

Arahath Mahinda after introducing Buddhism to Sri Lanka, worked tirelessly on two vital aspects, the practice of the Dhamma and the study of the Pāli canonical texts. Historical remains of the facilities made available for the pursuit of these two aspects bear witness to the fact that people were interested in both. Ruins of libraries, lecture theatres and meditation cubicles abound in the country. Practice of the Dhamma was based on the three main features of the Ñāna Mārga (Path of Wisdom), "Dhāna, Sīla, Bhāvana". There were no rituals. Age old oral tradition was employed for the study of the suttas with designated disciples, in the ancient tradition of the Bhanakas who memorized the suttas and recited them at meetings for their revision. Arahath Mahinda facilitated the teaching process by arranging to make available the Sinhala commentaries on the suttas.

It is this version of Buddhism that was written down at Aluvihare. Ven.Mahinda was careful to see that this Dhamma was established in Sri Lanka. In order to make sure that the correct tenets and dogma were studied he provided Sinhala commentaries. It was these Sinhala Commentaries that were translated into Pāli by Ven Buddhaghosa. But what was the need for this translation? One cannot think of any valid reason. Sinhala commentaries were needed for the teaching of the Dhamma to Sinhala people, and the original Pāli version was available in the TriPiṭaka for reference when necessary. If Buddhagosa wanted to write his own commentaries in Pāli he could have done that instead of translating the Sinhala version. He had a command of the Pāli language but there is no evidence of how or where he learnt Sinhala with sufficient proficiency to translate complex works to Sinhala. Moreover, what has happened to the Sinhala commentaries is a mystery. Chronicles say they were burnt. Was it done to destroy the evidence? Were they destroyed by invaders? If so why only the

Sinhala commentaries, why not all the written works? Did Mahaviharins collude with Buddhagosa in these activities?

Buddhagosa in his translations had made changes, added stories and anecdotes, which is not the accepted function of a translator or even a commentator. These additions are meant to raise the Buddha to a transcendental being, above the realm of this world, who is god like and could grant to humans what they pray for. Some stories describe people offering flowers and incense to Buddha (see Buddhagosa's Commentary on Kalinga Bodhi Jataka). What benefit did Buddhagosa and Mahaviharins, if they were involved, expect from these activities? In this connection Prof. Marasinghe (2015) says; "The hard work of Buddhagosa and the Mahavihara fraternity culminated in the formulation of a new ritual structure with attractive advantages to keep both the lay followers and the members of the Sanga happy and content. As a result, when we pass from the canonical Pāli texts to the post-canonical Pāli texts and the Pāli commentaries we come into a totally new teaching different from the original".

Buddha was a normal human being who gave up lay life and went in search of an answer to the eternal suffering of humans and led a very simple life, often resting or sleeping under a tree. What he achieved did not make him a larger than life being or make him or his Dhamma a transcendental or metaphysical phenomena. The Pāli canonical texts still depict this Theravāda Buddha (Prof Marasinghe's words) who is totally different to the glorified Buddha of the Buddhagosa's Commentaries. Buddhagosa's Buddha had accumulated merit in innumerable eons of samsara to achieve what he achieved. Here Buddhagosa asserts that achieving Nirvāna is not possible without such accumulation of merit. Buddha has never said merit is necessary for achieving Nirvāna, merit could be accumulated or that merit could be transferred from one person to another. Sri Lankan Buddhists make the futile attempt to do all this and the blame must lie with Ven. Buddhagosa.

Before the advent of Buddhagosa there were no rituals, during a period of 700 years from the 3rd Century BC to the 5th Century AD. Though there were stupas like Thuparamaya and statues of Buddha and the Bodhi Tree, people treated these as objects of veneration for recollection of the Buddha and his attainment, and not for ritual worship of the theistic kind which is performed in expectation of benefit. Buddha advised people to offer alms or give away their possessions to help them get rid of attachment to these objects that are impermanent, for it was the cause of suffering. But Buddhists of today offer alms expecting an accumulation of merit as an insurance for a better life in the next birth. The concept of accumulation of merit and its transfer were discussed and rejected at the Third Dhamma Saṅgāyanāva referred to above, and therefore these concepts were not brought to Sri Lanka by Mahinda.

Practice of ritual worship is associated with theistic religions and was never advocated by Buddha, who said that one could attain freedom from suffering by one's own effort and not by the intervention of an external agent. Buddhagosa paved the way for the entry of ritual worship into the practice of Buddhism, and the belief that worship of stupas, statues, and Bodhi trees would result in the accumulation of merit and rewards. The uniqueness of Buddhism was ruined. To quote Prof. Marasinghe; "Thus all aspects of the new ritual Buddhism which changed the Theravāda Buddhism into a system of worship, offering and prayer, like any other theistic religion, has been very carefully planned and smuggled into practice with several bonus packages for the operators".

Chapter 29

Controversies related to Abhidhamma

Abhidhamma may be considered as an attempt to further analyze the Dhamma. Except Sautrāntika all other schools of Buddhism have attempted to develop their Abhidhamma versions. The word "Abhidhamma" may mean "about Dhamma" or "concerning Dhamma". Ven. Buddhagosa in his Commentary "Dhammasangithi" refers to Abhidhamma as "extra" or "special" Dhamma. Sarvāsthivādins had attempted to give a greater degree of importance to the word Abhidhamma by saying that it means "on the threshold of Nibbāna" or "on the verge of attaining Nibbāna". Schools such as Mahisashaka and Dharmagupthika had indicated that the word Abhidhamma means it surpasses all other Dhammas. In China too it is considered as the supreme Dhamma. All this shows how Abhidhamma assumed greater importance than the Suttas (Potter et al, 1999).

In Theravāda tradition Abhidhamma is accepted as a preaching of the Buddha. He had preached all the seven texts in the Abhidhamma. How a highly venerated status had been bestowed on the Abhidhamma could be found from the two references made in Attasalini, the Commentary on the Abhidhamma text Dhammasangini, written by Buddhagosa. One reference says that Abhidhamma was one of Buddha's ambitions which he developed when he was a Bodhisathva and which was fulfilled after he attained Buddhahood. The other says Abhidhamma was preached by Buddha to his mother who was born in Thavthisa heaven. Further, according to this Commentary, at times when he wanted to go out for alms Buddha had created a "manokāya" of himself and got this image to preach Abhidhamma to the deities and after partaking his meal he would preach Abhidhamma to Ven. Sariputta. The latter after learning the Abhidhamma from the Buddha himself had taught it to his pupils Baddaji, Sobitha, JayaPāli, Piyadassi and others. These pupils had preserved and transmitted the Abhidhamma in the usual oral tradition until it was revised at the Third Buddhist Council and then brought to Sri Lanka where it was committed to writing during the Fourth Council at Aluvihare.

Though the Theravāda Commentaries give the above account as the history of Abhidhamma there is evidence that may suggest a different origin of Abhidhamma. Very early texts like Suttanipatha do not make any reference to Abhidhamma. What is plausible is that Abhidhamma is a compilation of interpretations by analysis that gradually accumulated and eventually came to be put together as a separate Piṭakaya. The fact that Kathavatthu, which is included in the Abhidhamma, was preached at the Third Council in the 3rd BC also points to the possibility that Abhidhamma was a later compilation though based on Buddha's original teaching. Sarvāsthivādins also subscribes to a similar point of view. Though it is said that Abhidhamma was also recited at the First Council this is unlikely, it was probably compiled at the Third Council. Abhidhamma was not discussed at the First Dharmasaṅgāyanāva nor at the Second. At the First Dhammasaṅgāyanāva most of the Nikāyas were assigned to Bhanakas who were responsible for learning and reciting the suttas by memory and carrying them by the oral tradition, but not Abhidhamma. Abhidhamma Piṭaka may have been composed after the 3rd Century BC. They were written down in the 1st CE at the time that the rest of the Tipiṭaka was written at Aluvihare, Sri Lanka.

However a modicum of these methods and formats of the Abhidhamma could be seen in some early discourses. For example Ithivuthaka (Kuddhaka Nikāya) and also the Vibanga sutta (Majjima Nikāya) show some resemblance to Abhidhamma technique. Abhidhamma had put together in a systematised and a catagorized manner the essence of the Dhamma that was scattered and submerged in embelishments in the discourses. Though different in the style of language and presentation, in the essential content the Abhidhamma is not different from the Suttas.

The canonical Abhidhamma Piṭaka gives simple lists of doctrines as found in the suttas and their explanations without the intricacies of language found in the suttas which sometimes introduce controversies. Later post-canonical Abhidhamma works are more philosophical and contain innovations and doctrines not found in the canonical Abhidhamma. A good example is Vasubandhu's "Abhidhammacosa" and Buddhagosa's Commentary on the Theravāda Abhidhamma.

By the 7th CE the Chinese pilgrim Xuanzang could find seven Abhidhammic works most of which however are extinct (Baruah, 2008). Only the Theravāda and Sarvāsthivāda Abhidhamma texts are extant as complete texts and remnants of few others are available as Chinese and Tibetan translations. Mahāyānists adopted the Abhidhamma of the Sarvāsthivāda and therefore Mahāyāna version may not be very different from that of Sarvāsthivāda.

Theravāda Abhidhamma has seven books and they are as follows;
DhammAsaṅgani

Vibhanga

Dhatukatha

Puggalapannati

Kattavattu

Yamaka

Patthana

The "Khuddaka Nikāya" also has three Abhidhamma type texts; "Patisambhidamagga", "Nettipakarana" and "Petakopadesa".

Abhidhamma technique employs a system consisting of what are called "matikas" (matrix, list). These are lists of doctrines and explanations which attempt to analyse and systematize the contents of the suttas.

If we are to look at the seven books of the Abhidhamma Piṭaka the "Dhammasaṅgani" is a manual of ethics for monks based on the Vinaya Piṭaka. "Vibhanga" has 18 chapters each dealing with a separate subject. The first for example analyses the aggregates. "Dhathukatha" analyzes and discusses topics drawn from "Vibhanga" with analytical questions that gradually increase in complexity which is a technique that may be seen in the Abhidhamma of Sarvāsthivāda also. "Puggalapannati" attempts to categorize persons based on the characteristics to be found in them when they progress in the path to Nibbāna. Kathavatthu contains more than 200 debates dealing with heretical questions which are answered in such a way that they are negated. "Yamaka" has ten chapters each dealing with different topics like 'root' and the discussion takes the form of questions and answers. "Patthana" deals with 24 Conditions and cause and effect relations in a detailed analysis of the "Paticcasamuppada". Early Buddhism and also Nāgārjuna, however, identify only four types of Conditions. Thus it is seen that the canonical Abhidhamma Piṭaka does not extend beyond the scope of the Sutta Piṭaka but keeps within its boundaries and attempts to analyse and systematize the subject matter for better understanding of the doctrines.

A closer scrutiny of the analysis of life phenomena in the Suttas may reveal that there is room for further analysis. For example the empirical person has been analyzed under five methods; "nama-rupa", five "skandas", five "dhāthu" (elements), twelve "ayathana" and eighteen "dhathu" analysis. The learned monks in their effort to see whether a further analysis is possible had attempted to analyze phenomena until they could not be divided anymore. According to Y.Karunadasa (1998) the Dhamma Theory of the Abhidhamma was the result of this endeavor and this theory is the corner-stone of the Abhidhamma. This theory indicates that all phenomena could be analyzed into Dhammas, the ultimate units which cannot be further analyzed and which arise with other Dhammas and may constitute the Condition for the arising of yet other Dhammas. However other thinkers (Kalupahana, 2008) are of the opinion that such a theory is not discernible and that Abhidhamma has only carried further the analysis achieved in the suttas. Further the Abhidhama composers realized that analysis of phenomena into Dhammas is inadequate to glean a correct understanding of the characteristics and functions of all objects. They thought that analysis has to be combined with synthesis and this system is known as "bedha-sangrha" method, "bedha" means analysis and "sangrha" means synthesis. This system of analysis and synthesis could be clearly seen in the Abhidhamma texts; analysis is well presented in the Abhidhamma text Dhammasaṅgani and synthesis in the Patthana (Y Karunadasa, 1998).

In the analytical method phenomena are first categorised into four basic dhammas; "chitta", "chaitasika", "rupa" and Nibbāna and then these four are further analysed into 82 Dhammas as follows :-

Chitta	01	Viññāna
Chaitasika	52	Vedana, Saññā, Saṅkara
Rupa	28	Rupa
Nibbāna	01	Asankatha dhamma

These Dhammas though presented as ultimate basic units they are not permanent and eternal, but subject to Buddhist principles of existence "anicca, dukha, anatta" and they arise, disappear and arise again. However, they are presented as "paramartha padartha" (ultimate essence or element) in the sense that they cannot be further analysed.

This method of analysis and synthesis is designed to focus on the "anithya-anathma" character of dhammas and also on their interdependent relationship. Moreover this method was aimed at refuting the two theories that were prevalent at that time that everything arises either from one single ultimate element or several separate elements. Abhidhamma method of analysis showed that phenomena did not arise from a single ultimate element. Further its method of synthesis proved that the elements were interdependently related to each other and they were not entirely independent and disparate elements (Karunadasa, 1998).

Abhidhamma method of analysis and synthesis also aimed at refuting the eternalist and nihilist theories that were in vogue at that time. The two extreme views; one which said that everything exists as permanent phenomena and the other which said that nothing exists were by this means negated. Avoidance of these two extremes established the middle path that Buddha took and reiterated in "paticcasamuppāda" as the basis of Buddha's teaching. "Paticcasamuppāda" is therefore the basis of the Abhidhamma as it is of almost all doctrines of Buddhism. Everything arises, declines and arises again but nothing exists permanantly nor do they not exist at all. Abhidhamma strengthens this point of view which was a basic empirical truth that Buddha realized early in his journey searching for an answer to the human predicament.

The analysis of the mind that is thorough in the Abhidhamma points to the importance of the mind in the quest for salvation and the need for its purification by methods of meditation. In this sense Abhidhamma is not purely a theoretical project that is isolated from the people but very much an exercise with enormous practical value. It presents the essence of the Buddha's teachings without the long discussions, similes, everyday language and repetitions employed to illustrate and elucidate difficult theories that are to be found in the Suttas. It has the same purpose as the Suttas in that it clearly explains the role of the mind in the human predicament and shows how the mind could overcome this problem and find freedom (Karunadasa, 1998, Tillakaratne, 1995).

But this does not mean Abhidhamma has not caused any problems and development of unwarranted issues. Its Dhamma theory which postulates on the presence of indivisible ultimate elements has led to the idea that Abhidhamma is contemplating on a substantialist theory. The idea that "pure dhammas exist" came into reckoning due to the analytical method employed by Abhidhamma which spoke about ultimate elements.

Sarvāsthavādins also produced a volumenous Abhidhamma consisting of seven books. Unlike the seven books of Theravāda the books of Sarvāsthavāda have their authors as given below;

Title	Author
Ngnanaprasthana	Arya Kathyayani Puthra
Sangithiparyaya	Mahakaushtila
Prakaranapada	Vasumithra
Viññānakaya	Devasharma
Dhathukaya	Purna
Dharmaskanda	Arya Shariputhra
Prangnapthishasthra	Arya Maudgalyana

Though similar in number the content of the Abhidhamma texts of Theravāda and Sarvāsthavāda is different except the similarity seen between Vibanga of Theravāda and Dharmaskanda of Sarvāsthivāda. Sarvāsthavādins accepted the Dhamma theory subject to the condition that Dhammas are subject to their "svabhāva" concept. They analysed the phenomena into five basic components and further divided them into 75 elements.

Chitha	01
Chaitha/Chaithasika	46
Rupa	11
Chitha Viprayutta Sanskara	14
Asanskrutha	03

It is seen that the basis of the Dhamma analysis in both Theravāda and Sarvāsthavāda is the "panchaskanda". Sarvāstivāda has an extra basic category in "chitha viprayutta sanskāra" under which there are 14 elements. This is something not found in Early Buddhist discourses in their description of "panchaskanda" and seems to be a creation of the Sarvāsthavādins. The "rupa" category has been anlysed on the basis of the sensory organs and their subjects. However Sarvāsthavādins have an extra element named "avingnapthi rupa". This is also not found in the Suttas and it was used initially to explain Karma but later they had changed the meaning of the word to "sanvaraya" and used it for some other purpose.

In the "chittha viprayutta sanskara" which as mentioned above is not found in the Suttas, there is a Dhamma named "prapthi". The function of this is to strengthen the relationship between a Dhamma and a person. In opposition to this there is another Dhamma called "aprapthi" which would attempt to break the bond between a person and a Dhamma. This system is used to explain the functioning of the "kusal-akusal" chaithasika. It is "prapthi"or "aprapthi" dhamma that binds or unbinds the kusal or akusal chaithasika. Theravādins use the "bavanga" chittha for this purpose.

Katyayaniputra (150 BC) launched the Sarvāsthavāda School by composing the "Ñānaprasthana", which means foundation of knowledge. As shown above this text is included in their Abhidhamma and it has influenced the other texts of their Abhidhamma quite significantly. It brings out the integrative and the coordinating function of the Dhammas (Dhammajoti, 2020). Though Dhamma is a central theme in both Theravāda and Sarvāsthivāda Abhidhamma works and represents the ultimate unit of all phenomena, the Dhammas in Sarvāsthivāda exists through the three temporal states; past, present and future preserving their intrinsic nature in keeping with the "svabhava" theory, though their mode of existence may change. In contrast Dhammas in Theravāda is subject to the laws of "paticcasamuppada" which has no extensions into the past or to the future. Only the present exists in Theravāda.

It can be seen that the subjects and topics analysed in the two Abhidhamma works are in the main different though some doctrines are similar such as aggregates. For instance in Theravāda all phenomena or Dhammas can be categorized on the basis of "skanda, dhātu and ayatana", whereas in Sarvāsthivāda the Dhammas are categorized on the basis of "rupa" (matter), "citta" (thought), "cetisika" (thought-concommitants) and "asamskrta" (unconditioned).

Further the "Ñāna-prasthana" of the Sarvāsthivāda Abhidhamma makes a special effort to support the theory of tri-temporal existence of Dhammas and thereby refute the Theravāda position that Dhammas exist only in the present. For example it attempts to show that defilements are binding in the past, present and in the future. This can be illustrated by the following discussion that appear in this text;

In the Ñāna-prasthana there is a discussion that takes the form of questions and answers;

Question - "Have all past sumyojana (fetters – synonym for defilement) bound to the object?"

Answer - "Past samyojanas have bound to the object. There are samyojanas which are not past. They are future and present that have bound".

Question - "Will all future samyojanas bind in the future"?

Answer - "There are four possibile cases …." And here the chatuscoti is applied.

Question - "Are the present samyojanas now binding"?

Answer - "Present samyojanas are now binding. There are samyojanas binding but not present. They are past and future samyojanas".

Question – "What is the purpose of this discussion"?

Answer – "The purpose is to refute the doctrinal position of others and demonstrate the true principle. There are some who claim the past and the future do not exist truly. To refute them it is demonstrated here that the past and the future exists truly" (Dhammajoti, 2020).

Thereafter the "Ñāna-prasthana" goes on to elaborate how defilements are bound to the past, present and the future. It seems to be a continuous process and not broken into three stages which attempts to strengthen their tri-temporal existence theory.

Apart from this tri-temporal existence theory Sarvāsthavāda had another major theory on causation. For the first time in the world of philosophy Katyayaniputra the effective founder of Sarvāsthavāda formulated a well-designed theory to show that cause and effect existed simultaneously which is known as "sathkaryavāda". The theory consists of a six- fold system of causality and it is the sixth that attempts to prove that the effect could be found in the cause. This theory was immediately adopted by the Mahāyāna Yogācāra School as it suited their idea of store-consciousness ("alaya-viññānaya").

Sarvāstavādins also compiled a gigantic commentary on their Abhidhamma titled "Abhidhamma-Mahavibasha" which further analysed and explained their Abhidhamma texts. It is said that this compilation may have taken 500 years to complete.

These analyses, discussions and debates culminated with the production of another excellent commentary by Vasubandhu titled "Abhidhammacosa-bhashya". Vasubandhu writes about the Sarvāsthavāda Abhidhamma, often criticising it from the Sautrāntika point of view. He criticises the tri-temporal existence of Dhammas saying that nothing could exist continuously in the past, present, and the future. However he tends to agree with the Sarvāsthavāda idea of simultaneous existence of cause and effect. His criticism of Sarvāsthavāda had prompted a junior contemporary named Samghabadra to write a treatise titled "Nyayanusara" on Vasubandhu's "Abhidhammacosa-bhashya" criticising the latter's point of view. These texts which are extant in Sanskrit, Chinese and also Tibetan are extremely important works on Buddhist Abhidhamma. Vasubanadhu's work greatly influenced Mahāyāna and Eastern and Tibetan Buddhism (Gold, 2015).

Mahāyānists also composed their Abhidharma based on the Sarvāsthavāda model to some degree. The Yogācāra compositions are to be found in the writings of Asaṅga, Vasubandhu, Stiramathi, Dharmapala, etc. The Yogācāra Abhidhamma expounds their main doctrines like the eight-fold causality theory that includes the "Alaya-Viññānaya", the three natures, mere cognizance, "dasa-bhumi", ten paramitās, "thrikāya" of the Buddha etc.

The main Mahāyāna Abhidhamma texts include;

Yogakarabhumi-sastra which has a strong Sarvāsthavāda influence,
Abhidhamma-samuccaya – written by Asaṅga
Abhidhamma-samuccaya-bhashya, a commentary on the above written by Sthiramathi Mahāyānasamgraha – written by Asaṅga
Mahāyānasamgraha-bhashya – a commentary on the above work written by Vasubandhu

Praññāparamithā-sūthras have drawn from the Abhidhamma texts, particularly ideas like the Dhamma theory. Therefore most of the texts in the Praññāparamithā series appear to be meaningless without a consideration of the Abhidhamma. Praññāparamithā means perfection of wisdom and these sūthras discuss subjects like emptiness, lack of "svabhāva", illusory nature of objects ("maya") etc (Sasanārathana, 1953).

Chapter 30

Controversy related to the Silence of the Buddha

Buddha, it is claimed had not answered certain questions posed by his contemporaries and disciples. These are known as "avyakrta" (unanswered) and also as "thapaniya" (set aside) questions. This apparent silence of the Buddha has been interpreted differently by different Schools of Buddhism. Theravāda texts has given a set of ten such questions while Mahāyāna writers have identified fourteen. These questions pertain mainly to the following issues; whether or not the world is eternal, whether the world is finite or infinite, whether or not the soul is same as the body and whether the Thathāgatha exists after death or does not exist after death or both or neither. In Theravāda texts the questions pertaining to the first three issues are presented in the form of two cornered logic ("dvicoti") while the fourth is four cornered ("chatuscoti") making a total of ten. The Theravāda interpretation of this silence of the Buddha is based on empiricism, whereas that of the Mahāyānists is based on metaphysics and transcendence. The former is based on Buddha's experience while the latter attempts to attribute Buddha's silence to a transcendental feature in Buddhism which words cannot explain. According to Mahāyānists Nibbāna cannot be explained and this is the main transcendental feature of Mahāyāna. They say Buddha had not explained the nature of Nibbāna and was similarly silent on the above mentioned issues as they are part of the Absolute Truth which is ineffable (Tilakeratne, 1993)).

According to Theravāda commentators Buddha being an empiricist of the highest order, had not attempted to speculate on these issues as they do not come into the realm of empirical existence and cannot be experienced. Buddha also had not claimed to be omniscient and therefore it is in order that he did not comment on things that could not be comprehended by experience. Buddha speaks about these matters in the "Cula Malunkya sutta" (Majjima Nikāya).

Malunkya Putta Thera tells Buddha he will not remain to lead the higher life under the tutelage of the Buddha if he refuses to answer these questions. Buddha tells Malunkya that it is not necessary to know the answers to these questions to lead the higher life that he teaches. Further he says that he has not preached on these aspects because such knowledge will not lead to freedom from suffering. What he has preached is the Four Noble Truths which will lead to freedom from suffering. Buddha admonishes Malunkya to retain what he has preached and to discard what he has not preached. He tells Malunkya that to contemplate about such matters is like the man who instead of allowing the surgeon to remove the poisoned arrow that had pierced him tries to find out the details about the person who shot the arrow and details about the make of the arrow etc. Main issue is suffering and how to achieve freedom from suffering.

The subject is further discussed in the "Aggi Vacchagotta sutta" (Majjima Nikāya). The wanderer Vacchagotta asks the Buddha whether it is his view that the world is eternal. Buddha replies that it is not so. Then Vaccha asks the Buddha whether it is his view that the world is not eternal. Buddha says it is not so. Vaccha repeats the question in relation to the other issues mentioned above and Buddha's response was similar indicating that he has no entrenched view on these matters one way or another. Buddha then tells Vaccha that such views are a thicket of a view, a wilderness of a view with suffering and will not lead to enlightenment and freedom. Vaccha asks the Buddha what is the view held by him. Buddha says his view is contained in the Four Noble Truths. Vaccha asks where an enlightened monk would arise. Buddha says the word "arise" is not appropriate. Vaccha asks whether such a monk would both arise and not arise. Buddha gives a similar answer. Vaccha then asks whether such a monk would neither arise nor does not arise and Buddha replies in the same way. This is the application of the four cornered logic or 'chatuscoti'.

When Buddha rejected all four possibilities of empirical existence of the enlightened monk, Vaccha said he was confused. Then the Buddha makes the allegorical reference to a fire which burns until it is extinguished when the fuel is totally burnt out. Buddha explains that the question where did the fire go is not appropriate. When all the fires of greed, hatred and ignorance are burnt out one would attain Nibbāna. Such an Arahath would not have an empirical existence and therefore the question whether he exists after death would not be appropriate.

In the above mentioned discourses Buddha clearly demonstrates his reluctance to speculate on matters that cannot be comprehended through experience. The extent of the Universe in time and space does not come within the scope of human experience. Contemplation on such issues which was the preoccupation of some of the contemporaries of the Buddha was thought to be a waste of time by Buddha in the context of his philosophy of life. The question whether the body was the same as the soul or different was also a subject of debate at that time which the Buddha thought was irrelevant. He had a comprehensive theory on the material-form of the body and how it arises and also how the mind arises as expounded in the 'Paticcasamuppādaya' or dependent co-origination. His anatta theory dealt with the question of soul and therefore, as explained by him in the Samyutta Nikāya it is meaningless to ask a further question on whether the body is same as soul or different.

Buddha in the Mahānidāna Sutta (Dhiga Nikāya) explains the nature of the Thathāgatha and why the question whether or not the Thathāgatha exists after death does not arise. He says such questions arise in the unenlightened mind and once the mind is liberated from all attachments the Thathāgatha understands everything and will not be troubled by such questions. The fact that Early Buddhist discourses do not mention of any Arahath who had asked these questions lends credence to this view point. Further the Arahaths have spoken about their freedom and liberation from suffering based on their own experience which could be considered as testimonial evidence about the nature of the Arahath and Nirvāna (Thera Gāthā, Theri Gāthā).

Hence it is clear that Buddha on many occasions had provided answers to these questions and given explanations why he refuses to answer some of the questions. It is in keeping with the empirical methods he employed to gain knowledge and the non-mystical nature of his Dhamma. He had refuted sixty four metaphysical theories on life in the Brahmmajāla Sutta (Dhiga Nikāya) and he had no intention of getting involved in such other metaphysical issues.

Yet it is claimed by Mahāyānists that the silence of the Buddha had started soon after his enlightenment at Buddhagaya. Buddha had contemplated on the ability of ordinary people to understand his Dhamma and whether or not he should preach his Dhamma to these people. Mahāyānists claim that by this silence soon after his enlightenment Buddha had provided a philosophical opening for the development of the concept of ineffability and transcendental doctrines. Starting with his silence extending up to Ven. Nāgārjuna's famous "Śūnyatha vada" which they claimed originates from this silence, both Yogācāra and Madhyamaka schools of Mahāyāna had extensively used the silence of the Buddha to develop their doctrines. In fact this distortion of facts has gone a long way and resulted in the development of such esoteric religions like Zen (Tilakaratne, 1993).

These Schools of Buddhism tend to believe that Buddha had used silence as a means of communication due to the inadequacy of language to explain the transcendental nature of enlightenment. This idea does not hold water because Buddha had always explained his silence or refusal to answer any question. Buddha for instance maintains silence when

Vacchagotta asks whether or not there is a soul. After Vaccha leaves Buddha explains to Ven. Ananda that if he had said there is a soul, it would support an eternalist view. On the other hand if he had said there is no soul, it would support a nihilist view. Buddha had avoided both these extremes. Further it would be contrary to his 'anatta' theory.

Buddha had a four-fold policy of answering questions. We have discussed these aspects in Chapter 4. The attitude he adopted regarding these ten questions is in conformity with his policy of dealing with questions.

Chapter 31

Controversies related to early Buddhism in Sri Lanka

Arahath Mahinda had come to Lanka two hundred and thirty years after the death of Buddha. This is recorded in both Dipawamsa and Mahawamsa. Arahath Mahinda is believed to be the son of King Dharmasoka and this is mentioned in the Mahawamsa. But the fact that his son would be the missionary to Lanka is not recorded in any of the Asoka edicts that are carved on the several stone pillars that he constructed. However one of his edicts mentions Lanka as one of the targetted countries where he would spread the Dhamma.

Mahawamsa describes the various religions that were practiced in Sri Lanka before the arrival of Arahath Mahinda, including Brahmanism, worship of Yaksas, Tree-deities, Patron-deities, Jainism and even Ajivika which compared to Buddhism had a much lesser following in India during that time. In fact all the religions that were practiced in India are mentioned except Buddhism. This is strange for in India during Asoka's time Buddhism was as popular as any of the other religions mentioned in the Chronicle and if all those religions had found their way to Lanka there was no reason why Buddhism had not. It is likely that the authors of Mahawamsa wanted to give all the credit to Arahath Mahinda for bringing an entirely new religion to Lanka. This would not have been possible if they said Buddhism was already present in Lanka (EW Adikaram, 1946).

Is there any evidence that Buddhism was practiced in Lanka before Arahath Mahinda brought it to the country? Mahawamsa describes three visits to Lanka by the Buddha, the first was to Mahiyangana which occurred five months after Buddha's enlightenment, the second to Nagadeepa took place five years after Buddha's enlightenment and the third three years later to Kelaniya. However, these visits by Buddha outside India are not recorded in the Tipiṭaka. Buddha's life and activity, particularly after enlightenment, are described in detail in the Sutta-Piṭaka and the Vinaya-Piṭaka. It is strange that three important visits by him are not mentioned.

Buddha's first visit to Lanka had been to Mahiyangana where a stupa has been built. Mahawamsa records that the stupa had been built long before Arahath Mahinda brought Buddhism to Lanka. A deity named Mahasumana had built it at the place where Buddha sat to preach to the Yaksas. Buddha's kesha-datu had been enshrined in the stupa. People may not have worshipped at this stupa for rituals were not practiced at that time. Yet at least a vestige of Buddhism and a degree of belief in it would have been present if the story about the stupa is true irrespective of whether or not Buddha had visited Sri Lanka. No attempt has been made to find the period to which this stupa belongs using modern technology like carbon dating.

Another Mahawamsa legend that supports the idea that Buddhism may have been present prior to Arahath Mahinda is the story of the Princess Bhadrakacchayana who was brought to Lanka as the queen for King Pandukabaya. This princes is supposed to be related to the Buddha and she and others in her retinue may have been Buddhists. And they have come disguised as nuns probably as Bikkhunis.

These are only legends and not historical facts supported by epigraphic or other archaeological evidence. Further there is no scientific evidence, epigraphic or archaeological, to prove that such a person as Arahath Mahinda came to Sri Lanka. What could have happened is that Buddhism may have found its way to Lanka in trickles like other Indian religions. Then during King Devanampiyatissa's time, which coincided with the resurgence of Buddhism in India under Dharmasoka who had sponsored the Third Dhamma-Saṅgāyanāva and initiated the spread of the Dhamma to other countries, there would have been a Buddhist mission sent to Sri Lanka which caused a rapid conversion of the Island into Buddhism. Such a sudden conversion of the people would not have been possible if Buddhism was totally unknown to them. The evidence that this may have happened could be gleaned from the fact that there was during this period a sudden increase in the building of stupas, monasteries, preaching halls, dwelling places for monks, alms halls, libraries and other structures related to the dissemination of the Dhamma, remains of which are present. Anuradapura blossomed as it were with religious as well as cultural activities. These things could not have happened without the leadership of an eminent and capable monk, or group of monks well versed in Buddhism. The writing of Sinhalese commentaries to the Tipiṭaka was undertaken under the auspices of these great monk or monks. This compilation had been enormous. The civilizational change that resulted from these activities was of great significance and these have become the heritage of the Sinhalese.

Bhanaka system that was employed to operate the oral tradition of preserving the Dhamma must have been brought to Lanka at the time this great missionary work took place. Without Bhanakas it would not be possible to compile such a large collection of Sinhalese commentaries which Ven. Buddhagosa translated to Pāli. Ven.Buddhagosa in his Samanthapasadika and also other commentaries makes reference to Bhanakas (EW Adikaram, 1946).

Mahavamsa describes how Buddhism spread very rapidly throughout the island and how people accepted the religion. This may have been due to the fact that there was strong royal patronage for Buddhism. The other reason may have been that Buddhism was not unknown to them though Mahavamsa does not subscribe to such a view. Most of the dissemination of the Dhamma was achieved during Devanampiyatissa's time (247 – 207 BCE) but most of the kings who followed him except a few helped in the propagation of the Dhamma.

Mahavamsa and also the Commentaries talk about several Arahats who seem to have attained Arahathhood soon after being sworn in as a monk. A good example is the Minister in King Devanampiyatissa's Court Aritta who entered the Order few days after the arrival of Arahath Mahinda and immediately attained Arahathhood together with fifty five of his brothers. The possibility of this happening has to be considered in the background of the strenuous and demanding nature of the path to Arahathhood that monks in Buddha's time had to follow. Ven Ananda Buddha's cousin and considered the treasurer of the Dhamma was not an Arahat at the time of Buddha's "pariNirvāna". Incidents of bikkhus attaining Arahathhood after listening to a sermon by another Arahat are to be found in the Sutta-Piṭaka too but it seems to be a more frequent occurrence in the Mahavamsa and the Pāli Commentaries. For example on the occasion of the consecration of the Mirisavetiya chethiya Thera Piyadassi had preached and Mahavamsa says thousands attained Arahathhood including fourteen thousand bikkhunis.

A religion that had flourished in this manner would be expected to be soon entrenched and would not undergo decay for a long period of time. However dissentient views and heretical doctrines had attempted to make an entry into the country and disrupt the doctrinal base of Buddhism. The foreign military invasions had been another problem. The changes occurring in India in Buddhist doctrine and practice had their reverberations in Lanka also. We will consider these matters in the discussion that follows.

After Devanampiyatissa's reign and during King Suratissa's time (187 – 177 BCE) the first Dravidian invasion by Sena and Guttika took place. The second invasion by Elara was during King Asela's time (145 BCE). None of these Tamil rulers, though they were Hindus, did any damage to Buddhism. In fact Elara was one of the most just kings and had Buddhists as his ministers. These Tamil Kings would have known that there was no possibility of survival if they attempted to subvert

Buddhism. Yet Elara was ousted by Dutugamunu a prince from Rohana in the extreme South. The Sinhala Buddhists had a strong national independent consciousness and would not submit to foreign rulers.

King Vattagamini Abaya (29 – 17 BC) had defeated the South Indian invaders after hiding from them for fourteen years. This was a time of decadence after the glorious times of King Dutugemunu followed by his brother Saddhatissa. The Brahmanatissa famine and also the decline in vinaya of the monks caused this decadence. King Vattagamini when in hiding had been greatly assisted by a Thera called Mahatissa. The King had built Abhayagiri Vihara in Anuradapura and in gratitude gifted it to the Thera. Thera Mahatissa had been later expelled from Mahavihara. The first signs of schism appeared subsequently as a rival school was formed at Abhayagiri monastery.

The monks at Mahavihara realized the need to write down the discourses. The Baminiya famine, which had caused the death of a large number of monks, had shown them the difficulty of preserving the Thri-Piṭakaya by the oral tradition. The conflict with Abhayagiri Vihara also was a reason for this decision. The relentless invasions from South India also caused problems for the preservation of the Dhamma. Further there was the entry of undesirables into the sanga sasana endangering the purity of the discourses. Mahaviharins decided to launch into the writing of the Pāli discourses outside Anuradapura and went to Aluvihare in Matale for the purpose. They received assistance from a chieftain and not the King which shows that they were not in good terms with the King. The rift thus caused and subsequent worsening of relations in the sanga was not resolved and had far reaching repercussions and made it easy for the entry of a major rival school Mahāyāna into the country at a later time.

The Nikāyasangraha (Theravāda lineage - 14 CE, by Sangarajah Dharmakirthi) which gives an account on the development of Buddhist sects, mentions that Mahadalitissa a dweller of the Abhayagiri accepted the teachings of the Dhamma-ruci Nikāya belonging to the Vajjiputtika sect in India. The seeds of dissent and sectarianism among the sanga was seen to be growing in the country which portended ill for the peaceful development of Buddhism.

The Mahavamsa after giving an account of the rift that occurred between Mahavihara and Abhayagiri in the First Century BC is silent about dissentient developments in the next three centuries. The Pāli Commentaries also do not refer to this matter except the incident where a disagreement over a Vinaya rule occurred between Mahavihara and Abhayagiri which had to be settled by the intervention of the King Bhathiya (38 – 66 AD). The dispute, it appears, was not related to a doctrinal matter but a linguistic one. This could be due to the acceptance of Sanskrit by the Abhayagiri sect as the language for their work on the religion (Adikaram, 1946). Pāli was the language of the Buddha and the Thervadins. Mahāyānists on the other hand had adopted Sanskrit as their language.

However both sects received assistance from the several kings who ruled the country after Vattagamini-Abhaya and Buddhism could exist without difficulty. During this period Abhayagiri sect could develop as a separate school. Though there was no open conflict the rivalry must have been present in a dormant state. Peace prevailed until the time of Voharaka-Tissa (269 – 291 BC). It was during this period that the Abhayagiri School took the strategic step and put forward the Vaitulya Piṭaka as the true teaching of the Buddha (Nikāyasangraha). Mahvihara monks rejected this position of the Abhayagiri as not in keeping with Buddha's original teaching. The King appointed his minister Kapila who was well learned in all fields to investigate into the matter. Kapila reported that the Abhayagiri assertion was baseless. King burnt the Vaitulya books and admonished the monks but the rift may have continued for during the reign of Gotabhaya (254 – 267 CE) they again attempted to introduce their heretical doctrine as the true Dhamma. The King banished the monks out of the country but the problem did not disappear.

The banished monks had gone to Kavirapattana in South India. There they had met a person called Sangamithra who having heard their story decided to go to Lanka with the intention of making Mahavihara monks accept the Vaitulyavada. This meeting and what followed may not have been accidental as later events discussed below would reveal. Sangamithra came to Lanka, befriended the King and became the tutor of the King's two sons but the King did not change his good relationship with Mahavihara. King's elder son Jethatissa was not kindly disposed towards Sangamithra but the younger son Mahasena was friendly with him. When Jethatissa ascended the throne Sangamithra went back to India but came back after ten years when Mahasena (277 – 304 CE) had succeeded his elder brother to the throne. Sangamithra got Mahasena to issue a proclamation prohibiting giving of alms to Mahavihara. When Mahavihara monks did not receive alms they decided to leave their monastery rather than accept heretical views. Sangamithra got the King to demolish several buildings of the Mahavihara monastery and the wealth therein were appropriated by the Vaitulyavadins.

One of the King's own ministers who did not approve what the King was doing fled to the South, raised an army and was planning to oust the King. King agreed to restore the buildings and war was averted. Meanwhile the Queen who also did not like what Sangamithra was doing got him killed. But the King did not change his attitude towards Mahavihara and built the Jetavana-vihara within the premises of the Mahavihara and gave it to a monk called Kohontissa who was not well disposed towards the Mahaviharins. Jetavana-vihara also was partial towards Abhayagiri and later became a center where both Theravāda and Mahāyāna were taught. Thus by this time there were three sectarian centers of Buddhism in Sri Lanka; Mahavihara which taught Theravāda, Abhayagiri which taught mainly Vaithulyavada and Jetavana which taught both.

Mahasena's son Siri Megavanna (352 -379 CE) who succeeded his father took steps to restore what his father destroyed and helped the Mahavihara to recover. The kings who followed Siri Megavanna treated Mahavihara and Abhayagiri-vihara equally and there was greater cordiality among the monks with different views. Chinese traveller Fa Hein who visited Anuradapura in the 1st Century CE says that dwellers at Abhayagiri studied both vehicles (Adikaram 1946).

However, King Mahanama (409 – 431 CE) had an antipathy towards Mahavihara and consequently Abhayagiri-vihara was benefitted. He had been a monk before he took up the kingship and probably had belonged to the Abhayagiri fraternity. During the reign of this king a highly significant event took place which had far reaching effect on Theravāda Buddhism. The Sinhalese commentaries that had existed from the time of Arahath Mahinda were translated to Pāli by Buddhagosa during this time. Two events of great significance, the writing down of the TriPiṭaka at Aluvihare and also the translation of Sinhalese Commentaries into Pāli had happened when kings ill-disposed towards Mahavihara were in power.

It could be seen that the seeds of Mahāyāna were laid with the proclamation of Vaithulyavada doctrine as the true Dhamma by the dwellers of Abhayagiri during King Voharaka-tissa's (269 – 291 CE) reign. Why did the Abhayagiri dwellers accept this foreign doctrine? Was it mainly to spite Mahavihara dwellers? Was it the rift between these two monasteries, which was personal in nature and not due to doctrinal differences that paved the way for Mahāyāna to gain a foothold in the Island?

That may have been one of the factors that helped Mahāyāna to force itself into Lanka. However what was happening in India had its influence here too. Mahāyāna was the dominant Buddhism in India by the 5th Century CE. Mahāyāna developed to be the dominant religion in Lanka also by the 5th Century CE. It declined and disappeared in India in the 10th Century and same happened in Lanka too.

5th Century was the time Buddhagosa who had been staying in South India came to Sri Lanka. Buddhagosa had introduced transcendental ideas into his translations of the Sinhalese commentaries which we have discussed in Chapter 27. Transcendentalism is a strong philosophical character in Mahāyāna. This could not have been done without the connivance of the Mahavihara monks, for Buddhagosa was their guest and he would not have had the freedom to write whatever he wanted. Mahavihara though maintaining their loyalty to Theravāda was found to be accommodative with regard to Mahayanist ideas and tenets. Theravāda monks under favourable conditions were more resistant and assertive. For example under King Mahasena they had the courage to resist the Vaitulyavadins and even leave their monastery rather than accept the Vaitulya doctrine. But in the 5th Century CE they connive with Ven Buddhagosa to introduce elements that are totally in disagreement with Buddha's Dhamma into important texts such as translations of Sinhalese Commentaries. We have discussed this matter, which is considered a great betrayal, in Chapter 28.

A special effort had been made by Indian Mahāyānists to introduce Mahāyāna into Sri Lanka where Theravāda had been thriving. The sūthra named "Lankavatara" (meaning "Entry into Lanka") was composed purposely to facilitate the spread of Mahāyāna in Lanka. What is of immense significance is that one of the texts among the Mahāyāna texts that were included in Vaitulya-Sūtras was the Lankavatara (Kalupahana 2008). We have mentioned above how Abhayagiri monks attempted to claim that Vaitulya doctrine was the Buddha's Dhamma. It is the same Vaitulya texts that had included within its sūthras the discourse titled "Lankavathara" ("Entry into Lanka"). Thus it shows how well the Abhayagiri monks were equipped to venture into the project to convert Lanka to Mahāyāna.

Further the Chapter 8 of Lankavatara is virtually a handbook which would be useful in converting Buddhists in Lanka to Mahāyāna. In Kalupahana's (1992) opinion it attempts to condemn the Sinhalese by derogatory reference to the legend that deals with the origin of the Sinhalese race involving a lion as the sire. This chapter also criticizes meat eating which could be an insinuation against the Theravādins who do not advise against meat eating.

Kalupahana (1992) is of the opinion that Lankavatara sūthra was compiled in India probably to be used by Sangamithra in his project to convert Lankan Buddhism to Mahāyāna. However Abhayagiri dwellers had made their first attempt to claim that Vaithulya doctrine was the true Dhamma of the Buddha during the reign of Voharaka-Tissa before the arrival of Sangamithra. It was during King Gotabhaya's time that Sangamithra had come to Sri Lanka for the first time and came again ten years later when King Mahasena was in power. Therefore it is probable that Abhayagiri monks had the Vaitulya sūthras before Sangamithra came to the country. It is yet possible that Sangamithra may have used Lankavatara sūthra for his proselytization project in Sri Lanka and the whole affair including the Abhayagiri proclamation regarding Vaitulya sūthra may have been orchestrated by the Mahāyānists in South India.

Lankavatara sūthra later came to be the main doctrinal text for the Mahāyānists in East Asia. It is strange that a book meant to be used for the conversion of Buddhists in Sri Lanka failed to be accepted in that country but was adopted as the main doctrinal text of Mahāyāna in East Asia (Kalupahana, 1992). The latter countries did not accept the fact that the book was intended to be used in Sri Lanka. And the Sri Lankan Buddhists were probably ardent in their attachment to Theravāda that they resisted the intrusion by other doctrines. When the Mahayanist influence that came from South India waned with the decline of that religion in India, Mahāyāna dominance in Sri Lanka also gradually decreased. The fact that Theravāda survived despite all these intrusions and pressure speaks volumes of the strength of that dhamma and the people's loyalty to it with 70% of the population remaining Buddhist until present times. Yet Sri

Lankans have adopted several Mahāyāna ideas which remain to date as part of their religious milieu. Buddhagosa's work and Mahavihara capitulation as mentioned earlier may have contributed to this state of affairs.

Chapter 32

Controversies related to Commentaries on Tipiṭaka

Writing of commentaries on religious and philosophical works had started as a tradition from the time an alphabet or script in the relevant language had been constructed. Pāli was the language used by Buddha but it did not have an alphabet for purposes of writing. Pāli was written in Brahmi script. Philosophers like Nāgārjuna, Asaṅga, Vasubandhu, Dignāga, Dharamakirti, Chandrakirti and later Buddhagosa had written commentaries in Sanskrit and Pāli which are very similar languages.

Commentaries on the Bible had been written by ancient, medieval, and modern commentators. Jewish commentaries on the Old Testament are also to be found. Commentaries on the RgVeda had started to be written in the 7th Century AD (Dandekar, 1990).

Several people had written commentaries on the Tipiṭaka texts. They are Buddhagosa, Dhammapala, Upasena, Mahanama and Buddhadatta. Buddhagosa had been a resident of South India before he came over to Sri Lanka. Dhammapala was a Thera who lived in Badaratitta a village in the South-east coast of India. Buddhadatta was a contemporary of Buddhagosa and had been living in Kavirapattana in South India. Upasena and Mahanama were monks living in Lanka at the time they wrote the commentaries.

Two of the commentators, Buddhadatta and Dhammapala, were from South India and they were living there at the time they translated the Sinhalese commentaries into Pāli. Buddhadatta wrote "Madhurattavilasini" the commentary on the Buddhavamsa. Dhammapala wrote "Paramattadipani" which contains commentaries on Udana, Itivuttaka, Vimanavattu, Petavattu, Theragatha, Therigatha and CariyaPiṭaka. Dhammapala is believed to be Tamil and he may have had access to Commentaries written in Tamil (Adikaram 1946).

It was to Kavirapattana in South India that the Vaithulyavada monks escaped when they were banished by King Gotabhaya and it was the same Kavirapattana where the commentator Buddhadatta lived. Kavirapattana in India could be a place where Mahāyānists were active in organizing the spread of Mahāyāna in the 3rd CE to the 5th CE. Further Mahavihara may have developed links with this place with the help of Buddhagosa who was a contemporary of commentator Buddhadatta who lived in Kavirapattana. Without such a link commentators living in South India could not have done the translation of Sinhalese texts which is a language that may have been strange to them.

That brings us to the question how did these South Indian commentators learn Sinhalese and gain competence in that language to the degree required to perform the difficult and responsible task of translating the Sinhalese commentaries. And some of them were living in India. Who was there to guide them and help them with the difficult task they had undertaken?

There is no information available on this aspect. Mahavamsa writes at length about Buddhagosa and also about other translators but it does not tell us how they mastered the Sinhalese language. Their own work does not give an explanation to this baffling question. Sri Lankans who had written on these commentaries and commentators eg. EW Adikaram (1946) and GP Malalasekera (1928) also have not looked into this matter.

Another question that has to be asked is; was there a need to translate Sinhalese commentaries to Pāli? Even if there was such a need, was there a need to burn the Sinhalese commentaries that were meant to be used by the Sinhalese who were the inhabitants of the Island? Some may say these may have been burnt by invaders. But would invaders selectively burn Sinhalese books only? Why didn't they burn the Tipiṭaka which had been written down by then and which was a much more valuable text?

G.P.Malasekera (1928) is of the opinion that though Mahavamsa says that a bonfire was made of the collection of Sinhalese Commentaries piled up "as high as seven averaged sized elephants" this should not be accepted in its literary sense but what may have happened is with the development of Pāli and Sanskrit the use of Sinhalese language would have waned and the Sinhalese Commentaries would have disappeared. How could books that had been kept in the custody of the Mahavihara monks disappear for no apparent reason? Isn't it their responsibility to preserve these Sinhalese books written in the language of their people? How could such a large collection of books disappear without a trace?

There was no need to translate Sinhalese commentaries into Pāli. It would not have been for the benefit of the Sinhalese people. If the translations were meant for people in India why translate the Sinhalese commentaries, why could not Buddhagosa write his own commentaries on the Suttas directly as the Suttas were in Pāli and Buddhagosa was conversant in that language? It would have avoided errors that may be caused due to lack of proficiency in Sinhalese.

Perpetrators of the despicable act of destroying the Sinhalese commentaries may have had two motives for burning the Sinhalese commentaries. One was the need to destroy the evidence that would prove the many alterations, additions, omissions and errors committed by the translators with the connivance of Mahaviharins who were their hosts. The other was to establish Pāli as the dominant language displacing Sinhalese. No Sinhalese literary work of value was produced for several centuries since this terrible act. We have discussed these matters in Chapter 27 on Buddhagosa.

Adikaram (1946) mentions etymological and also chronological errors in these commentaries. But more importantly he shows the metaphysical and transcendental features that Buddhagosa's translations contain. These would not have been present in the original Sinhalese versions. Sinhalese commentaries were supposed to have been brought to Lanka by Arahath Mahinda. This may not be true for Arahath Mahinda was living in India and could not have arranged Sinhalese commentaries in such large quantities to be written while in India. However what actually could have happened is that after he came to Lanka he must have got the commentaries written in Sinhalese by local scholars so that the Dhamma he brought to Lanka could be taught and easily understood by the people. Arahath Mahinda in his mission had concentrated on two aspects, the learning of the Dhamma and the practice of it. For both these activities Sinhalese texts would be an essential need.

Adikaram identifies two types of discrepancies in the Pāli Commentaries. There were discrepancies between Suttas and Commentaries and also between Commentaries themselves. Further there were three types of differences between Suttas and Commentaries. There were textual errors, enlarging of a point by the Commentary and addition of new facts by the Commentary. These errors, enlargements and additions very often were of a metaphysical and transcendental nature. As a result Buddha was made into a larger than life being who did not belong to the realm of this world but a transcendental phenomenon that was eternal, omniscient and God-like.

Such features would not have been present in the Sinhalese commentaries which were based on the Buddhism that was brought to Lanka by Arahath Mahinda. Buddhism was cleansed of all such material at the 3rd Dhammasaṅgāyanāva thanks to Ven. Moggalliputtatissa before it was brought to Lanka. The Dhamma that was written down at Aluvihare, before Buddhagosa came to Lanka, was the Dhamma brought by Arahath Mahinda. Moreover the major Suttas that were written down do not have these features. Therefore in all probability all this distortion has been done by Buddhagosa and his successors.

Some of these errors are mentioned in the Commentaries themselves. A mistake in one Commentary is pointed out in another. Amplification of facts is more numerous. Buddha's conceivement and birth are described in the Acchariyabbhutadhamma Sutta (Majjima Nikāya) without much deviation from normal reality though certain amount of fantasy is present. In the Commentary ("Papancasadani") this is amplified to such an extent that the description does not fit the birth of a normal human being.

Apart from amplification the deliberate addition of facts could also be seen frequently in the Commentaries. For instance in the Visuddimagga the number of aggregates ("panchaskanda") is not given as five as in the Sutta but an additional four are mentioned. Aggregates are central to the teaching of Buddha and they feature in several doctrines. An alteration in this concept cannot be made by a responsible Commentator if he is to do justice to the original version.

In the Commentary on the Kalinga Bodhi Jataka there is an additional story which is not found in the original where Ven Ananda makes a request that Buddha leaves some object which could be worshipped by people of Savatti. This obviously is an example of the effort Buddhagosa made to start rituals in Lanka.

According to Kalupahana (2008) Visuddhimagga attempts to bring together tenets found in the Suttas and ideas that Buddhagosa may have collected in his sojourn in South India drawn from Theravāda, Sarvāsthavāda, Sautrāntika and Mahāyāna. This task of harmonizing these widely different theories has made Visuddhimagga an extremely cumbersome text and there may not be any originality in it except that it demonstrates the fact that the author possessed vast knowledge.

Thus it is seen that translation of Sinhalese Commentaries into Pāli was an unnecessary exercise from the point of view of the Sinhalese people and may have resulted in the destruction of the invaluable Sinhalese Commentaries which would have been most useful in the study of the history of early Buddhism in Sri Lanka. It may have also caused an irreparable damage to the Sinhalese language.

Chapter 33

Controversies related to Vajarayāna

Vajarayāna, another school of Buddhism also known as, Manthrayana, Tantrayana etc. has come to be the main religious tradition in Tibet. Its origin is not very clear but what is known is that it came out into the open in the 300 CE in India and spread until about the 700 CE. Though the names of Nāgārjuna and Asaṅga are mentioned as its authors there is no evidence to support this viewpoint. There are several views regarding where it started in India. As Nāgārjuna's name is linked to its authorship some believe that it may have started in South India. Others are of the view that it may have originated in North-west in the Peshawar region (Santina, 1998).

The term Vajra has both the meaning of "thunderbolt" and "diamond". Thunderbolt represents the ability of Vajarayāna to cleave through defilements in a flash and diamond is the hardest substance which represent the steadfast nature of Vajarayāna. "Yana" means vessel as in Mahāyāna and Hinayana the other two vessels in Buddhism. This concept of vessel and its inclusion in the nomenclature could be attributed to Mahāyāna ideologists who in their attempt to derogate Theravāda and its various Schools called them Hinayana, the word "hina" here meant small and inferior.

Vajarayāna is called Manthrayana probably because it employs various kinds of chanting, "mantra", incantations etc. when following the "paramithā" process. We know that Buddha had not approved such practices in Buddhism. In Brahmmajāla-sutta (Dhiga Nikāya) he rejects such practices as forms of magic that charlatans make use of to swindle the gullible and make money.

The reason for the birth and development of Vajarayāna could be that the schools of Buddhism, Theravāda, Madhyamaka and Yogācāra had taken the form of highly developed deep philosophies and there was no simple rendering or version of Buddhism that could resonate with the simple intellect of the common people. Further the path to freedom and the final goal in all these branches of Buddhism was long and tedious particularly the Bodhisattva stream in Mahāyāna. People may have been in need of a method that achieve quick results. Vajarayāna may claim to have a short-cut way to reach Nibbāna. Though this is often given as a reason for the development of Vajarayana the possibility of a significant input by Hindu influence cannot be ruled out. This would be discussed below.

The preceptive path to salvation in Vajarayāna is significantly different from those of Theravāda and Mahāyāna though there are philosophical similarities. In Theravāda it is the Ariyaṭṭhaṅgikamagga and in Mahāyāna it is the Bodhisattva "paramithā" stream. In Vajarayāna the method involves incantation of "manthra" and such chanting, various formations of hands and fingers called "mudra" and "yogic" postures. This complexity is necessitated due to the requirement of physical, verbal and mental application in a practical manner in the process of development of "jhana". The physical application may even take the form of sexual activity to achieve final renunciation of all that is physical (Snellgrove, 1987).

Some may argue that these features were present in Early Buddhism in an attempt to show that Vajarayāna was the result of the linear development of Early Buddhism. They may give as examples chanting of "pirith", Buddha's "mudra" formations with fingers, symbolic use of "dhamma-chakra" etc. But these methods are not recommended in Early Buddhism for the attainment of Nibbāna in the Ariyaṭṭhaṅgikamagga.

Some believe that the mystical elements like chanting of incantations, yogic postures, may have been practices in the regions where Vajarayāna developed and which may have been adopted by Vajrayanists. As mentioned above, in this regard, the influence of Hinduism cannot be ruled out. Practices such as chanting of verses, yogic methods are recommended in Hinduism and are part of their ritualistic system. Hinduism was a very strong presence in the regions where Vajarayāna developed in the 600 to 800 CE. Hinduism employed aggressive methods to introduce their tenets to Buddhism and consequently Mahāyāna was the casualty. Similarly Hindu features may have been introduced into Vajarayāna. To say that characteristic features of Vajarayāna is closer to Hinduism than to Early Buddhism is no exaggeration. This may have been a gradual process where Mahāyāna adopted several critical characteristics of Hinduism and then Vajarayāna, developing on the basis of Mahāyāna, may have gone further and absorbed more of Hinduism (Lu, 2017).

Vajarayāna evolved in this manner and subsequently formed its base firmly on Madhyamaka and Yogācāra philosophy and developed further. However Vajarayāṇa differs from most of these schools in that it is more mystic, reticent and secretive. It has no TriPiṭaka but it has a large collection of "tantras" which describe the philosophy and precepts of Vajarayāna. In the practice of Vajarayāna precepts emphasis is given to the physical body and here Yoga methods are employed. The basis for this is the belief that the human body has mystic powers that circulate in systems of tubules within the body. Three of these systems are more important and they are named; "ali" or "lalana", "kali" or "rasana" and "avaduti". "Ali"and "kali" are positioned on the right and left side of the spine and "avaduti" is right in the middle. All these systems are directed towards the top of the head. What is expected in yogic exercise is the development of spiritual mystic power of the body and to direct it towards the head. "Ali" symbolizes wisdom, "kali" symbolizes compassion and strategic means of wisdom. "Avaduti" symbolizes the association of wisdom and compassion. Apart from these systems of tubules there are four vital centers in the body known as cycles or lotus. Function of all these is the direction of mystic power towards the head employing yogic and breathing exercises.

Vedic scripture speaks about similar energy centers present in the body in relation to the brain and spine (Subash Kak, 2016). These descriptions appear in the Vedic Tantra which are also called "Manthramārga" as they employ "manthras". Vajarayāna may have borrowed these ideas from Vedic and Hindu tradition.

During yogic exercise the body is equated with the universe. Buddha is considered the "Vishvakāya". The body, the universe and the "Buddhakāya" are symbolically joined together. The reality of everything is this "Buddhakāya" or "Dhammakāya". "Buddhaswabhava" (Buddha-nature) is present in everything and everybody. The Yogi must realize the systemic balance in this reality and it can only be done by the method that Vajarayāna teaches that include mystic rituals, yoga means, "manthra" etc. The final goal is this realization (Santina, 1998).

The similarity between Mahāyāna and Vajarayāna could be seen in the "trikāya" system which the latter has borrowed from the former. However it has gone further in the path of mysticism. How different all this is from Early Buddhism can easily be understood.

Further Vajarayāna identifies five Buddhas called "Jeena-Buddhas" who are features of the "Vishvakāya". Apart from all this a concept of an ancient Buddha also has been created which is a manifestation of "Dharmakāya" and which is considered as the font of all phenomena. "Dharmakāya" is equal to emptiness and it is the reality of everything. The realization of the unity of the human body, the universe and the "Dharmakāya" is the realization of "śūnyatava". All this was done to enable Vajarayāna to fall in line with Madhayamaka theory which has emptiness as its core philosophy.

Another development is the "Mandala" which is a graphic representation of the unity between person, universe and

"Buddhakāya" which is made use of in the yogic practice. We discuss all this to elucidate the process of distortion of Early Buddhism, how Buddhism has been mutilated beyond recognition.

The fact that the damage is far worse than all that is described above could be realized when one sees how sexual relationship has been incorporated into a religion that is recognized by name as Buddhism. Sexual relationship has been introduced as a means of realization of the Bodhisattva mentality and nature. Whether this is symbolic only or is part of the precepts that lead to the final goal is not clear. But even a symbolic inclusion of sex as part of the method of attaining Nibbāna is something abhorrent and detestable in the context of a religion that is even distantly connected to Buddhism. Buddha had specifically said that all pleasure senses have to be eliminated before embarking on the path to Nibbāna (Samaññaphāla-sutta).

In the drawings and paintings of Buddhas and Bodhisathvas of Vajarayāna these figures appear with their respective concubine in physical embrace. These motifs are made use of in the yogic methods. Female consorts of gods is a feature of Hinduism. Mahāyāna gods and Bodhisattvas too have their female partners. Vajarayāna has taken the matter to its logical end as it were. One of the main reasons for the decline of Buddhism in India may have been the introduction of this element of sex into a school of religion that identified itself with Buddhism. This was a most reprehensible act of treachery.

However what is strange and astonishing is the acceptance in Tibet of all that was Vajarayāna and its further development with state sponsorship. The religion that developed in Tibet is a mixture of Vajarayāna, Madhayamaka, Yogakara and their indigenous traditions. The system of governance with the Dalai-Lama as its head is something that Buddha would not approve if he had been alive. In fact he would not approve most of what has happened to Buddhism that he preached. Dalai-Lama is accepted as one of the Buddhist leaders in the world but the pertinent and basic question in the first instance is whether what he preaches is Buddhism.

Chapter 34

Was the decline in Science caused by the decline of Buddhism in India ?

It is often said that Buddhism is scientific. Buddha is said to be the first person who had said that one must not believe anything unless one could convince oneself by personal experience. In this regard Kālāma Sutta (Aṅguttara Nikāya) is often quoted as the earliest pronouncement on scientific method. In this Sutta empiricism was recommended as the method of gaining knowledge in preference to other methods like scripture, hearsay, testimony, reason and authority. In the evolution of scientific method two of the above methods have remained as acceptable tools in the armamentarium of science and they are empiricism and reason. Why Buddha did not rely on reason as a method of gaining knowledge is discussed in Chapter 4 on Knowledge.

In this Chapter how science progressed in India in the Buddhist period will be discussed. The apparent mystery in nature and the inquisitive mind of the human being had worked as a stimulus for man to investigate into his surroundings. As a result inquiry into nature had begun very early in the life of man. This could be seen in the ancient civilizations that developed in relation to river basins in Mesopotamia, China, India and Egypt. Due to the difficulty in finding plausible explanations to some of the mysteries in nature metaphysical and superstitious beliefs originated and took root in some societies. These proved to be a fetter to the development of science. For instance when theories based on god and creation were resorted to explain natural phenomena scientific inquiry was suppressed. Religions based on belief in God developed instead of free inquiry.

In ancient India Brahmanism discouraged free inquiry into nature by taking up the position that everything happens according to Brahma's will. It did not allow freedom of thought to take root and prosper. It in fact introduced fetters of caste denying access to knowledge to those considered low caste. Access to knowledge was given only to high caste people.

The Golden Era of science in ancient India corresponds to the Golden Era of Buddhism in ancient India. From about the 5th Century BC till about the 6th Century AD Buddhism flourished in India and so did science. The main reason for this was the fact that Buddhism encouraged science while other religions like Brahmanism and later even Hinduism discouraged science. Christianity also when it developed in Rome during the same period suppressed the growth of science and paved the way for the emergence of the Dark Ages. It is said that if Indian science was allowed to freely develop India today would have been in the forefront in the field of science and Buddhism would have been the religion of the world and most of today's ills would not have deteriorated to an extent that the very existence of the world is now under threat.

For science to grow there has to be freedom of thought and encouragement of the enquiring mind. There has to be a facilitation of observation, investigation and experimentation. The Buddha was a person who did all this and encouraged others to do the same. He wanted others to examine thoroughly any opinion or theory including his own Dhamma before accepting them. He mentions ten grounds on which any view should not be accepted; Vedic authority, tradition, hearsay, textual authority, agreeability, authority of the holder of the view, logicality, accepted by others, agrees with one's own view. In the Vimamsaka sutta (Majjima Nikāya) Buddha expands this freedom of enquiry to include the nature of the Buddha himself and says that this enquiry should be done not for a short period but for a long period of time.

In contrast Brahmanism maintained that all knowledge comes from God (Jayatilake, 1998). It claimed that Vedic texts were not written by man but originated from god. Formal education was confined to the study of Vedas only and even that only for the high caste. The Vedic literature is divided into four parts which belong to four periods of Indian history. They are as follows; 1) Veda, 2) Brahmana, 3) Aranyaka and 4) Upanishad. The word Brahmana here means the writings of a teacher who is well versed in the "science "of sacrificial rituals. The main subject of discourse in these texts is the methods of sacrificial rituals known as "yoga homa", offering to gods for favours, deletion of sin, acquiring of supernatural powers etc. Brahmanism was based mainly on these texts. The caste system reached its zenith during the period of Brahmanism (Fowler, 2002). Thus there was no scientism in the men who practiced Brahmanism.

Whereas most of the scientists in India during this period were Buddhists. Indian science made radical, significant and lasting contributions to world science mainly in the fields of mathematics, medicine and to a lesser degree in astronomy. The scientists who made these contributions were Buddhists. The kings who supported science and education were Buddhists. There were six Buddhist universities which thrived during this period as they received assistance and patronage from kings; Nalanda (King Gupta 415 -455 AD), Vickramasila (King Dharmapala 770 – 810 AD), Odantapura (King Gopala 660 - 705 AD), Somapura (King Devapala 816 – 850 AD), Jagaddala (King Ramapala 1077 – 1129 AD) and Vallabhi (King Maithra 7th Century AD). Some of these universities were Mahāyāna oriented and Mahāyāna like Theravāda encouraged scientific thought. Most of these universities were in Magadha country which is considered the cradle of Buddhism.

Indian mathematics is considered mother of all mathematics. Basic rule of numerical mathematics, the concept of zero, algebra, logarithm etc. were constructed by Indian mathematicians. Most of them were the work of the famous mathematician, astronomer and philosopher Aryabhatha who was born in 476 AD and lived in the Buddhist heartland, capital of Maghada Empire, Pataliputhra. He constructed formulae to determine area, volume and designed intermediate equations of the first degree. He authored the famous book called "Aryabhatiya" in 499 AD which described all this work. Indian mathematics found its way to Arab from where it went to Europe in the 12th Century AD as part of the process that took all Arab science to Europe made possible by the Great Latin Translation. It was Aryabhatha who first said that the Earth rotated in its own axis and that eclipse was not the work of mythical Rahu but was due to the shadow of the Earth falling on the Moon.

In the field of medicine, particularly in surgery, Indian physicians excelled and led the world. Their methods of treatment were adopted by many physicians in the world China, Arab, Greece, Sri Lanka and Europe. Most of the Indian physicians were Buddhists. King Dharmasoka had sent medical missions to five Hellenistic states in Europe. Teaching of medicine was compulsory in all Buddhist universities such as Nalanda. The famous Buddhist philosopher Nāgārjuna who was also a physician had made valuable contributions to medical texts such as the Sushrutha Samhitha written by the famous ancient Indian surgeon Sushrutha. Jeevaka was appointed the physician to Buddha and his achievements in the field of medicine is described in the Vinaya Piṭaka.

Buddhist scientists were a threat to the Brahmins who made use of the caste system and ignorance of the people to exploit them. Even in a court of law Brahmins had to be considered always right and were above the law and no punishment could be carried out against them. Brahmanism considered women to be an inferior species. Buddhism fought against all these negative attitudes and oppressive treatment of categories of human beings for no fault of theirs. This was the bone of contention between Buddhism and Brahmanism. The history of India during this period could aptly be described as an acrimonious struggle between these two religions. Buddha in his condemnation of Brahmanism had said that Brahmins who claim that they are superior by virtue of the fact that they were borne out of the mouth of Brahma have wives who menstruate, become pregnant and give birth (Aggañña sutta, Dīgha Nikāya).How could Brahmins who are thus born claim they are superior to others who are similarly born? This statement had shaken the very core of Brahmanism and it is no exaggeration to say that Brahmins were seething with anger and were determined to destroy Buddhism and all it stood for including freedom of thought which forms the foundation of science.

Brahmins attacked both Buddhism and science for both stood for freedom and emancipation from all kinds of bondage including caste and also because most of the scientists were Buddhists. All vocations related to science were declared sacrilegious, blasphemous and heretical. Support from Buddhist universities to the chemical and medical science in the hospitals was stopped. The practice of obstetrics and maternity science which had been scientifically developed to a very high standard was denigrated as dirty and relegated only to be practiced by low caste women. Caste rules were made stricter. Aryabhatha the greatest Indian mathematician was ridiculed and his theories were branded as false. If the Earth is moving they asked, where is it going? They fabricated a book which said the Earth is stationary and claimed that that was the original thesis of Aryabhatha.

Charaka was a physician to King Kanishka who contributed a lot to the development of Sarvāsthavāda school of Buddhism in Kashmir, North-West of India in about the 1st Century AD. Charaka authored a text on medicine called Charaka Samhitha. He had developed physiological concepts on digestion, metabolism and immunity. His book remained the standard text for two centuries. It was translated to Arab and later to Latin in the 12th Century AD. The Brahmins attempted to denigrate the work of Buddhist physicians Sushrutha, Nāgārjuna, Charaka and Vagbhata. They attempted to show that the texts on

Ayurveda were the works of mystical "Irshi" and created a god of medicine called Dhanavanthari who came out of the "churning ocean of milk" and who was the author of those Samhitha mentioned above (Gavin Flood, 1996).

In around the 10th to the 12th Century AD Buddhism started to decline in India due to the reasons we have discussed in Chapter 36 on "Decline of Buddhism in India". With the waning of Buddhism Indian science also went into decline. No scientist of repute, in the caliber of Aryabhatha for instance, was produced in India in any of the fields it excelled in, such as mathematics, medicine and astronomy, since the decline of Buddhism until modern times.

Chapter 35

Controversies related to Buddhist Councils (Dhamma Saṅgāyanā)

Buddha had encouraged discussion as a method of settling disputes. Whenever dissent arose within the Sanga community he discussed the matter and settled the issue amicably. Though there were dissentient views during his life time there was no schism and formation of splinter groups. Some monks such as Ven. Sathi and Ven. Aritta Sunkkatha had even criticized the Dhamma and the Buddha himself during his life time (Mahāthanhāsankaya-sutta, Majjima Nikāya). After his death several schools of Buddhism came into being but these were due to interpretational differences and not schismatic. Arising of Mahāyāna and Vajarayāna however may be considered as schismatic change as totally different doctrines had been developed. Serious dissent that could not be settled by talking to each other had necessitated the convening of a council or Dhamma Saṅgāyanāva where a large gathering of monks would peruse the Dhamma and arrive at consensus. Some councils were held to review the Dhamma and Vinaya while others were necessary to iron out differences which on some occasions resulted in groups of monks breaking away and forming their own schools.

The first Saṅgāyanāva held soon after Buddha's demise (early 5th Century BC) is the most important of all the Councils as it was at this council that the oral transmission method and preservation of the Dhamma was organized and launched as a major project of the Sanga community. There may have been other reasons for the need to hold a council like the comment of monk Subaddha and also the arising of various interpretations of the teaching of Buddha and the tendency for the development of sects. Senior monks had come to realize that as the authoritative source of the Dhamma was no more it was time to revise the Dhamma and Vinaya and take steps to organize a system to preserve them for posterity. The oral tradition that was begun at this Council had been maintained for about six centuries until the Tipiṭaka was written down in the 1st BCE. Facilities for writing was scarce during those times and preservation of texts and scripture were usually done by memorizing them by assigned groups who would recite them periodically and teach it to younger groups so that the material is handed down from generation to generation (Sasanārathana, 1952).

The first council was held at Rajagāha chaired by Ven. Mahākassapa. They had recited, classified and arranged the teachings of the Buddha. The discourses were classified according to their length and the four main Nikāyas were identified as Dīgha, Majjhima, Samyutta, and Aṅguttara. These were assigned to groups of monks headed by a senior monk. These reciters of the discourses were known as Bhanakas.

According to EW Adikaram (1946) the Pāli Commentaries mention Bhanakas who were assigned with the above mentioned four major Nikāyas, two Vibhangas, Dhammapada and the Maha-Ariyavamsa but there is no mention of Bhanakas assigned to work on the Khuddaka-Nikāya (Small Collection). Khuddaka Nikāya is the fifth of the Nikāyas which are included in the Canon. There are fifteen Suttas and separate books in the Khuddaka Nikāya but whether they had been compiled at the time of the first council is not known. If they were available there is no reason why they were omitted when Bhanakas were assigned with the work. How these were preserved and handed down until they were committed to writing is not known. Oliver Abeynayake (1984) is of the opinion that some of the texts in the Kuddhaka Nikāya belong to early times and others are later additions.

It is said that at the First Council Ven Ananda recited all the Suttas that the Buddha had taught. The number of Suttas go into thousands. It is difficult to believe that one person could remember all the Suttas and recite them at a convention. As an explanation for this extraordinary feat the theory has been put forward that an Arahath who has no influx of defilements and has a purified mind empty of carnal desires could retain the wealth of goodness contained in the discourses.

Vedic texts also have been preserved by the oral transmission method until they were written down. They were memorized by Brahmins who possessed a talent for that and were recited at meetings and were handed down to their next generation pupils. Most of the religious texts of that period were preserved using this method. This process was well established even before Buddha came into the picture. Buddha always wanted his preaching to be preserved for the good of the future generations. In all probability Buddha also may have initiated such a system for the preservation of his Dhamma. The process probably was not started at the First Council but it may have been organized and the responsibility of implementation may have been assigned to senior monks on that occasion. Therefore Ven Ananda would not have been required to recite all Suttas.

Moreover Buddha was travelling around and preaching his Dhamma to a large number of people. Thus the system was open to the society and many people would have remembered the discourses. Buddha may have repeated the discourses several times particularly the essence of his Dhamma. These preaching would have been etched in the memory of his disciples and followers. On the other hand Vedic texts were a closed system. Only the learned Brahmins of high caste had access to them. Therefore if discrepancies and errors were to occur in the process of transmission it is likely that Vedic texts were more affected than Buddhist texts.

The Second Buddhist Council was held in Vaisali hundred years after Buddha's parinirvāna. Information on the history of Buddhism during this period is scanty. Kings who supported Buddhism were on the wane. King Ajathasattu after Buddha's demise took up the role of a warrior king and after a long war conquered Vaisali. Ajathasattu was killed by his son Udayabadda, a wicked tradition started by Ajattasattu himself and continued for several generations of kingship so much so that they are known as Patricidal Dynasty. These patricidal kings were not religious minded for obvious reasons. By the time of King Kalasoka (393 - 365 BC) Buddhism was considerably weakened. There was a dearth of quality monks and the kings were not interested in the welfare of Buddhism. Monks in Vaisali and Vajji were in difficulty and faced problems of survival and they were forced to accept money.

Maghada and Kosala had been the states where Buddhism was well established. Vaisala and Vajji were situated north of the river Ganges and therefore separated from Maghada and Kosala which were in the south bank. Vaisala and Vajji were also strong Buddhist states. Though these states were keen on Buddhism they were separated from the main centers of Buddhism and the monks felt independent after Buddha's death. Forced by the economic and social pressures they put forward ten demands to amend the Vinaya Piṭaka which included handling of money, partaking of food after sunset using two fingers, taking alcohol when ill and some other minor issues. The Theravāda text Chulavagga-Pāliya gives an account of these ten issues ("dasa vasthuva"). Other schools such as Mahāsāṅgika and Dharmaguptha give different versions particularly with regard to the first six of the ten issues (Sasanārathana, 1952).

These ten points were accepted by the people of Vaisala and Vajji probably because they could see the difficulties faced by the monks. Thereafter the monks started to put into practice what was allowed by the amendments. After the lapse of a period of time a leading and high ranking monk named Yasa Maha-sthavira visited this region. He tried to tell the people that the ten points violate the edicts of the Vinaya-Piṭaka but the people did not accept his point of view and were supportive of the Vaisala – Vajji monks. These monks took umbrage at Ven.Yasa's attempt to admonish to them and meted out a punishment to him and were planning more action against him. A conflict had resulted which needed to be resolved.

During that time there was one Ven.Revatha who was often called upon to settle such conflicts. The conflict regarding the "Dasa-vasthuva" was also referred to him. It is said that Vaisala – Vajji monks tried to bribe Ven Revatha by giving him robes but he did not side with them and stayed neutral. Two other issues also came up to complicate the problem, these were regarding the question; in which state would Buddhas be born and who are identified as disciplined monks. A representative committee was appointed to decide on these issues. The committee looked at only the "Dasa-Vasthuva" and were silent on the other two issues. They had decided to convene a council and as a result the Second Buddhist Council was held. Ten thousand monks wanted to participate but only seven hundred were selected. These were said to be the monks who were senior and advanced in meditation practices. The Council was held at Valukaramaya in Vaisala and lasted for eight months. After the Council ten thousand monks who accepted the "Dasa-vasthuwa" were banished with the help of King Kalasoka. These monks had gone to Kosambi and with the help of a regional ruler had held their own council. It is recorded that all the discourses which were discussed at the First Council had been reviewed at the Second Council held at Vaisala. However nothing is known about what was discussed at the council held by the breakaway group. The chronicle Deepavamsa says that the Suttas and the Vinaya were turned upside down at the council of the breakaway group of monks. These monks who broke away formed themselves into a new School of Buddhism called Mahāsāṅgika. This was the first schismatic change that occurred in the Buddhist Sanga Community which was a matter of great significance.

The Third Buddhist Council was convened at Asokarama in Pataliputra in the year 247 BCE. King Asoka had been crowned in about 230 BCE but at the beginning he was indifferent to Buddhism though he helped all religions equally. After listening to a preaching by Ven. Nigrodha King Asoka was converted to Buddhism and started to spend lavishly for its development. As a result undesirable people with no religious incline and also monks with heretical views mainly of the Mahāsāṅgika sect joined the main Theravāda school for personal benefits that came from King's generosity. Senior pious monks did not like what was happening and refused to perform the rituals in the presence of heretical bogus priests. The King heard about this and he sought the advice of senior monk Ven. Moggalliputtatissa who advised the King to hold a council to get rid of the heretical and impious monks and to revise the Dhamma.

Nine hundred monks participated in the council which was chaired by Ven. Moggalliputtatissa and it lasted nine months. Ven. Moggalliputtatissa employing logical methods refuted the heretical views such as "Puggalavāda", "Lokotharavada", and several other views. His preaching was compiled into the text "Kathavatthu" which is included in the Abhidhamma Piṭaka. We have discussed Ven. Moggalliputtatissa's logic in Chapter 26. Thousands of monks most of them belonging to the Mahāsāṅgika sect were banished with the approval of the King. Sarvāsthavādins also had to leave Asoka's kingdom as they did not receive his assistance. They went to Kashmir region. Dharmasoka organized the spread of the Dhamma, sent missionaries to several parts of India and also foreign countries including Burma and Sri Lanka, which were very successful.

There were two Fourth Councils, one in Sri Lanka and the other in Kashmir organized by Sarvāsthavādins. The former was held in the 1st BCE and the latter in 1st CE. The Fourth Council held in Sri Lanka is of interest as the writing down of the TriPiṭaka was carried out concurrently. Deepavamsa says the Council and the committing to writing of the Tipiṭaka was held during the reign of Vattagamini-Abaya (29 – 17 BCE) at Aluvihare in Matale. We have discussed this matter in Chapter 36 on the "Decline of Buddhism in India and its spread in other countries".

The other Fourth Council convened by the Kushan emperor King Kanishka (78 CE – 105 CE) in Kashmir is not officially recognized by the Theravādins. However the event is recorded in Mahāyāna texts. The council discussed mainly the Sarvāsthavāda Abhidhamma. Main outcome of the council was an extensive commentary, known as "Mahavibhasha", on a portion of the Sarvāsthavāda Abhidhamma (Sasanārathana, 1952).

King Kanishka belongs to the Kushan community that migrated from North-Western China. Several communities from various parts of this region had migrated into India after the demise of Asoka and one of the largest groups who could get a foot hold and build a kingdom was the Kushan community. After Asoka Kanishka was the most powerful King in the Central and North-West India. His kingdom extended into Afghanistan, Bactria, Punjab, Kashmir and Himalaya and his capital was Peshawar. Sarvāsthavādins received King Kanishka's sponsorship. He regularly got down priests to his palace and listened to their preaching. He found that their views were not consistent and differed to a significant degree. This made him call for a council to iron out these differences. Some believe that Mahāyāna originated during King Kanishka's time with the coming together of several views and schools including Sarvāsthavāda (Vehihene Paññāloka 1966, Moratuwe Sasanārathana 1952). But this theory may not hold water, for Sarvāsthavāda continued to exist as an independent and separate religious entity after the birth of Mahāyāna and for a long time thereafter. In fact there are others who believe Mahāyāna originated in Andra Pradesh and that Ven Nāgārjuna to a significant degree was its author. We have discussed the origin of Mahāyāna in Chapter 23 on "Important differences between Theravāda and Mahāyāna".

Fifth Buddhist Council was held in Mandalay, Burma in 1871 under the auspices of King Mindon. It was chaired by three senior monks; Ven. Jagabhivamsa, Ven Narindhabhidhaja and Ven Sumanagalasami. Purpose of the Council was to review the Pāli Tipiṭaka to see whether there were any errors of omission or commission or whether any heretical material had been introduced. 2400 monks had participated and it had lasted five months. The Fifth Buddhist Council was a Burmese affair and other countries were not involved. However it helped to get the Burmese Pāli Tipiṭaka revised and cleared of errors.

The Sixth Buddhist Council is of great significance as several countries participated in it and it was timed to end on the Vesak day of 1956 which was the 2500th anniversary of Buddha's parinirvāna. It began on the Vesak day in 1954 and was held in a specially built cave and pagoda complex in Yangon, Burma. It was sponsored by the Government of Burma led by Prime Minister U Nu. Countries which participated were Thailand, Burma, Cambodia, Sri Lanka, Vietnam, Laos, Nepal and India. All the countries had brought their Pāli TriPiṭaka for review except India. The discourses were thoroughly examined to see that they tallied and differences were ironed out. Each country rendered the Pāli Cannon into their native scripts except India. The TriPiṭaka was also fully printed employing modern technology. The Council lasted two years and was terminated as the Vesak full moon rose on the 17th May 1956. It is ironical that India where Buddhism originated could not take a leading role at this event of great importance and it was left to the other countries, to which it had secondarily spread from India, to take the lead role.

There had been Buddhist Councils in Thailand as well. The first had been in the year 1477 and these were mainly Thai affairs for the purpose of revising the Pāli Canon.

Chapter 36

Decline of Buddhism in India and its survival in other countries

After the death of the Buddha Buddhism spread throughout India and beyond its borders to China, Sri Lanka, and also to Central Asia. During Mayura Dynasty (3rd BCE) under King Asoka Buddhism was in the ascendency and this trend continued until about the 12th CE but with a gradual downturn. Total Buddhist population in the 10th CE in the Indian subcontinent excluding Sri Lanka, Nepal and Burma was 10 Million and 90% of these Buddhists lived in India. In Bangladesh there were 7% and 1% in Pakistan. State patronage and monastic organization was responsible for the successful survival of Buddhism despite many challenges.

Under Gupta rule (4th – 6th CE) Buddhism started to lose its popularity and Hinduism became more assertive. People turned to Hinduism as it offered them means of solace through ritual while Buddhism confined to monastic activity was being gradually separated from the people. Nevertheless Gupta rulers extended sponsorship to Buddhism and built monasteries like the Nalanda. However the difference between Buddhism and Hinduism became less discernible and Mahāyāna became more ritualistic. Brahmins developed new relationships with the rulers and Buddhist monasteries lost control over its followers. These changes did not happen suddenly or over a matter of few years, rather it was a gradual process spread over several centuries.

Hun invasions from Afghanistan had caused considerable damage to Buddhism. These invaders had destroyed Buddhist monasteries and temples including those at Nalanda. Apart from the impact of Hinduism Hun invasions were the other major cause of the decline of Buddhism. There was no means of rebuilding the destroyed monasteries as rulers'support was not forthcoming and people also were indifferent (B Hans, 2917).

Another reason for the decline of Buddhism was the competition among the religions. Hinduism and later Islam were making inroads into the areas of Buddhist influence. Mahāyāna had moved away from Theravāda and was getting closer to Hinduism and the difference between Mahāyāna and Hinduism was less clear. This made Mahāyāna doctrinally and philosophically weak and vulnerable to incursion by other religious doctrines. Finally Mahāyāna also completely disappeared in India by about the 12th CE (Sasanarathana 1952). The development of Vajarayāna with its mystic rituals besmirched with carnal elements also would have contributed in a major way to the total disappearance of Buddhism in the country where it originated, and at that, a Buddhism that stood for purity of mind without defilements particularly carnal desire that a person in quest of Nibbāna must develop.

In Sri Lanka Theravāda had taken root from the time it was brought here in 3rd BC. Arahath Mahinda had taken steps to see that Buddhism would develop into a religion which would fulfill the religious needs of the people. Further he had fostered a cultural milieu comprising arts, craft and literature based on Buddhism that was imbibed and assimilated by the people. This religious-cultural milieu had paved the way for the development of a great civilization which got entrenched in the consciousness of the people (Adikaram, 1946).

It was difficult if not impossible to displace such a religious base of a civilization. Adversaries may come but the Buddhist civilization would not be dislodged from the consciousness of the people. Invasions accompanied by intention to convert came from South India, Portugal, Holland and Britain but though foreign occupation was long and grossly oppressive Buddhism escaped with little damage. Similarly Mahāyāna came but could not achieve its goals. Vajarayāna also may have made a short visit. Theravāda may have been accommodative to a degree and some of the Mahāyāna tenets may have been accepted and assimilated into the system and may be present to date.

One is somewhat nonplussed when one considers the fact that Buddhism lost ground and disappeared in India, the country of its origin, whereas in several other countries where it had spread to from India it had taken root and flourished despite obstacles and attempts to suppress. It is difficult to find reasons for this. Vedic tradition which influenced all religions that originated in India had later grown into Hinduism. The ancient Vedas may have been firmly imbued in the consciousness of the Indian people. As a result Hinduism which had the closest affinity to the Vedas would have resonated with the religious aspirations of the people more than any other religion. Hinduism thus could survive the Islamic and other foreign invasions and finally displace Buddhism also.

Legend has it that during King Asoka's time missionaries were sent to the mainland South East Asia called "Swarnabhumi" (Golden Land) where several kingdoms and independent states existed. This region later broke up into several countries; Burma (later Myanmar), Thailand, Cambodia, Laos and Vietnam. Brahamanism too may have spread to these countries. Mahāyāna and Vajarayāna also had found its way to these countries (Paul Williams, 2005).

In Southern Burma, in the 3rd CE in the Mon Kingdom and Pyu State the population consisted mainly of Theravāda Buddhists. Though the influence of Brahmanism and Mahāyāna were present these religions could not make a significant impact. An ancient Theravāda Buddhist text written on gold plates has been found in the Pyu city-state. The script of this text resembles that of Andhra-Pallava region in South India. Epigraphic inscriptions are also of this same script. Theravāda Buddhism may have come to this country from South India. Pyu state had been a flourishing Buddhist city and was contemporary of Anuradhapura.

In the Bagan Kingdom in Burma Theravāda came to be well established by the 11th CE under King Anaravrtha. The King had given preference to Theravāda over Mahāyāna and Vajarayāna. Before this a religion called Ari-Buddhism which was a mixture of Theravāda, Mahāyāna and Vajarayāna had been in practice. The King had implemented several religious reforms throughout the country to blunt the influence of Ari-Buddhism and also banished several monks belonging to that religion.

Today 90% of people in Burma are Theravāda Buddhists. It was the state religion before the army took over power. It appears that Theravāda was more appealing to the people in this region and was preferred over other religions that were present in the regional countries and which were vying with each other in the effort to spread into other countries (Paul Williams, 2005).

Thailand was inhabited by Chinese migrants and they adopted the religions that were in practice at that time. King Dharmasoka's Buddhist missionaries had come to South-East Asia in the 3rd BC and Theravāda Buddhism was in existence along with other religions. The first Thai Kingdom, Sukhothai was formed in the 13th CE. At the beginning Theravāda and Mahāyāna both were being practiced and also Brahmanism. During this period Thai monks travelled to Sri Lanka for ordination and learning Theravāda at Mahavihara which was known as Lankavong among Thai Buddhists. Monks from Mahavihara travelled to Thailand to teach Theravāda. Most of the Kings supported Theravāda and consequently the latter religion grew to be the main religion in Thailand with 95% practicing it. Thus in Thailand too the preferred religion was Theravāda which received royal patronage and which succeeded in overcoming competition from other religions like Mahāyāna and Brahmanism (Paul Williams, 2005).

In the case of Cambodia too it is believed that Buddhism was brought to the region during King Dharmasoka's time. However in the 100 BC – 200 CE period when the Funan Kingdom was flourishing Hinduism was the religion in practice. Kings worshipped Vishnu. Buddhism was also present as a secondary religion. Kingdom of Chenia replaced Funan and was in power till 700 CE. Buddhism was further weakened during this time but survived. Statues and images of Mahāyāna and even Sarvāsthavāda belonging to this period have been found. This was followed by Angkhor Kingdom and a gradual transition from the worship of Vishnu to the worship of Buddha and Bodhisathva Avalokethisvara took place. Under King Suryavarman (1009 – 1050 CE) Mahāyāna became stronger. King Jayavarman followed and he developed Mahāyāna further. At this time something very significant happened. A person named Tamalinda believed to be son of King Jayavarman went to Sri Lanka to be ordained as a monk and learn Theravāda. He returned to Angkhor after ten years and taught Theravāda. He organized and regrouped Theravāda Buddhism that had been scattered throughout the country. Buddhism in Sri Lanka during this time (1180 -1190 CE) had gone through turbulent times due to South Indian invasions and had become more resilient and disciplined. These changes have had a far reaching effect in the countries that were struggling to develop Theravāda Buddhism. Burma, Cheng Mai, The Mon Kingdoms, Laos and Cambodia could organize and become Theravāda countries. Famous Mahavihara in Sri Lanka may have played a crucial role in this gigantic phenomenon which had a far reaching effect on the Buddhist world.

Transformation of Cambodia from Mahāyāna to Theravāda was rapid and peaceful. Scholars find it difficult to explain this sudden change. It was probably due to the fact that Theravāda Buddhism was more liberal and much less metaphysical than the other religions that were present in those countries at that time such as Mahāyāna and Hinduism.

Buddhism came to China during Han Dynasty (202 BC) from the Kushan Empire during the time of King Kanishka 1. Several sects of Buddhism such as Dharmaguptaka, Mahisasaka, Sarvāsthavāda , Mahāsāṅgika etc. were keen on spreading along the Silk Road to China, Central Asia, Afghanistan and other regional countries. A form of Mahāyāna Buddhism developed in China acquiring aspects of Confucianism, Taoism and native Chinese religions and it had been adopted in Korea, Vietnam and Taiwan too. This religion with features mainly of Mahāyāna has not changed due to the influence of Theravāda or Hinduism. A large amount of Buddhist texts both Theravāda and Mahāyāna had been translated to Chinese. Chinese travelers came to India in search of Buddhist scriptures. Fa-Hien who came to Gandhar and who was the first to have come, Xuanzang who took away as much as 657 texts and Faxian were among pioneers who took away these scriptures and got them translated to Chinese. Some of the very important Buddhist Pāli and Sanscrit texts are extinct and would have been lost to the world if not for this massive undertaking by these historical Chinese travelers (Paul Williams, 2005).

Late stage Buddhism which included Vajarayāna tenets and also Yogācāra and Madhayamaka doctrines were taken to Tibet and was further developed with assimilation of local religious traditions. Today this religion is followed not only in Tibet but also in Mongolia, Bhutan, parts of Siberia, and Northern China.

Buddhism was brought to Korea in the 3rd CE from China. Korean thinkers carried out a revision in order to iron out inconsistencies in the Mahāyāna Buddhism and a unique form of Mahāyāna called Tongbulgyo (interpenetrated Buddhism) was formulated. This religion grew to be popular but was suppressed during Japanese invasions. After the invasion was overcome there was a revival and it developed several sects. At present it is more a philosophy than a practicing religion and about 70% of the population are believed to be influenced by

Buddhism including people in North Korea which is officially atheist (Lee Injae et al, 2014).

Chinese and Korean versions of Buddhism were introduced into Japan in the 6th CE. Several sects of Buddhism developed in Japan. Though about 60% of the population have Buddhist shrines in their homes much less are practicing Buddhists. Yet Buddhism has had a significant influence on the development of the Japanese culture (Lee Injae et al, 2014).

Buddhism had arrived in Vietnam in the 2nd BC either from India or from China. It is the main religion in the country and is a mixture of Mahāyāna, Taoism and Vietnamese folk religion. The country was split into North and South in 1954 and remained so until 1975. South Vietnam was controlled by pro-Western Christians and Buddhism was subject to discrimination. After the country was united the Communist party favoured Buddhism although no religion was accepted officially. Later Theravāda Buddhism was brought from Cambodia to South Vietnam and it has developed to a significant extent in that part of the country.

Buddhism is one of the official religions of Indonesia at present. Buddhism came to Indonesia in the 1st CE along with Hinduism. Both Theravāda and Mahāyāna are present among the 0.8% Buddhist population. Some of the most stupendous Buddhist monuments like Borobudur exists in Indonesia. Borobudur was built in the 9th CE during Seilendra Dynasty. Later Buddhism in Indonesia declined due to Islamic invasion.

Buddhism is the second largest religion in Malaysia with about 20 % of the population practicing it. Buddhism came to Malaysia as early as 200 BC with the migration of Chinese. Majority of Buddhists are of Chinese ethnicity. Thus it is the Chinese form of Buddhism that is practiced in Malaysia.

Buddhism spread to Central Asian countries, Afghanistan, and Iran due to the development of travel along the Silk Road. Sects like Dharmaguptaka, Sarvāsthavāda and Mūlasarvāsthavāda made a successful effort to spread their version of Buddhism to these countries (Mūlasaravasthavada, according to some, was an offshoot of Sarvāsthavāda while others say it is an independent school. It spread in Central Asia and also had been present in Indonesia). A syncretization of Greko-Western and Indian Buddhist philosophies had taken place as the Greek kingdom extended to Bactria (modern Tajikistan, Uzbekistan and Afghanistan) in Central Asia. This was a development consequent to the several invasions mounted by Alexander the Great into the Central Asia and Punjab region of India. These regions were converted to Buddhism with the syncretized philosophy facilitating the change and a type of Buddhism called Greco-Buddhism resulted. An event of great significance and symbolic of the union of philosophies is the conversion of King Menander 1 of Bactria into Buddhism as a consequence of intense discussions he had with a Buddhist monk Ven.Nagasena. King Menander was born into a Greek family in Alexandria and came to be an Indo-Greek King who controlled Bactria. The discussions he had with the monk are included in the text "Milinda-Panha" which is included in the Theravāda Sutta Piṭaka. Ven.Nagasena was a Theravāda monk and due to his influence King Menander, who was a Sarvāsthavāda Buddhist, may have been converted to Theravāda. It is said that he took up robes in later life. In spite of these changes of immense importance eventually Buddhism in these countries sadly were destroyed by Islamic invasions (A Berzin, 2006).

Thus it can be seen that Theravāda had spread to the South East Asia mainly due to missionary efforts of King Asoka and Mahavihara dwellers in Sri Lanka. In some of these countries Theravāda could triumph over Mahāyāna and Hinduism.

On the other hand Mahāyāna had spread during the time of the Kushan Kingdom in the North-West of India under King Kanishka along the Silk Road to China in the Far East and also to Central Asia, Afghanistan and Iran.

Decline of Buddhism in India and its survival in other countries

Buddhism has survived in most of these countries though it had almost disappeared in the country of its origin, India. In the countries where it survived it has contributed to the development of the spiritual, moral and cultural aspects of the lives of the people in a unique way. However some of the schools and sects of Buddhism that developed in these countries could hardly be recognized as Buddhism.

Bibliography

Discourses, (Sutta Piṭaka)   Source :–

    Pāli Text Society, United Kingdom
    Buddha Jayanthi Tipiṭaka, Sri Lanka
    Translations by Bikkhu Sujatho
    Translations by Bhikku Bodhi

Dīgha Nikāya :-

    Sangiti Sutta
    Aggañña Sutta
    Brhamajāla Sutta
    Mahānidāna Sutta
    Mahāpadāna Sutta
    Mahāparinibbāna Sutta
    Mahāsatipattāna Sutta
    Sāmaññaphala Sutta

Majjima Nikāya :-

    Madupundika Sutta
    Cūlasuññata Sutta
    Accharayabuta Sutta
    Ariyapariyasena Sutta
    Tevijjavachchagotta Sutta
    Cūlamalunkya Sutta
    Mūlapariyaya Sutta
    Vimamsaka Sutta
    Dhammadayada Sutta

Bibliography

Aṅguttara Nikāya :-

Nibbedikapariyaya Sutta
Kesaputtiya/Kalama Sutta
Sattasurya Sutta

Samyutta Nikāya :-

Loka
Sabbam Sutta
Bara-Hara Sutta
Jara Sutta
Kaccānagotta Sutta
Aselakassapa Sutta
Pathavi Sutta
Anattalakhana Sutta
Salayatana Vagga

Kuddhaka Nikāya :-

Udana
Dhammapada
Itivuttaka
Thera gātha
Theri gātha
Bodivamsa

Vissuddhimagga
Buddhacarita
Mahāvastu
Nidāna katha
Nikāyasaṅgraha

Abhidhamma :-

Comprehensive Manual of Abhidhamma, Translation by Bhikkhu Bodhi, 1993 Buddhist Publication Society

Mahāyāna Sūthra : -

Source :–

    Mahāyāna English Translation Resource

    The Buddhist Text Translation Society

Texts :-

Saddharmpundarika Sūthra
Vajradchedika Praññāparamithā Sūthra
Praññāparamithā Hardaya Sūthra (Heart Sūthra)
Lalithavisthara Sūthra
Lankavatara Sūthra
Thathgathagarba Sūthra
Mahāpariniravāna Sūthra
Astasashrika Praññāparamithā
Yogācāra bhumisasthra
Sandhinirmocana Sūthra
Updasaka Sūthra

Authored By Nāgārjuna :-

  Mūlamadhyamaka-karikā
  Vigrahavyavartani
  Surhlekha

Translations by DJ Kalupahana in A Source Book of Later Buddhist Philosophy (see below)

Authored by Vasubandhu:-

Vingnaptimatratasiddhi, Trimsatika, Vimsathika, Translations by DJ Kalupahana in "A Source Book of Later Buddhist Philosophy" (see below)

Abhidharma Kosa Bashyam 4 vols Translated into English by Leo Pruden, 1988, Asian Humanities Press, Berkeley, USA

Anacker Stephan, 1984, The Seven Works of Vasubandhu, Motilal Banarsidass, Delhi, India

Authored by Asaṅga:-

Abhidharma samuccaya, The Compendium of The Higher Teaching (Philosophy), Trans. Rahula Walpola 2001 Asian Humanities Press, Berkeley, USA

Compendium of the Mahāyāna: Asanga's Mahayanasamgraha, Trans. Karl Brunnholzi 2019, Snow Lion, Colarado, USA

Authored by Dignāga

Pramānasamuccaya, Trans. Masaki Hattori, 1968 Harvard University Press. USA

Veda

Four Vedas Translated in English Trans. R T Griffith & Bloomfield M, Kindle Edition, Hindu-ebooks

Bhagavadgita - English translation, by A C Bhakthivedanta, Bhakthivedantha Trust, Karnataka, India

Modern authors :-

Adams B & Petrucione F, 2021, Do quantum effects play a role in consciousness?, Physics World, 26 Jan. 2021

Adikaram EW, 1946, Early History of Buddhism in Ceylon, Buddhist Cultural Centre, Dehiwela, Sri lanka

Aristotle, 350 BCE, Metaphysics, Trans. W D Ross 1924

Bakker Hans, 2017, Monuments of Hope, Gloom and glory in the age of Hannic Wars, J Gando Fund foundation, Amsterdam

Basham AL, 1951, History and Doctrines of the Ājīvikas, Luzac, University of California

Bertrand Russel, 1945, A History of Western Philosophy, Simon & Schuster, New York

Berzin A, 2006, History of Buddhism in Afghanistan. Study Buddhism, Berzin Archives at Oxford Bodlean Electronic Archives

Bhante Henepola Gunaratana, 1992, Mindfulness in Plain English, Wisdom Publications, Sommervil, MA, USA

Bhathacharya K, Johnston E H, A Kunst, 1978, Dialectical method of Nāgārjuna - Vigrhavyavarthani, Motilal Banarsidass, Delhi

Bhikkhu Katukurunde Ñanananda, 2012, Concept and Reality in Early Buddhist Thought, Dharma Grantha Mudrana Bharaya, Sri Lanka

Bibhuti Baruah, 2000, Buddhist Sects and Sectarianism, Sarup & Sons, New Delhi

Bibliography

Bikkhu Dhammajoti KL, 2009, Sarvāstivāda Abhidhamma, Centre for Buddhist Studies, University of Hong Kong

Bikkhu Bodhi, 1994, Dhamma and Non-duality, Dharma Net Edition, Buddhist Publication Society, Kandy, Sri Lanka

Burch GB, 1964, Seven-valued Logic in Jain Philosphy, Philosophy, International Philosophical Quarterly, Feb. 1964

Burnet J, 1930, Early Greek Philosophy, A & C Black, London

Christian Lindtner, 1983, Nāgārjuna: Studies in the writings and philosophy of Nāgārjuna, Akademisk forlag, Copenhagen,

Coburn TB, 1984, Scripture in India, Journal of the American Academy of Religion, Houston, USA

Collins Steven, 1998, Nirvāna and other Buddhist Felicities, Cambridge University Press, UK

Dan Lusthaus, 1990, Retracing human nature Vs world nature- Journal of Chinese Philosophy, June 1990

Dandekar R N, 1990, Commentators of the RgVeda, A Recapitulation, Deccan College Postgraduate and Research Institute, Pune

Dawkins Richard, 2006, The God Delusion, Transworld Publishers, UK

Debiprasad Chattopadhya, 2001, What is Living and what is Dead in Indian Philosophy, People's Publishing House, New Dehi

Dundas P, 2003, The Jains, Routledge London

Emanuel SM, 2015, A Campanion to Buddhist Philosophy, John Wiley & Sons, New Joursey, USA

Flood Gavin D, 1996, An Introduction to Hinduism, Cambridge University Press, UK

Fowler Jeanean D, 2012, The Bhagavadgita, A Text and Commentary for Students. Sussex Academy Press, UK

Ibid 2002, Perspectives of Reality – An Introduction to the Philosophy of Hinduism, Sussex Academic Press, UK

Gold JC, 2015, Paving the Great Way : Vasubandhu's Unifying Buddhist Philosophy, Columbia University Press, New York

Gomperze T, 1905, Greek Thinkers, Nabu Press, USA

Hajime Nakamura, 1980, Indian Buddhism, A survey with bibliographical notes, Motilal Banarsidass, Delhi, India

Haldane JBS, 1928, The Origin of Life, The Rationalist Journal, Poland

Hankinson RJ, 1998, Cause and Explanation in Ancient Greek Thought, Oxford University Press, U K

Hirakawa Akira, 1993, A History of Early Buddhism, From Sakyamuni to Early Mahāyāna, (Trans. Paul Groner), Motilal Banarsidass, Delhi, India

Bibliography

Jainfu Lu, 2017, Chinese and Tibetan Esoteric Buddhism, Studies on East Asian Religions, Brill, Leiden, Netherlands

Jayatilake KN, 1963, Early Buddhist Theory of Knowledge, Motilal Banarsidass, Delhi, India

Ibid 1975, The Message of The Buddha, Buddhist Publication Society, Kandy, Sri Lanka

Kalupahana DJ, 2008, Source Book of Late Buddhist Philosophy, Buddhist Cultural Centre, Dehiwela, Sri Lanka

Ibid 2007, Source Book of Early Buddhist Philosophy, Buddhist Cultural Centre, Dehiwela, Sri Lanka

Ibid 1992, A History of Buddhist Philosophy – Continuities and Discontinuities, Motilal Banarsidass, Delhi

Ibid 1995, Nāgārjuna's Moral Philosophy and Sinhala Buddhism, Postgraduate Institute of Pāli and Buddhist Studies – University of Kelaniya, Sri Lanka

Ibid 2006, Karma and Rebirth, Buddhist Cultural Centre, Dehiwela, Sri Lanka

Ibid 1991, Mūlamadhyamaka-karikā of Nāgārjuna – Philosophy of the Middleway, Motilal Banarsidass, Delhi

Ibid 1975, Causality – Central Philosophy of Buddhism, University Press of Hawai, USA

Kant E, 1781, Critique of Pure Reason, Trans. P Guyer & A Wood, 1999, Cambridge University Press, UK

Karunadasa Y, 1983, Vibhajyavada versus Sarvastivada : The Buddhist Controversy on Time, Kalyani, J Hum & Soc Sc. University of Kelaniya, Sri Lanka

Ibid 2010, Theravāda Abhidhamma, Its inquiry into the nature of Conditioned Reality, Centre of Buddhist Studies, University of Hong Kong

Ibid 2015, The Buddhist Analysis of Matter, Centre of Buddhist Studies, University of Hong Kong

Ibid 2013, Early Buddhist Teachings, Centre of Buddhist Studies, University of Hong kong

Keenan J, 2003, Prospects for a Mahāyāna Theology of Emptiness, J Bud & Chris Studies, University of Hawai, USA

Larson EJ & Witham L, 1968, Scientists and Religion in America, Scientific American, Vol 281 No. 3 Sept. 1999

Lee Injae, Miller O, Johnson P & Hyun-Hae Yi, 2014, Korean History in Maps. Cambridge University Press, UK

Lindenfors P & Svensson J, 2021, Evolutionary Explanations for Religions, ResearchGate, Berlin, Germany

Long CH, 1963, Myths of Creation, Scholars Press, Indiana University, USA

Malasekera GP, 1928, Pāli Literature of Ceylon, M D Gunasena, Colombo, Sri Lanka

Marasinghe MMJ, 2014, "Bududhama Devamagak Keerima", (Sinhala) Sarasavi Publishers, Colombo, Sri Lanka

Matilal BK, 1968, Nyaya-Nyaya Logic of Negation, Harvard Oriental Series, Harvard University Press, USA

Max Mueller, 1859, A History of ancient Sanscrit Literature, Williams & Norgate, London, UK

Moratuwe Sasanaratana, 1952, "Lakdiva Mahāyāna Adahas", (Sinhala), Visidunu Prakashakoya, Nugegoda, Sri Lanka

Murti TRV, 1955, A Study of the Madhyamaka System, George Allen & Unwin, UK

Nagao GM, 1991, Madhyamika and Yogācāra : A Study of Mahāyāna Philosophies, Trans. L S Kawamura, State University of New York Press, USA

Nanayakkara S, 2003, "Mul Bududhame sita Vajarayānaya dakva" (Sinhala), Buddhist Cultural Centre, Nedimala, Dehiwela, Sri Lanka

Nietzsche F, (19th CE), The Will to Power Trans. Walter Kaufman, 1968, Vintage Books, New York, USA

Operin AI, 1838, The Origin of Life, Trans. S Morgulis, 1953, Dover, Mineola, New York, USA

Padmanabh J S, 1988, The Jain Path of Purification. Motilal Banarsidass, Delhi, India

Potter KH, Buswell RE & Jaini PS, 1999, Abhidhamma Buddhism to 150 AD, Encyclopedia of Indian Philosophies Vol VII, Motilal Banarsidass, Delhi, India

Premasiri PD, 2018, Early Buddhist Concept of Truth, A study based on Pāli Cannonical Sources, J Postgr Inst Pāli and Bud Studies, University of Kelaniya, Sri Lanka.

Ibid   1975, Moral Evaluation in Early Buddhism, The Sri Lankan J of the Humanities Vol 1 No 1 pp 31 – 45

Prior AN,   1969, Formal Logic, Oxford University Press, UK

Radakrishnan S, 1957,   Source Book in Indian Philosophy, Princeton University Press, USA

Ramanuj Prasad, 2008,   Veda: A Way of Life, Pustak Mahal, Delhi, India

Roderick Hindery,   2004,   Comparative Ethics in Hindu and Buddhist Traditions, Motilal Banarsidass, Delhi, India

Rudolph Otto, 1917,   The Idea of the Holy, Trans. J W Harvey, 1923 , Oxford University Press, New York, USA

Sacks M,   2001,   Objectivity and Insight, Clarendon Press, Oxford University Press, UK

Santina P D,   1998,   The Tree of Enlightenment,   Chico Dharma Study Foundation, California, USA

Sarathchandra E,   1952,   Buddhist Psychology of Perception, Ceylon University Press, Sri Lanka

Schopenhauer A, 1818, World as Will and Representation, Trans. R B Haldane & J Kemp, 2020, Routledge, UK

Sharma C,   1997,   A Critical Survey of Indian philosophy, Motilal Banarsidass, Delhi, India

Smith C de M, 2021, Can Consciousness be explained by Quantum Physics, The Conversation, United Kingdom

Snellgrove G, 1987, Indo-Tibetan Buddhism, Indian Buddhists and Their Tibetan Successors, Shambala Publications, Colarado, USA

Stephen Hodge, 2004, Textual History of Mahāyāna-Mahaparinirvāna-Sūthra, Buddha Nature, Tsadra Foundation, New York, USA

Subash Kak, 2016, Matter and Mind: Vaisheshika Sūtra of Kanada, Mount Meru Publishing, Toronto, USA

Susan Haack, 1978, Philosophy of Logics, Cambridge University Press, New York, USA

Swami Bhaskarananda, 1994, Essentials of Hinduism, Viveka Press, Washington, USA

Taranatha J, 16th CE, The Essence of Other Emptiness, Trans. Jeffry Hopkins, 2007, Snow Lions, Shambala Publications, USA

TH Stcherbatsky, 1932, The Doctrine of the Buddha, Bulletin de l Academie des Sciences de Russie, Petrograd

Thakchoe S, 2017, The Two Truths Debate, Simon & Schuster, New York, USA

Tillakaratne A, 2001, "Śūnyathavadayehi Darshanaya ha Charanaya", (Sinhala), Thivira Prakashana, Nugegoda, Sri L

Ibid 1993, Nirvāna and Ineffability, A Study of the Buddhist Theory of Reality and Language, Post Graduate Institute of Pāli and Buddhist Studies, University of Kelaniya

Ibid 1995, "Abhidhamma Adhyayana", (Sinhala) Karunaratne & Sons Ltd. Homagama, Sri Lanka

Tilleman TJF, 2011, Dharmakirti, Aryadeva and Dharmapala on Scriptural Authority, Tetsugaku Felicitation Volume for Professors A Uno and K Ogura, Hiroshima, Japan

Uswatte-aratchi G, 2020, Buddhagosa, Mahaviharins and the stunting of Sinhala, The Island (News Paper) 24th May 2020 Warder AK, 1991 – Introduction to Pāli, Pāli Text Society, London, UK

Uswatte-aratchi G, 2020, Buddhagosa, Mahaviharins and the stunting of Sinhala, The Island (News Paper) 24th May 2020 Warder AK, 1991 – Introduction to Pāli, Pāli Text Society, London, UK

Ibid 2000, Indian Buddhism, Motilal Banarsidass, Delhi, India

Wayman A, 1971, Buddhist Dependent Origination, History of Religions, Vol. 10, Number 3, Feb. 1971

William P, 2005, Buddhism, Critical Concepts in Religious Studies, Routledge, London, UK

Ibid 1989, Mahāyāna Buddhism - Doctrinal Foundation, Routledge, London, UK

Williams E & Brown CR, 2019, On David Hume, Stanford Encyclopedia, Cali. USA

Ziegfried Morenz, 1960, Egyptian Religion, Methuen Publishing, UK